VEGETARIAN

VEGETARIAN

CREATE GREAT-TASTING DISHES THROUGH THE SEASONS

Carla Bardi, Rachel Lane, Ting Morris

Reader's Digest

THE READER'S DIGEST ASSOCIATION, INC.
Pleasantville, New York / Montreal / Sydney / Singapore

A READER'S DIGEST BOOK

This edition published by
The Reader's Digest Association, Inc.,
by arrangement with McRae Books Srl

Copyright © 2010 McRae Books Srl

Vegetarian was created and produced by
McRae Books Srl
Via Umbria 36, 50145 Florence, Italy
Info@mcraebooks.com

FOR MCRAE BOOKS
Project Director: Anne McRae
Art Director: Marco Nardi
Photography: Brent Parker-Jones
Texts: Carla Bardi, Rachel Lane, Ting Morris
Food Styling: Lee Blaycock, Briony Bennet,
 Jackie Middleton, Rebecca Quinn
Layouts: Aurora Granata
Prepress: Filippo Delle Monache

FOR READER'S DIGEST
U.S. Project Editor: Andrea Chesman
Canadian Project Editor: Pamela Chichinskas
Senior Art Director: George McKeon
Executive Editor, Trade Publishing:
 Dolores York
Associate Publisher, Trade Publishing:
 Rosanne McManus
President and Publisher, Trade Publishing:
 Harold Clarke

LIBRARY OF CONGRESS CATALOGING-IN-PUBLICATION DATA

Morris, Ting.
 Vegetarian : create great-tasting dishes through the
 seasons / Ting Morris, Rachel Lane, and Carla Bardi.
  p. cm.
 ISBN 978-1-60652-111-3 (U.S. edition)
 ISBN 978-1-60652-158-8 (international edition)
 1. Vegetarian cookery. I. Lane, Rachel. II. Bardi,
 Carla. III. Title.
 TX837.M677 2010
 641.5'636−dc22

                                        2010004578

We are committed to both the quality of our
products and the service we provide to our
customers. We value your comments, so please
feel free to contact us.

 The Reader's Digest Association, Inc.
 Adult Trade Publishing
 Reader's Digest Road
 Pleasantville, NY 10570-7000

NOTE TO OUR READERS
Eating eggs or egg whites that are not
completely cooked poses the possibility of
salmonella food poisoning. The risk is greater
for pregnant women, the elderly, the very young,
and persons with impaired immune systems. If
you are concerned about salmonella, you can
use reconstituted powdered egg whites or
pasteurized eggs.

For more Reader's Digest products and
information, visit our website:
 www.rd.com (in the United States)
 www.readersdigest.ca (in Canada)
 www.rdasia.com (in Asia)

Printed in China

1 3 5 7 9 10 8 6 4 2

On the cover: (Main image) potato, eggplant, and spinach curry; (top left) pasta salad with feta
and olives; (top center) linguine with cherry tomatoes and pesto; (top right) whole-wheat
spaghetti with pesto, potatoes, and beans

Spine: paella

Back cover: (Top left) tagliatelle with pine nut and walnut pesto; (top right) pizza with onion and
pesto; (center left) zucchini fritters; (center right) sweet butternut squash soup; (bottom) mixed
bean and spelt soup in bread rolls

The level of difficulty for each recipe is given on a scale from
1 (easy) to 3 (complicated).

CONTENTS

INTRODUCTION

INTRODUCTION

What do Plato, Leonardo da Vinci, Saint Catherine of Siena, and Frankenstein's monster have in common with Paul McCartney, Paris Hilton, and Jonathan Safran Foer? You guessed it—vegetarianism! History is filled with the stories of famous vegetarians, or at least, would-be eschewers of meat. The great German scientist Albert Einstein once said in a letter to a friend, "Although I have been prevented by outward circumstances from observing a strictly vegetarian diet, I have long been an adherent to the cause in principle. Besides agreeing with the aims of vegetarianism for aesthetic and moral reasons, it is my view that a vegetarian manner of living by its purely physical effect on the human temperament would most beneficially influence the lot of mankind." By the final year of his long life Einstein was happily "living without fats, without meat, without fish, but... feeling quite well this way. It always seems to me that man was not born to be a carnivore."

As you can see, there is nothing faddish or even especially modern about vegetarianism. People have followed vegetarian diets for a long time and for a wide variety of good reasons, including the desire for better health, a safer and cleaner environment, a more ethical treatment of animals, and a fairer division of the Earth's dwindling resources. Still others are vegetarians for their religious or cultural beliefs or their political convictions. In many cases, these reasons overlap. Vegetarians are equally diverse in

the ways they follow their plant-based diets. The strictest vegetarians, called vegans, enjoy fruits, vegetables, whole grains and cereals, legumes, seeds, and nuts, but they exclude all animal products, including dairy, eggs, and honey. However, the majority of vegetarians do include at least some dairy or egg products or honey in their diets. There is also another, rapidly growing, group of people who—like Einstein—are not strict vegetarians, because they still eat some fish and chicken, or even small amounts of red meat, but they do try to limit the amount of animal products in their diets. These "semi-vegetarians" would prefer not to eat meat at all but for practical reasons have not entirely eliminated it. This book, with its wealth of simple and delicious recipes, will be especially useful to them since it makes following a vegetarian diet so easy.

A vegetarian diet is generally associated with a range of health benefits, including a lower incidence of obesity, high blood pressure, coronary heart disease, stroke, type-2 diabetes, and many forms of cancer. Vegetarians are also believed to suffer less from constipation, gallstones, diverticular disease, and high cholesterol.

Maintaining optimum health on vegetarian fare is not difficult, but there are one or two things to bear in mind if you are new to a meat-free diet. Variety is key: Be sure to eat a wide range of foods, including fruits, nuts, vegetables, legumes, and whole grains, so that you get all the nutrients you need from nonmeat sources. Nutrients that vegetarians may need to focus on include protein, iron, calcium, zinc, and vitamin B12. Protein can be found in beans, nuts, peas, and soy products, as well as in milk and eggs, if you allow them in your diet. Iron-rich foods include spinach, kidney beans, black-eyed peas, lentils, turnip greens, molasses, whole-wheat breads, and some dried fruits, such as dried apricots, prunes, and raisins. Calcium is found in dairy products but also in soy foods and some dark, leafy vegetables, such as collard greens and bok choy. Beans and milk products are good sources of zinc. Vitamin B12 is found in dairy products and eggs, but if you are a vegan, you may need to consume foods that have been fortified with B12, such as soy-based drinks, breakfast cereals, and nutritional yeast. You should also remember not to overload meals with high-fat cheeses to replace meat. Build your meals around low-fat protein sources, such as beans, lentils, whole-wheat pasta, and rice.

In this book we have tried to make things easier for you by gathering a wide variety of gourmet recipes for mouthwatering vegetarian dishes, ranging from soups and salads, through pasta, rice, and grains to stews, curries, baked dishes, and breads.

To help you stay on track, we have provided key nutritional information for each dish, including calories, fat, protein, fiber, and salt (see example below). This will allow you to plan balanced snacks and meals for every occasion. Enjoy!

Nutritional Facts
Amount per serving
Percentage of Daily Values
based on 2,000 calories

CALORIES

400
19%

PROTEIN

22g
48%

FAT
3g
4%

FIBER

10g
40%

SALT

0.9g
16%

SALADS

A HANDFUL OF GREEN LEAVES

Salad: Separate the leaves of the endive and romaine lettuce and discard the outer bitter leaves of the frisée. Tear the salad greens into manageable lengths. Combine all the greens in a bowl and toss well.

Dressing: Whisk the oil, vinegar, salt, and pepper in a small bowl. Drizzle over the salad and toss well. • Drizzle with a little more oil and add an extra grinding of pepper, if liked. Serve immediately.

■ ■ ■ *There is nothing simpler—or more delicious— than a bowl of crisp, fresh salad greens lightly tossed with an olive oil dressing. Feel free to use any combination of lush-looking salad greens that appeal to you at the market or that grow in your garden.*

Salad

- ¹/₂ **head crispy romaine (cos) lettuce**
- ¹/₂ **head frisée (curly endive)**
- 1 **cup (50 g) baby spinach or lamb's lettuce**

  Handful of arugula (rocket)

  Handful of watercress, tough stems discarded

  Handful of red radicchio or chard
- 2 **fresh flat-leaf parsley sprigs, leaves only**

Dressing

- ¹/₄ **cup (60 ml) extra-virgin olive oil, + extra to drizzle**
- 2 **tablespoons balsamic vinegar**

  Salt and freshly ground black pepper

Serves: 6
Preparation: 10 minutes
Level: 1

Nutritional Facts
Amount per serving
Percentage of Daily Values
based on 2,000 calories

CALORIES	PROTEIN	FAT	FIBER	SALT
109	2g	10g	1.2g	0.1g

SPRING CABBAGE SALAD WITH MINT

Salad: Combine the cabbage, onion, carrots, mint, and cilantro in a large serving dish. • Drizzle with the dressing. • Toss everything together with your fingers. Check the seasoning, and garnish with the whole mint leaves.

Dressing: Whisk the lemon juice, sugar, and salt in a small bowl until the sugar and salt are dissolved. Whisk in the oil and lemon zest.

Salad

1   green or white cabbage, finely shredded

1   red onion, thinly sliced

2   carrots, grated

3   tablespoons coarsely chopped fresh mint leaves + a few whole leaves, to garnish

2   tablespoons coarsely chopped fresh cilantro (coriander) leaves

Dressing

2   tablespoons freshly squeezed lemon juice

2   teaspoons sugar

1/2 teaspoon salt

3   tablespoons peanut (groundnut) oil or grapeseed oil

1/2 teaspoon finely grated lemon zest

Nutritional Facts
Amount per serving
Percentage of Daily Values
based on 2,000 calories

 CALORIES **97**

 PROTEIN **2g**

FAT **6g**

 FIBER **3.6g**

 SALT **0.5g**

Serves: 6
Preparation: 15 minutes
Level: 1

ASIAN SLAW

Salad: Combine the cabbage, carrots, snow pea shoots, peanuts, bell pepper, scallions, mint, and cilantro in a large bowl.

Dressing: Whisk the lime juice, sesame oil, soy sauce, garlic, ginger, and palm sugar in a small bowl. Pour over the salad and toss to combine. Season with salt and pepper and serve.

Salad

- 1/2 **Chinese cabbage (wom bok), finely shredded**
- 2 **carrots, julienned**
- 2 **cups (120 g) snow pea shoots, trimmed**
- 1/2 **cup (80 g) peanuts, toasted and chopped**
- 1 **red bell pepper (capsicum), julienned**
- 5 **scallions (spring onions), thinly sliced**
- 1/4 **cup (25 g) finely chopped fresh mint**
- 1/4 **cup (25 g) fresh cilantro (coriander)**

Dressing

- 3 **tablespoons freshly squeezed lime juice**
- 1 1/2 **tablespoons Asian sesame oil**
- 1 **tablespoon soy sauce**
- 1 **clove garlic, minced**
- 1 **teaspoon finely grated fresh ginger**
- 1 **teaspoon finely grated jaggery (palm sugar) or brown sugar**

Salt and freshly ground black pepper

Serves: 4
Preparation: 15 minutes
Level: 1

Nutritional Facts
Amount per serving
Percentage of Daily Values
based on 2,000 calories

CALORIES	PROTEIN	FAT	FIBER	SALT
234	8g	16g	5.3g	0.6g

CRUDITÉS WITH SAFFRON DIP

Cut each scallion from the middle, sliding the knife toward the greener end. Repeat this cut several times on each scallion and then place in a bowl of iced water. Let rest until the sliced ends curl, about 20 minutes. Drain well. • Cook the cauliflower in a large pot of salted boiling water until just tender, 3–5 minutes. Drain well and let cool. • Slice the celery, zucchini, and radishes, if using, lengthwise to make long sticks. Slice the onions into rings. Tear the radicchio into manageable pieces. • Arrange the prepared vegetables on a large serving dish. • Combine the saffron, lemon juice, and horseradish in a small bowl. Season with salt and pepper. Add the oil and ricotta and beat until all the ingredients are well mixed. Stir in the pistachios. • Place the bowl of dip on the serving dish with the vegetables and serve.

4 scallions (spring onions), trimmed
1 small cauliflower, cut into florets
4 tender celery sticks, taken from the heart
8 baby zucchini (courgettes), with flowers, if possible
12 radishes (optional)
2 small red onions
2 small heads red radicchio
Pinch of saffron threads
2 tablespoons freshly squeezed lemon juice
1 tablespoon prepared horseradish
Salt and freshly ground black pepper
1/3 cup (90 ml) extra-virgin olive oil
1 cup (250 g) fresh ricotta cheese, drained
4 tablespoons blanched pistachios, chopped

Serves: 6
Preparation: 30 minutes
Cooking: 3–5 minutes
Level: 1

Nutritional Facts
Amount per serving
Percentage of Daily Values
based on 2,000 calories

 CALORIES **283**
 PROTEIN **10g** 22%
 FAT **23g** 28%
 FIBER **3.3g**
SALT **0.3g**

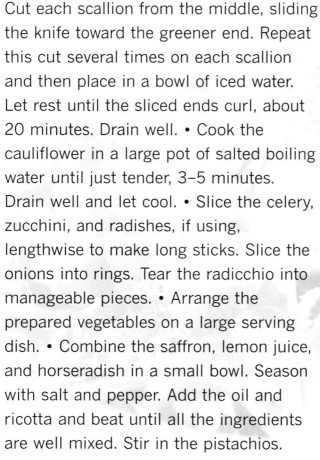

SPINACH SALAD WITH ORANGE AND AVOCADO

30

Peel the oranges using a sharp knife, removing all the bitter white pith. Break the fruit into segments. • Put the spinach leaves in a large salad bowl. Top with the oranges and avocados. • Beat the lemon juice and oil in a small bowl with a fork. • Add the scallions and orange zest and season with salt and pepper. Beat well. • Drizzle the dressing over the salad and toss carefully. • Serve at once.

2 large ripe oranges

8 ounces (250 g) baby spinach leaves

2 large ripe avocados, peeled, pitted, and sliced

Freshly squeezed juice of 1 lemon

1/4 cup (60 ml) extra-virgin olive oil

2 scallions (spring onions), trimmed and sliced

Finely grated zest of 1 orange

Salt and freshly ground black pepper

Serves: 4
Preparation: 15 minutes
Level: 1

Nutritional Facts
Amount per serving
Percentage of Daily Values
based on 2,000 calories

 CALORIES 375 18%

 PROTEIN 15g 33%

 FAT 37g 42%

 FIBER 4g 16%

 SALT 0.4g 7%

SPINACH WITH STRAWBERRIES AND ALMONDS

32

Salad: Toast the almonds in a large frying pan over medium heat until golden brown, about 5 minutes. Remove from the heat and let cool. • Combine the spinach, strawberries, fennel, and almonds in a large salad bowl.
Toss gently.

Dressing: Beat the lemon juice, orange juice, oil, vinegar, and mustard in a small bowl with a fork. Season with salt and pepper. • Drizzle the dressing over the salad and toss gently. • Serve immediately.

Salad

- 2/3 cup (100 g) blanched almonds
- 12 ounces (350 g) baby spinach leaves
- 12 ounces (350 g) strawberries, sliced
- 1 fennel bulb, thinly sliced

Dressing

- Freshly squeezed juice of 1/2 lemon
- Freshly squeezed juice of 1 orange
- 1/4 cup (60 ml) extra-virgin olive oil
- 2 tablespoons balsamic vinegar
- 1 teaspoon Dijon mustard
- Salt and freshly ground black pepper

Serves: 4
Preparation 15 minutes
Cooking: 5 minutes
Level: 1

Nutritional Facts
Amount per serving
Percentage of Daily Values
based on 2,000 calories

 CALORIES 330 16%
 PROTEIN 9g 20%
 FAT 28g 35%
 FIBER 6.7g 27
 SALT 0.4g

CHEESE SALAD WITH FRESH FRUIT AND HERBS

Combine both cheeses in a large salad bowl. • Add the radicchio, frisée, apple, pear, grapes, golden raisins, orange, grapefruit, and shallot. Toss well. • Beat the oil and vinegar in a small bowl with a fork. Add the mustard, dill, chives, and parsley. Season with salt and white pepper and beat again. • Drizzle the salad with the dressing and toss gently. • Serve at once.

4	ounces (125 g) Emmental, diced
4	ounces (125 g) Parmesan, in flakes
1	small radicchio, torn
1	head frisée (curly endive), chopped
1	apple, peeled, cored, and diced
1	pear, peeled, cored, and diced
1/2	cup (75 g) green grapes, halved
2	tablespoons golden raisins (sultanas)
1	orange, peeled and cut in segments
1	grapefruit, peeled and cut in segments
1	shallot, finely chopped
1/4	cup (60 ml) extra-virgin olive oil
1	tablespoon balsamic vinegar
1	tablespoon whole-grain mustard
2	tablespoons each finely chopped fresh dill, chives, parsley
	Salt and freshly ground white pepper

Nutritional Facts
Amount per serving
Percentage of Daily Values
based on 2,000 calories

CALORIES **340** • PROTEIN **19g** • FAT **23g** • FIBER **2.7g** • SALT **0.7g**

Serves: 6
Preparation: 20 minutes
Level: 1

PINEAPPLE SALAD

Salad: Combine the pineapple, bean sprouts, peanuts, carrots, cucumber, and scallions in a large salad bowl. Toss gently.

Dressing: Combine the peanut butter, oil, soy sauce, vinegar, and chile in a small saucepan over low heat. Stir gently until well mixed, adding enough water to obtain a smooth, creamy dressing.

• Spoon the dressing over the salad, or serve separately in a small bowl so that guests can serve themselves.

Salad

8   ounces (250 g) fresh or canned pineapple, drained, cut into bite-size pieces

8   ounces (250 g) bean sprouts

1   cup (100 g) toasted peanuts

2   large carrots, grated

1   small cucumber, peeled and diced

2   scallions (spring onions), trimmed and thinly sliced

Dressing

6   tablespoons smooth peanut butter

2   tablespoons vegetable oil

2   teaspoons light soy sauce

1   teaspoon white vinegar

1   teaspoon ground chile (or 1 fresh red chile, thinly sliced)

About $1/2$ cup (125 ml) cold water

Nutritional Facts
*Amount per serving
Percentage of Daily Values
based on 2,000 calories*

CALORIES	PROTEIN	FAT	FIBER	SALT
442	16g	33g	5.6g	1.2g

Serves: 4
Preparation: 20 minutes
Cooking: 5 minutes
Level: 1

GRILLED SUMMER SALAD

Salad: Place the mozzarella on a large plate. • Mix 2 tablespoons of oil with the garlic, salt, pepper, and Tabasco in a small bowl. Drizzle over the mozzarella and sprinkle with half the chopped basil and lemon zest. Leave to marinate while you prepare the vegetables. • Place the bell pepper halves, skin side up, under a very hot broiler (grill), until blackened. Place in a plastic bag and let cool. Remove the skins, core, and seeds. Tear the peppers lengthwise into quarters and set aside. • Preheat a ridged grill pan on top of the stove for about 10 minutes, or use a very hot broiler (grill). • Pour the remaining 6 tablespoons of oil into a large shallow dish. Dip the eggplant slices in the oil to coat each one on both sides. • Grill until lightly browned, then turn over. Turn frequently to get a scorched pattern. They are done when soft and crisscrossed with grill marks.
• Transfer to a large plate, and season with

Salad

8 ounces (250 g) mozzarella cheese, cut into $^{1}/_{2}$-inch (1-cm) slices

8 tablespoons (125 ml) extra-virgin olive oil + extra to drizzle

1 clove garlic, finely chopped

Salt and freshly ground black pepper

Dash of Tabasco

2 tablespoons finely chopped fresh basil

1 teaspoon finely grated lemon zest

2 red bell peppers (capsicums), halved

1 yellow bell pepper (capsicum), halved

1 eggplant (aubergine), cut lengthwise into $^{1}/_{4}$-inch (5-mm) slices

5 zucchini (courgettes), cut lengthwise into $^{1}/_{4}$-inch (5-mm) slices

1 fennel bulb, trimmed, cut into $^{1}/_{4}$-inch (5-mm) slices

4 plum tomatoes, cut into $^1/_2$-inch (1-cm) slices

Dressing

$^1/_3$ cup (90 ml) extra-virgin olive oil

2 tablespoons balsamic vinegar

2 scallions (spring onions), trimmed and thinly sliced

Salt and freshly ground black pepper

Squeeze of fresh lemon juice

$^1/_4$ cup (25 g) basil leaves, coarsely torn

Serves: 6
Preparation: 35 minutes
Cooking: 15–20 minutes
Level: 2

salt and pepper. Repeat until all the eggplant is cooked. • Repeat with the zucchini and fennel. • Drizzle the tomatoes with oil. Grill on both sides, until lightly charred (but not burned!), 1–2 minutes. Transfer to a plate and season with a pinch of salt and the remaining basil. • Arrange the cheese and vegetables attractively in a wide salad bowl.

Dressing: Whisk the oil and vinegar in a small bowl. Stir in the scallions, and season with salt and pepper. • Drizzle the dressing over the vegetables about 15 minutes before serving. • Add a squeeze of lemon juice and freshly ground black pepper, and scatter the basil on top when you bring the salad to the table.

(See photograph on the following page.)

Nutritional Facts
Amount per serving
Percentage of Daily Values
based on 2,000 calories

CALORIES	PROTEIN	FAT	FIBER	SALT
455	11g	30g	3.3g	0.4g
				7%

LENTIL AND HERB SALAD

Rinse the lentils under running cold water. Place in a saucepan, cover with cold water about 1 inch (2.5 cm) above the level of the lentils, and add the garlic. Bring to a boil, then turn down the heat and simmer until tender, 25–30 minutes. • Meanwhile, chop half the watercress and add to the other fresh herbs. • Drain the lentils and remove the garlic. Stir in the oil and vinegar and season with salt. • Add the herbs to the lentils while they are still warm and toss well. • Mix the remaining watercress leaves and pecorino into the salad. • Divide among individual salad bowls or arrange on a large serving plate, making sure you don't break up the fragile cheese shavings. • Drizzle with a little extra oil and serve with the lemon wedges.

³/₄ cup (150 g) Le Puy lentils

1 clove garlic, peeled

3 tablespoons finely chopped fresh parsley

3 tablespoons finely chopped fresh basil

2 tablespoons finely chopped fresh arugula (rocket)

1 cup (50 g) watercress, thick stems discarded

¹/₄ cup (60 ml) extra-virgin olive oil, + extra to drizzle

1 tablespoon sherry or red wine vinegar

Salt and freshly ground black pepper

¹/₂ cup (60 g) pecorino cheese, shaved

2 lemons, cut into wedges, to serve

Serves: 4
Preparation: 10 minutes
Cooking: 25–30 minutes
Level: 1

Nutritional Facts
Amount per serving
Percentage of Daily Values
based on 2,000 calories

 CALORIES 316 15%

 PROTEIN 15g 33%

 FAT 20g 25%

 FIBER 4g 16%

 SALT 0.3g 5%

ORANGE AND WATERCRESS SALAD

Salad: Put the watercress in a salad bowl. • Grate the orange zest and set aside. • Peel the oranges and pare off the white pith. Cut the flesh crosswise into thin slices, removing any seeds, and add to the bowl. Add the carrots and radicchio. • Open the pomegranate, cut into sections, and remove the seeds. Carefully discard the bitter pith and add most of the seeds to the bowl, reserving a few for juicing. • Toast the sunflower and pumpkin seeds in a pan over high heat until nutty, 1–2 minutes.

Dressing: Combine the lemon juice, pomegranate juice, and mustard in a screw-top jar. Add the orange zest and oil. Season with salt and pepper. Cover and shake well. • Drizzle over the salad and toss. Garnish with the seeds and serve.

■ ■ ■ *To extract the pomegranate juice, press the seeds that are not added to the salad through a sieve.*

Salad

2	cups (100 g) watercress
2	large oranges
3	carrots, grated
1	head green or red radicchio, torn
2	tablespoons fresh pomegranate seeds
1	tablespoon sunflower seeds
1	tablespoon pumpkin seeds

Dressing

2	tablespoons freshly squeezed lemon juice
1	tablespoon pomegranate juice (from the seeds)
1	teaspoon Dijon mustard
1/4	cup (60 ml) grapeseed oil or sunflower oil
	Salt and freshly ground black pepper

Serves: 4
Preparation: 10 minutes
Cooking: 1-2 minutes
Level: 1

Nutritional Facts
Amount per serving
Percentage of Daily Values
based on 2,000 calories

CALORIES 306
PROTEIN 15g 35
FAT 25g 3
FIBER 2.6g 10
SALT 0.2g

TOMATO MEDLEY

Salad: Combine all the tomatoes in a large bowl.

Dressing: Heat all but 1 tablespoon of oil in a large frying pan over low heat. Add the onion and sauté until tender, 3–4 minutes. • Add the garlic and parsley. Stir in the lemon zest, 4 tablespoons of lemon juice, and the vinegar. • Add the sun-dried tomatoes and cook until the dressing is warm, about 2 minutes. • Remove from the heat and add the basil leaves.
• Season the tomatoes lightly with salt and pepper, spoon the warm dressing over the top, and toss gently. • Transfer to a large serving dish. • Put the arugula in a small bowl and drizzle with the remaining 1 tablespoon each of oil and lemon juice. • Mix the arugula in with the tomatoes and serve.

Salad

3	plum tomatoes, sliced
2	green tomatoes, sliced
12	cherry tomatoes, halved
6	grape or baby plum tomatoes, quartered
8	yellow cherry tomatoes, halved
	Salt and freshly ground black pepper
1	cup (50 g) arugula (rocket) leaves

Dressing

8	tablespoons (125 ml) extra-virgin olive oil
1	sweet white onion, finely chopped
2	cloves garlic, minced
2	tablespoons coarsely chopped fresh parsley
1	teaspoon finely grated lemon zest
5	tablespoons freshly squeezed lemon juice
1	tablespoon red wine vinegar
1/4	cup (40 g) sun-dried tomatoes, drained
2	tablespoons coarsely torn fresh basil leaves

Nutritional Facts
Amount per serving
Percentage of Daily Values
based on 2,000 calories

CALORIES	PROTEIN	FAT	FIBER	SALT
306 / 15%	3g / 7%	28g / 35%	2.8g / 11%	0.1g / 3%

Serves: 4
Preparation: 20 minutes
Cooking: 3–4 minutes
Level: 1

MUSHROOM, APRICOT, AND ENDIVE SALAD

Salad: Whisk the Gorgonzola, cream cheese, and butter with a handheld blender until smooth. • Remove the endive leaves from their cores. Reserve the small cores. Spread the inside of each leaf with cheese mixture, then sandwich them back together into their original endive shape. Wrap each filled endive in plastic wrap (cling film) and chill for 2 hours. • Slice the reserved cores thinly and put in a bowl with the mushrooms and apricots. Drizzle with oil and lemon juice. Season with salt and pepper and set aside.

Dressing: Whisk the mustard, vinegar, sour cream, and a squeeze of lemon juice in a small bowl. Taste for seasoning. • Unwrap the endives and cut into rounds about 1 inch (2.5 cm) thick. Divide among four plates with the apricot mixture. • Top with dressing and garnish with walnuts.

Salad

- 3 ounces (90 g) Gorgonzola dolce
- 3 ounces (90 g) cream cheese, softened
- 2 tablespoons unsalted butter, softened
- 2 heads Belgian endive (witloof chicory)
- 12 button mushrooms, thinly sliced
- 4 apricots, pitted and sliced, or soaked dried apricots, sliced
- 1 tablespoon walnut oil
- 2 teaspoons freshly squeezed lemon juice
- Salt and freshly ground black pepper
- 2 tablespoons toasted walnuts, crushed

Dressing

- 1 teaspoon Dijon mustard
- 1 tablespoon white wine vinegar
- 3 tablespoons reduced-fat sour cream
- Fresh lemon juice

Nutritional Facts
Amount per serving
Percentage of Daily Values
based on 2,000 calories

 CALORIES 522 25%

 PROTEIN 10g 22%

 FAT 39g

 FIBER 2.7

 SALT 1g 8%

Serves: 4
Preparation: 30 minutes + 2 hours to chill
Level: 2

THREE-BEAN SALAD WITH ASPARAGUS

Salad: Cook the fava beans in a pan of unsalted boiling water and simmer for 3–4 minutes. Drain, refresh in cold water, and peel off their tough skins. If using frozen beans, cook according to instructions on the package. Set aside. • Cook the green beans in a medium pan of salted boiling water until crunchy tender, 4–6 minutes. Drain, rinse in cold water, and set aside. • Cook the snow peas in a small pan of salted boiling water for 2 minutes. Drain, rinse under cold water, and set aside. • Blanch the asparagus spears in salted boiling water until just tender, 4–5 minutes. Drain and let cool.

Dressing: Chop the basil, vinegar, oil, garlic, salt, and pepper in a blender. Transfer to a small bowl. • Combine the vegetables, borlotti or red kidney beans, olives, and cheese in a salad bowl. Drizzle with the dressing. • Toss lightly. Sprinkle with the basil and serve.

Salad

1	pound (500 g) fava (broad) beans in shells, or 8 ounces (250 g) frozen beans
8	ounces (250 g) green beans, trimmed
5	ounces (150 g) snow peas (mangetout), trimmed
16	green asparagus spears, trimmed
1	(14-ounce/400-g) can borlotti or red kidney beans, drained
15	black olives, pitted
8	ounces (250 g) feta or mozzarella cheese, cut into small cubes
5	basil leaves, torn

Dressing

1/4	cup (25 g) basil
2	tablespoons white wine vinegar
1/3	cup (90 ml) extra-virgin olive oil
1	clove garlic, peeled
	Salt and freshly ground black pepper

Nutritional Facts
Amount per serving
Percentage of Daily Values
based on 2,000 calories

CALORIES	PROTEIN	FAT	FIBER	SALT
381	20g	25g	12g	2.2g
8	3%	5	5	3

Serves: 6
Preparation: 30 minutes
Cooking: 13–17 minutes
Level: 1

WINTER ROOT VEGETABLE SALAD

Salad: Cut the parsnips lengthwise into halves or quarters, depending on size, and then into 2-inch (5-cm) pieces.
• Keep the skin on the potatoes and cut them into 6 wedges. • Top and tail the sweet potato, keep the skin on, and halve it widthwise. Cut each half into 3–4 wedges. • Preheat the oven to 350°F (180°C/gas 4). • Combine the parsnips, potato, sweet potato, and garlic in a large roasting pan. Sprinkle with the salt and drizzle with the oil. Mix to coat in the oil, spreading the vegetables out in the pan.
• Roast for 35–40 minutes, until the vegetables are golden, crisp on the outside and soft inside.

Dressing: While the vegetables are in the oven, make the dressing. Whisk the orange juice with the vinegar, oil, and honey in a bowl. • Finely chop the rosemary and add to the dressing. Season with salt and pepper. • Remove the roasting pan from the oven and

Salad

3	parsnips, peeled
6	medium potatoes, scrubbed clean
1	sweet potato, about 10 ounces (300 g), scrubbed clean
4	cloves garlic, peeled
1	teaspoon salt
1/4	cup (60 ml) canola (rapeseed) oil or extra-virgin olive oil
10	cherry tomatoes, halved
2	ripe pears
1	cup (50 g) arugula (rocket)

Dressing

- 1/3 **cup (90 ml) freshly squeezed orange juice + extra to drizzle**
- 2 **teaspoons balsamic vinegar**
- 2 **tablespoons extra-virgin olive oil**
- 1 **scant tablespoon wildflower or other honey**
- 3 **sprigs fresh rosemary, leaves only**

   Salt and freshly ground black pepper

Garnish

- 2 **tablespoons pine nuts, toasted**

Serves: 4
Preparation: 30 minutes
Cooking: 45–50 minutes
Level: 2

drizzle half the dressing over the vegetables. • Add the tomatoes and return to the oven. Roast for another 10 minutes. • Leave to cool slightly while preparing the pears. • Peel, core, and slice the pears into 6–8 pieces. Mix with the arugula in a bowl and toss with the remaining dressing. • Transfer the roasted vegetables with their juices to a large bowl. Top with the pears and arugula, and toss gently. • Arrange the salad on individual salad plates or in a large serving dish.

Garnish: Toast the pine nuts in a dry, nonstick pan over high heat for 1 minute. • Sprinkle over the salad and serve warm or at room temperature.

53

(See photograph on the following page.)

Nutritional Facts
Amount per serving
Percentage of Daily Values
based on 2,000 calories

CALORIES	PROTEIN	FAT	FIBER	SALT
466	6g	24g	7.8g	1.3g
22	3	C	1%	24

BOHEMIAN CUCUMBER AND GHERKIN SALAD

56

Salad: Lightly peel the cucumbers, removing the coarse skin only and leaving as much green as possible.
• Slice them thinly in a food processor with a blade attachment or use a potato peeler. • Spread out in a shallow bowl, sprinkle with salt, and tuck bits of the crushed garlic between the cucumber slices. Let drain for 30 minutes.
Dressing: Mix the sour cream with 1 tablespoon lemon juice, the sugar, paprika, salt, and most of the dill. Taste and add a little more paprika and lemon, if wanted. • Take the cucumber out of the water it has produced and place in a shallow serving bowl. Add the gherkin.
• Spoon the dressing over the top and toss lightly. Taste the salad for seasoning and sprinkle with the remaining dill. Serve immediately.

Salad

2   **cucumbers**
3/4   **teaspoon salt**
1   **clove garlic, crushed**
3   **pickled gherkins, thinly sliced**

Dressing

1/3   **cup (90 ml) sour cream**
1–2 tablespoons freshly squeezed lemon juice
     Pinch of sugar
     Pinch of paprika
     Salt
1   **tablespoon finely chopped fresh dill**

Serves: 4
Preparation: 10 minutes + 30 minutes to rest
Level: 1

Nutritional Facts
Amount per serving
Percentage of Daily Values
based on 2,000 calories

 CALORIES **45** 2%
 PROTEIN **1g**
 FAT **4g**
 FIBER **0.5g**
 SALT **1g**

CORINTHIAN APPLE, PINEAPPLE, AND SAUERKRAUT SALAD

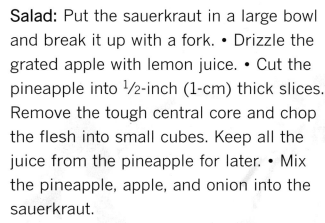

58

Salad: Put the sauerkraut in a large bowl and break it up with a fork. • Drizzle the grated apple with lemon juice. • Cut the pineapple into 1/2-inch (1-cm) thick slices. Remove the tough central core and chop the flesh into small cubes. Keep all the juice from the pineapple for later. • Mix the pineapple, apple, and onion into the sauerkraut.

Dressing: Whisk the oil, vinegar, cream, sugar, and salt in a small bowl. • Pour the dressing over the salad and toss well. Add more salt and white pepper, if needed. • Cover and marinate in the refrigerator for 30 minutes. • Taste again and adjust the seasoning. Stir in 1 tablespoon of the reserved pineapple juice, more vinegar, or a pinch of sugar, if wanted, before serving.

Salad

1 pound (500 g) sauerkraut, drained

1 large tart apple, peeled, cored, and coarsely grated

1 tablespoon freshly squeezed lemon juice

1 small pineapple, skin removed

1 onion, finely grated

Dressing

2 tablespoons grapeseed oil or sunflower oil

2 tablespoons white-wine vinegar + extra if needed

3 tablespoons half-and-half (single cream)

Pinch of sugar

Pinch of salt and freshly ground white pepper

1 tablespoon pineapple juice (optional)

Serves: 4
Preparation: 20 minutes + 30 minutes to marinate
Level: 1

Nutritional Facts
Amount per serving
Percentage of Daily Values
based on 2,000 calories

CALORIES	PROTEIN	FAT	FIBER	SALT
124	2g	6g	4.6g	2.4g

PESTO POTATO SALAD

Salad: Put the eggs in a saucepan, cover with cold water, and boil for 5 minutes. Refresh in cold water, peel, and set aside.
• Cover the potatoes in a medium pan with cold water, bring to a boil, and cook until tender, 12–18 minutes. Drain well and let cool a little. • Cut the potatoes in cubes and put them into a salad bowl.
Pesto: Combine the parsley, watercress, garlic, cheese, and pine nuts in a food processor and chop until smooth. • Slowly add the oil and pulse until you have a runny paste. • Pour the pesto over the potatoes. Stir in the capers, half the parsley, and lemon juice. Add the water if the potatoes are too dry. Season with salt and plenty of pepper. • Coarsely chop the eggs and gently mix into the salad. Garnish with the remaining parsley.
• Serve warm or at room temperature.

Salad

3   large eggs
1³/4 pounds (800 g) small waxy salad potatoes, scrubbed
2   tablespoons capers
2   tablespoons finely chopped fresh parsley leaves
1   tablespoon freshly squeezed lemon juice
1   tablespoon warm water (optional)
     Salt and freshly ground black pepper

Pesto

1   cup (50 g) fresh parsley leaves
1/2 cup (25 g) watercress leaves
1   large clove garlic
     Salt
1/4 cup (30 g) freshly grated Parmesan
1/3 cup (60 g) pine nuts
2/3 cup (150 ml) extra-virgin olive oil

Serves: 6
Preparation: 30 minutes
Cooking: 20–25
Level: 2

Nutritional Facts
Amount per serving
Percentage of Daily Values
based on 2,000 calories

 CALORIES 445 / 2
 PROTEIN 10g / 22
 FAT 35g / 4
 FIBER 2.8g /
 SALT 0.2g /

WHITE ASPARAGUS SPRING SALAD

Bring a large pan of salted water to a boil with the sugar and add the asparagus. Cook until tender, 4–6 minutes. Drain, refresh in cold water, and set aside. • Peel 2 oranges and remove the pith. Divide into segments, removing the seeds and catching any juice in a small bowl. Place the segments on a plate. • Put the snow peas in a colander and pour boiling water over them. Rinse in cold water and drain. • Squeeze the remaining orange and combine the juice with the reserved juice. Whisk in 2 tablespoons of oil and a pinch of sugar. Season with salt and pepper and stir in the shallot. • Warm the remaining 1 tablespoon oil in a small frying pan and stir in the walnuts. Fry over medium heat until golden, 1–2 minutes. • Place the salad greens on four plates and top with the oranges and asparagus. • Drizzle with the dressing and sprinkle with walnuts.

1 teaspoon sugar

1³/4 pounds (800 g) white (or green) asparagus, trimmed

3 oranges

3 ounces (100 g) snow peas (mangetout), trimmed

3 tablespoons Asian sesame oil or sunflower oil

Salt and freshly ground black pepper

1 shallot, finely chopped

1 cup (100 g) walnuts

2 cups (100 g) mixed peppery salad greens, such as watercress, mizuna, radicchio, or arugula (rocket)

Serves: 4
Preparation: 30 minutes
Cooking: 5–8 minutes
Level: 1

Nutritional Facts
Amount per serving
Percentage of Daily Values
based on 2,000 calories

 CALORIES 334 16%
 PROTEIN 12g 26%
 FAT 25g 31%
 FIBER 7g 28%
 SALT 0.1g 1%

SUMMER LEEKS IN VINAIGRETTE

Leeks: Bring a large saucepan of water with the salt to a boil. Add the leeks and cook until tender, 6–8 minutes. • Refresh in a bowl of iced water. Place the leeks on paper towels to drain, gently pressing on them to squeeze out any water.

• Ladle some cooking liquid for the vinaigrette into a measuring cup or jug, both to measure and to cool.

Vinaigrette: Pour the vinegar and oil into a screw-top jar. Add the sugar, mustard, and $2/3$ cup (150 ml) leek-cooking liquid. Put on the lid and shake vigorously to combine. • Transfer to a small bowl and season generously with pepper. • Mix in the olives, sun-dried tomatoes, and parsley. • Cut the leeks into pieces about 3 inches (8 cm) long. • Arrange on a serving dish and pour the vinaigrette over the top.

64

Leeks
1   teaspoon salt
6   thin leeks, trimmed and green outer leaves discarded

Vinaigrette
2   tablespoons white wine vinegar
$1/3$ cup (90 ml) extra-virgin olive oil
    Pinch of sugar
1   teaspoon Dijon mustard
    Freshly ground black pepper
$1/2$ cup (50 g) pitted black olives, chopped
2   ounces (50 g) oil-packed sun-dried tomatoes, drained and chopped
3   tablespoons finely chopped fresh parsley

Serves: 4
Preparation: 10–15 minutes
Cooking: 6–8 minutes
Level: 1

Nutritional Facts
Amount per serving
Percentage of Daily Values
based on 2,000 calories

CALORIES	PROTEIN	FAT	FIBER	SALT
251	4g	23g	5.3g	1.6g

BEET, FAVA BEAN, AND GOAT CHEESE SALAD

Salad: Put the beets in a pan of cold salted water and boil until tender, 30–50 minutes, depending on size. • Drain, put under cold running water, and rub off the skins while still warm. • Boil the beans in unsalted water until tender, 3–4 minutes. Drain and refresh in cold water. Peel off the tough skins of the large beans by gently squeezing with your fingertips. • Season the goat cheese with salt, pepper, and a squeeze of lemon juice.

Dressing: Whisk the oil, vinegar, sugar, and salt in a small bowl. • Cut the beets into thin wedges. Put in a bowl and toss with the dressing. Add the beans, scallions, and tarragon, and toss again. • Arrange the salad greens on a serving dish with the beets and beans. Drizzle with a little oil and a generous squeeze of lemon juice. Top with the goat cheese.

Salad

1   pound (500 g) beets (beetroot), trimmed and gently scrubbed

1¹/₃ cups (200 g) shelled fava (broad) beans or frozen fava (broad) beans

¹/₃ cup (100 g) chèvre or other fresh goat cheese, crumbled

   Salt and freshly ground black pepper

1   lemon, halved

5   scallions (spring onions), thinly sliced

2   tablespoons coarsely chopped fresh tarragon

1   cup (50 g) mixed salad greens

Dressing

¹/₄ cup (60 ml) extra-virgin olive oil + extra to drizzle

1   tablespoon balsamic vinegar

   Pinch of sugar

   Salt

Nutritional Facts

Amount per serving
Percentage of Daily Values
based on 2,000 calories

CALORIES
165
8%

PROTEIN
6g
13%

FAT
11g
14%

FIBER
2.7g
11%

SALT
0.3g
6%

Serves: 6
Preparation: 20 minutes
Cooking: 33–54 minutes
Level: 1

MINTED RADISH AND GOAT CHEESE SALAD

Dressing: Combine the cream, yogurt, chopped mint, and parsley in a bowl and whisk well. Add the lemon juice, salt, and white pepper. Transfer to a small serving bowl, garnish with mint leaves, and chill until needed.

Salad: Peel the cucumber lightly, to remove the coarse skin only, leaving as much green as possible. Cut in half lengthwise and scrape out the seeds with a teaspoon. Halve each half lengthwise again, and cut into 1½-inch (4-cm) pieces. Put into a large salad bowl.

• Slice the radishes to a thickness of ¼ inch (5 mm) or thinner, or cut into 6 wedges, and add to the cucumber.

• Slice the onion thinly and separate into rings. Add to the bowl. • Tear the mint leaves into the bowl. Mix in the parsley leaves and the cheese. • Drizzle with oil

Dressing

⅓ cup (90 ml) heavy (double) cream

¼ cup (60 ml) plain nonfat yogurt

3 tablespoons finely chopped fresh mint leaves + 3–4 mint leaves to garnish

1 tablespoon finely chopped fresh parsley

1 teaspoon freshly squeezed lemon juice

Salt and freshly ground white pepper

Salad

1 medium cucumber

12 radishes (1 large bunch), trimmed

½ red onion, peeled

68

Handful of fresh
mint leaves

1/4 cup (15 g) (1 small
bunch) flat-leaf
parsley leaves

1/3 cup (100 g)
crumbled soft fresh
goat cheese

3 tablespoons extra-
virgin olive oil

1 scant tablespoon red
wine vinegar

Freshly ground black
pepper

Crusty, freshly
baked bread,
to serve

and vinegar, and top with freshly ground black pepper. • Mix everything together. • Serve the salad with crusty, freshly baked bread and pass the dressing in a bowl on the side for everybody to help themselves.

69

Serves: 4
Preparation: 15 minutes
Level: 1

(See photograph on the following page.)

Nutritional Facts
Amount per serving
Percentage of Daily Values
based on 2,000 calories

 CALORIES **250**

 PROTEIN **6g**

 FAT **23g**

 FIBER **1.8g**

 SALT **0.3g**

DANDELION AND GARDEN FLOWERS WITH QUAIL EGGS

Put the quail eggs in a saucepan, cover with cold water, and boil for 2 minutes. Refresh in cold water and set aside. • Put all the leaves and flowers in a shallow glass bowl. Sprinkle with the lemon zest and Parmesan, and season with salt and pepper. Drizzle with the lemon juice and grapeseed oil and lightly toss with your fingers. • Top with the eggs and serve.

8 quail eggs

1 cup (50 g) arugula (rocket) or lamb's lettuce

1 cup (50 g) young dandelion leaves, torn

Handful of red radicchio or purple basil

20 borage flowers

1 rose, petals only

1/2 cup (25 g) arugula

15 nasturtiums

4 dill fronds

4 fennel fronds

Marigold petals

Zest of 1 lemon, finely chopped

2 tablespoons freshly grated Parmesan

Salt and freshly ground black pepper

Freshly squeezed juice of 1/2 lemon

3 tablespoons grapeseed oil

Serves: 4
Preparation: 15 minutes
Cooking: 2 minutes
Level: 1

Nutritional Facts
Amount per serving
Percentage of Daily Values
based on 2,000 calories

CALORIES
194
9%

PROTEIN
10g
22%

FAT
17g
21%

FIBER
0.6g
2%

SALT
0.1
2%

VEGETARIAN SALADE NIÇOISE

Salad: Put the eggs in a small saucepan, cover with cold water, and bring to a boil. Decrease the heat to medium and gently simmer for 6 minutes. Drain and cool under cold running water. Peel and quarter. • Steam the potatoes for 10–15 minutes, until tender. Cut in half and set aside. • Meanwhile, bring a medium saucepan of water to a boil, add the beans, and blanch until just tender, 2–3 minutes. • Combine the eggs, potatoes, and green beans in a medium bowl and add the tomatoes, artichokes, onion, olives, and parsley.

Dressing: Whisk together the lemon juice, oil, garlic, and mustard in a small bowl. Season with salt and pepper. • Drizzle the dressing over the salad, toss to combine, and serve.

Salad

- 4 large eggs
- 8 ounces (250 g) baby potatoes
- 8 ounces (250 g) green beans, trimmed
- 3 tomatoes, quartered
- 3 marinated artichokes, quartered
- 1 red onion, sliced
- 1/4 cup (25 g) small black olives
- 1/4 cup fresh flat-leaf parsley leaves

Dressing

- 2 tablespoons freshly squeezed lemon juice
- 2 tablespoons extra-virgin olive oil
- 1 clove garlic, finely chopped
- 1/2 teaspoon Dijon mustard

  Salt and freshly ground black pepper

Nutritional Facts
Amount per serving
Percentage of Daily Values
based on 2,000 calories

 CALORIES 248
 PROTEIN 14g
 FAT 14g
 FIBER 3.5g
 SALT 0.4g

Serves: 4
Preparation: 15 minutes
Cooking: 18–24 minutes
Level: 1

RAW ENERGY SALAD

Salad: Toast the pumpkin, sunflower, sesame, and cumin seeds in a medium frying pan over medium heat until golden brown, 3–5 minutes. • Combine the red cabbage, carrot, beet, spinach, onion, currants, mint, and toasted seeds in a large salad bowl.

Dressing: Whisk the orange zest and juice, pomegranate molasses, and oil in a small bowl. Pour over the salad and toss to combine. Season with salt and pepper and serve.

Salad

- ¼ cup (45 g) pumpkin seeds
- ¼ cup (45 g) sunflower seeds
- 2 tablespoons sesame seeds
- 2 teaspoons cumin seeds
- ¼ red cabbage, finely shredded
- 1 large carrot, grated
- 1 cooked beet (beetroot), grated
- 2 cups (100 g) baby spinach leaves, finely chopped
- 1 red onion, thinly sliced
- ¼ cup (45 g) dried currants
- 3 tablespoons finely chopped fresh mint

Dressing

- Finely grated zest and juice of 1 orange
- 3 tablespoons pomegranate molasses
- 1 tablespoon extra-virgin olive oil
- Salt and freshly ground black pepper

Nutritional Facts
Amount per serving
Percentage of Daily Values
based on 2,000 calories

 CALORIES 270 13%
 PROTEIN 9g 20%
 FAT 18g 22%
 FIBER 5g 20%
 SALT 0.2g 3%

Serves: 4
Preparation: 15 minutes
Cooking: 3–5 minutes
Level: 1

FRUIT AND NUT QUINOA SALAD

Combine the water and quinoa in a medium saucepan and bring to a boil. Decrease the heat to low, cover, and cook until all the water is absorbed, 15 minutes. Fluff the grains with a fork and transfer to a medium bowl. • Add the apricots, almonds, pistachios, raisins, currants, mint, cilantro, lemon zest and juice, oil, orange zest, and cinnamon. Stir to combine. Season with salt and pepper and serve.

2	cups (500 ml) water
2	cups (400 g) quinoa, rinsed
1¹/₂	cups (270 g) dried apricots, sliced
¹/₃	cup (50 g) almonds, coarsely chopped
¹/₃	cup (50 g) pistachios
¹/₄	cup (45 g) raisins
¹/₄	cup (45 g) currants
2	tablespoons finely chopped fresh mint
2	tablespoons finely chopped fresh cilantro (coriander)
	Finely grated zest and juice of 1 lemon
2	tablespoons extra-virgin olive oil
1	teaspoon finely grated orange zest
¹/₂	teaspoon ground cinnamon
	Salt and freshly ground black pepper

Serves: 4
Preparation: 15 minutes
Cooking: 15 minutes
Level: 1

Nutritional Facts
Amount per serving
Percentage of Daily Values
based on 2,000 calories

 CALORIES 700 34%
 PROTEIN 23g 50%
 FAT 25g 31%
 FIBER 16g 64%
 SALT 0.4g 7%

SPELT SALAD WITH TOMATOES, CORN, AND CAPERS

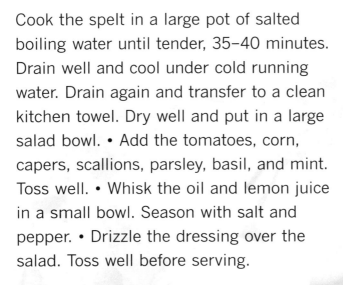

Cook the spelt in a large pot of salted boiling water until tender, 35–40 minutes. Drain well and cool under cold running water. Drain again and transfer to a clean kitchen towel. Dry well and put in a large salad bowl. • Add the tomatoes, corn, capers, scallions, parsley, basil, and mint. Toss well. • Whisk the oil and lemon juice in a small bowl. Season with salt and pepper. • Drizzle the dressing over the salad. Toss well before serving.

1	pound (500 g) spelt (or pearl barley)
24	cherry tomatoes, halved
1	cup (150 g) canned corn (sweet corn), drained
2	tablespoons capers preserved in brine, drained
2	scallions (spring onions), trimmed and sliced
1	tablespoon finely chopped fresh parsley
1	tablespoon finely chopped fresh basil
1½	teaspoons finely chopped fresh mint
⅓	cup (90 ml) extra-virgin olive oil
	Freshly squeezed juice of 1 lemon
	Salt and freshly ground black pepper

Serves: 4
Preparation: 15 minutes
Cooking: 35–40 minutes
Level: 1

Nutritional Facts
Amount per serving
Percentage of Daily Values
based on 2,000 calories

 CALORIES **690** 35

 PROTEIN **12g** 26

 FAT **23g** 28

 FIBER **9.9g**

 SALT **0.4g**

BULGUR SALAD WITH SNOW PEAS AND HERBS

Combine the bulgur and 2–3 pinches of salt in a medium bowl and pour the boiling water in over the top. Stir gently, then cover with a clean cloth. Let stand until the bulgur is tender, 20–25 minutes. • While the bulgur is soaking, boil the snow peas in a small saucepan of lightly salted water until tender, 5–7 minutes. Drain and let cool. • Squeeze any excess water out of the bulgur and put into a salad bowl. • Add the snow peas, scallions, cucumber, tomatoes, onion, parsley, and mint. Toss gently. • Beat the oil, lemon juice, salt, and pepper in a small bowl. Drizzle over the salad and toss gently. • Chill the salad in the refrigerator for 1 hour before serving.

1 cup (150 g) medium bulgur

Salt

2¹/2 cups (625 ml) boiling water

4 ounces (125 g) snow peas (mangetout), trimmed and thinly sliced

2 scallions (spring onions), trimmed and thinly sliced

1 cucumber, peeled and finely diced

2 ripe tomatoes, cut into small dice

1 small sweet red onion, finely chopped

4 tablespoons finely chopped fresh parsley

1 tablespoon finely chopped fresh mint

¹/4 cup (60 ml) extra-virgin olive oil

Freshly squeezed juice of 1 lemon

Freshly ground black pepper

Nutritional Facts
Amount per serving
Percentage of Daily Values
based on 2,000 calories

CALORIES
280
13%

PROTEIN
6g
13%

FAT
13g
16%

FIBER
9.2g
37%

SALT
0.7g
13%

Serves: 4
Preparation: 35 minutes
+ 1 hour to chill
Cooking: 5–7 minutes
Level: 1

BAKED RICE SALAD

Preheat the oven to 350°F (180°C/gas 4).
• Stud the onion with the cloves. • Heat 2
tablespoons of oil in a Dutch oven over medium
heat. Add the onion and sauté until transparent,
3–4 minutes. • Stir in the rice, bay leaf, and
broth. Cover and bake for about 20 minutes,
until the rice has absorbed the broth and is al
dente. Let cool. • Cook the green beans in
salted boiling water until tender, 5–7 minutes.
Drain. • Cook the peas in salted boiling water
until tender, 3–5 minutes. Drain. • Preheat the
broiler (grill) to high. Grill the bell pepper until
charred all over, 10 minutes. Put in a plastic
bag, seal, and let rest for 10 minutes. Peel off
the skin and remove the seeds. Wipe clean with
paper towels and slice thinly. • Blend the
gherkins, capers, remaining oil, and vinegar in a
food processor until smooth. • Put the rice in a
salad bowl. Discard the onion, cloves, and bay
leaf. Add the green beans, peas, corn, pepper,
and arugula. • Toss gently with the dressing.

84

1	small onion
3	cloves
6	tablespoons extra-virgin olive oil
1¹/₂	cups (300 g) short-grain rice
1	bay leaf
	Generous 2¹/₃ cups (600 ml) vegetable broth, boiling
1	cup (150 g) frozen chopped green beans
1	cup (150 g) frozen peas
1	large red bell pepper (capsicum)
6	pickled gherkins, drained
1	tablespoon salt-cured capers, rinsed
3	tablespoons white wine vinegar
	Salt
1	cup (150 g) canned corn (sweet corn), drained
2	cups (100 g) arugula (rocket)

Serves: 4
Preparation: 30 minutes
Cooking: 45–60 minutes
Level: 2

Nutritional Facts
Amount per serving
Percentage of Daily Values
based on 2,000 calories

 CALORIES **560** 27%

 PROTEIN **12g** 26%

 FAT **24g** 30%

 FIBER **5g** 20%

 SALT **1.8g** 32%

PASTA SALAD WITH FETA AND OLIVES

86

Combine the tomatoes, onion, garlic, feta, oil, basil, mint, and lemon zest in a large salad bowl. Toss well and season with salt and pepper. Let rest for 30 minutes. • Cook the pasta in a large pot of salted boiling water until al dente. • Drain well and cool under cold running water. Drain again and dry on a clean kitchen towel. • Add the pasta to the bowl with the dressing. Add the olives and toss well. • Garnish with basil and serve.

1¹/₂ pounds (750 g) cherry tomatoes, quartered

1   small red onion, thinly sliced

1   clove garlic, finely chopped

8   ounces (250 g) feta cheese, cut into small cubes

¹/₃ cup (90 ml) extra-virgin olive oil

1   tablespoon finely chopped fresh basil + extra leaves to garnish

1   tablespoon finely chopped fresh mint

Finely grated zest of 1 lemon

Salt and freshly ground black pepper

1   pound (500 g) penne or other short pasta

1   cup (100 g) black olives, pitted

Serves: 6
Preparation: 15 minutes + 30 minutes to rest
Cooking: 15 minutes
Level: 1

Nutritional Facts
Amount per serving
Percentage of Daily Values
based on 2,000 calories

 CALORIES 500 24

 PROTEIN 17g 37

 FAT 26g

 FIBER 2.5g

 SALT 2.4g

ROAST BEETS WITH BALSAMIC VINEGAR

If the beets have their greens attached, remove them and set aside. • Preheat the oven to 400°F (200°C/gas 6). • Place the beets in a large bowl and drizzle with the oil. Toss well. Place in a baking dish. Cover with foil and roast for 30–45 minutes (depending on size) until tender. • Remove from the oven and let cool a little. Peel and discard the skin. Slice lengthwise and season with salt and pepper. • Heat 1 tablespoon of butter in a large frying pan over medium heat. Add the beet greens and toss until wilted, 1–2 minutes. Set aside. • Add the balsamic vinegar to the pan and bring to a boil. Whisk in the remaining butter. Add the beets to the pan and toss until the beets are covered in a shiny sheen. • Transfer to a bowl and top with the wilted leaves. Sprinkle with the dill and hazelnuts.

18 small beets (beetroots), with peel, green stems attached if possible

3 tablespoons extra-virgin olive oil

Salt and freshly ground black pepper

2 tablespoons butter

2 tablespoons balsamic vinegar

3 tablespoons fresh dill, snipped

1/2 cup (70 g) hazelnuts, roasted and chopped

Serves: 6
Preparation: 15 minutes
Cooking: 30–45 minutes
Level: 1

Nutritional Facts
Amount per serving
Percentage of Daily Values
based on 2,000 calories

 CALORIES **215** 10%
 PROTEIN **3g** 7%
 FAT **20g** 25%
 FIBER **1.9g** 8%
 SALT **0.2g** 4%

SOUPS

SPICY PUMPKIN AND CHILE SOUP

Melt the butter in a large soup pot over medium-low heat. Add the onion and garlic and sauté until softened, 3–4 minutes. • Add the pumpkin, potato, and chiles. Cook until the pumpkin turns golden at the edges, 5–6 minutes. • Toast the coriander and cumin in a small pan over low heat until fragrant, 1–2 minutes. Grind with a pestle and mortar. • Stir the toasted spices, red pepper flakes, and paprika into the pumpkin mixture and simmer for 1–2 minutes. • Add the broth, cover, and simmer until the pumpkin is tender, about 20 minutes. • Purée the soup in a food processor. Return to the pan and stir in the lime juice. Season with salt and pepper, and additional pepper flakes for extra spice, if desired. • Reheat the soup gently and stir in most of the cilantro. • Sprinkle with the remaining cilantro, add a swirl of yogurt, and serve.

¹⁄₄	cup (60 g) butter
1	large onion, chopped
2	cloves garlic, sliced
2	pounds (1 kg) pumpkin or butternut squash, peeled, seeded, and cubed
1	potato or sweet potato, diced
1	mild green chile, seeded and sliced
1	fresh red chile, seeded and sliced
2	teaspoons whole coriander seeds
1	tablespoon cumin seeds
1	teaspoon crushed red pepper flakes
1	teaspoon smoked paprika (pimentòn)
5	cups (1.25 liters) vegetable broth
	Freshly squeezed juice of 1 lime
	Salt and freshly ground black pepper
2	tablespoons chopped fresh cilantro (coriander)
2	tablespoons plain yogurt, optional

Serves: 6
Preparation: 20 minutes
Cooking: 40 minutes
Level 1

Nutritional Facts
Amount per serving
Percentage of Daily Values
based on 2,000 calories

CALORIES	PROTEIN	FAT	FIBER	SALT
128	2g	9g	2.3g	0.5g

CHILLED SPANISH ALMOND SOUP

Crush the garlic and sea salt to a paste with a pestle and mortar. • Finely grind the almonds in a food processor. Add half the water and the vinegar and process briefly, until combined. • Add the bread crumbs to the paste. Blend for 1–2 minutes, until smooth. Continue to blend while adding the oil and garlic. • Pour in the remaining water and blend until you have a creamy liquid. • Transfer to a serving bowl and season with salt, white pepper, and more vinegar, to taste. • Chill the soup for at least 1 hour or up to 2 hours. Serve in individual bowls with the grapes evenly distributed. Sprinkle each bowl with almond flakes.

3	cloves garlic, peeled
1	teaspoon coarse sea salt
1¹/₄ cups (200 g)	blanched almonds
2²/₃ cups (650 ml) iced water	
¹/₄	cup (60 ml) sherry vinegar or white wine vinegar + more as needed
1	cup (75 g) fresh bread crumbs
3	tablespoons extra-virgin olive oil
	Salt and freshly ground white pepper
20	seedless green grapes (Muscat preferably), halved
2	tablespoons toasted almond flakes, to sprinkle

Serves: 4
Preparation: 10 minutes + 1–2 hours to chill
Level: 1

■ ■ ■ *Ajo blanco is a kind of white gazpacho from Andalusia. Invented by the Moors, it was traditionally made by pounding the ingredients together, but a food processor makes light work of this refreshing soup.*

Nutritional Facts
Amount per serving
Percentage of Daily Values
based on 2,000 calories

CALORIES	PROTEIN	FAT	FIBER	SALT
177	177	177	177	177
9				9%

PEA SOUP WITH MINT PESTO TOASTS

Soup: Heat the oil in a soup pot over medium heat. Add the onions and sauté until softened, 3–4 minutes. Stir in the garlic, leek, potato, curry powder, and lemon zest and simmer over low heat for 5 minutes. • Add the peas and broth. Bring to a boil, then cover the pan. Simmer until the potato is soft, 10–15 minutes. Remove from the heat and stir in the mint.

Mint Pesto Toasts: Chop the pine nuts, mint, parsley, garlic, and oil in a food processor until puréed. Transfer to a small bowl and stir in the pecorino. Add a pinch of salt. Cover with plastic wrap (cling film) and refrigerate. • Purée the soup in a food processor until smooth. • Return to the pot and stir in the cream. Gently reheat. • Spread the pesto on the toasts and float on the soup. Serve hot.

Soup

- 2 tablespoons extra-virgin olive oil
- 2 onions, chopped
- 2 small cloves garlic, coarsely chopped
- 1 leek, finely chopped
- 1 potato, peeled and diced
- 1/2 teaspoon curry powder
- 1/2 teaspoon finely grated lemon zest
- 1 pound (500 g) frozen peas, thawed
- 2 cups (500 ml) vegetable broth
- 3 tablespoons chopped fresh mint
- 1/4 cup (60 ml) cream
- Salt

Mint Pesto Toasts

- 2 tablespoons pine nuts
- 1/2 cup (25 g) fresh mint
- 1/2 cup (25 g) fresh parsley
- 1 clove garlic, peeled
- 1/4 cup (60 ml) extra-virgin olive oil
- 2 tablespoons freshly grated pecorino
- Baguette (French loaf) sliced and toasted

Serves: 6
Preparation: 20 minutes
Cooking: 25 minutes
Level: 1

Nutritional Facts
Amount per serving
Percentage of Daily Values
based on 2,000 calories

 CALORIES 300 14

 PROTEIN 9g 20

 FAT 22g 7

 FIBER 7.6g 30

SALT 0.6g

SUN-BLUSHED VICHYSSOISE

Melt the butter in a large soup pot over medium heat. Add the leeks, onion, and sweet potato and sauté until softened, 4–5 minutes. • Stir in the chile, salt, and broth. Cover the pan and bring to a boil. Decrease the heat and simmer with the lid half on, until the vegetables are soft, about 20 minutes. Remove from the heat and let cool. • Purée in batches in a food processor or push through a fine strainer. Let cool. • Whisk in the cream mixture (leaving a little to garnish) and season with white pepper. The soup should be light and creamy. If it is too thick, add a little iced water. • Chill for at least 1 hour before serving. Sprinkle with chives and garnish with the reserved cream mixture.

■ ■ ■ *This classic soup was created by a French chef in New York in the early 20th century. The chef, who grew up near Vichy in France, based his recipe on one of his mother's soups. This version uses sweet potatoes, which gives it a sun-blushed look.*

Nutritional Facts

Amount per serving
Percentage of Daily Values
based on 2,000 calories

 CALORIES **256** 12%
 PROTEIN **4g** 9%
 FAT **19g** 23%
 FIBER **3.7g** 15%
 SALT **1.3g** 24%

1/4 cup (60 g) unsalted butter

3 large leeks (white part only), cut into quarters lengthwise and thinly sliced

1 small (mild) red onion, chopped

1 large sweet potato (about 14 ounces/ 400 g, peeled and cut into 1/2-inch (1-cm) cubes

1 mild green chile, seeded and thinly sliced

1 teaspoon salt

5 cups (1.25 liters) vegetable broth

2/3 cup (150 ml) sour cream mixed with 2/3 cup (150 ml) light (single) cream, or 1 1/3 cups (300 ml) light (single) cream

White pepper

2 tablespoons snipped fresh chives

Serves: 6
Preparation: 15 minutes
Cooking: 25 minutes
Level: 1

FAVA BEAN, PASTA, AND GRILLED BELL PEPPER SOUP

If the fava beans are big, remove the tough skins: Put the beans in a pan of boiling water, bring to a simmer, and drain at once. Refresh under cold water, let dry a little, then press gently to slip off the skin. • Place the bell pepper halves skin side up under a very hot broiler (grill) until blackened. Put in a plastic bag and leave for 10 minutes. • Peel off the charred skin. Cut the peppers into thin strips and set aside. • Heat the oil in a large pan over medium heat. Add the onion and sauté until just golden, about 5 minutes. • Add the beans and peas and sauté for 2 minutes. Pour in the broth, bring to a boil, and simmer over low heat until tender, 10–12 minutes. • Add the pasta, bring back to a boil, and simmer for 2 minutes. • Stir in the bell peppers and season with salt and pepper. Serve with Parmesan sprinkled on top.

1 pound (500 g) shelled fresh fava (broad) beans (about 3 pounds/ 1.5 kg in pods)

1 large or 2 small red bell peppers (capsicums), halved lengthwise and seeded

2 tablespoons light extra-virgin olive oil

2 medium onions, finely chopped

1 cup (150 g) frozen peas

4 cups (1 liter) vegetable broth, warmed

2 cups (100 g) cooked pasta, chopped if large or long

Salt and freshly ground black pepper

Freshly grated Parmesan cheese

Serves: 6
Preparation: 30 minutes
Cooking: 30 minutes
Level: 2

Nutritional Facts
Amount per serving
Percentage of Daily Values
based on 2,000 calories

 CALORIES 153

 PROTEIN 8g

 FAT 5g

 FIBER 7.5g

 SALT 0.3g

PORTUGUESE CALDO VERDE WITH CROUTONS

Soup: Heat the oil in a large soup pot over medium heat. Add the onion, garlic, carrots, celery, salt, and paprika. Decrease the heat, cover the pan, and sweat the vegetables until almost tender, 8–10 minutes, stirring once or twice. • Add the potatoes and water. Bring to a boil, cover, and simmer over low heat until tender, about 15 minutes. • Place the cabbage in a colander and pour boiling water over to wilt. Set aside. • Purée the soup with a handheld blender until almost smooth. • Add the cabbage and bring back to a boil. Simmer until the cabbage is tender, 6–8 minutes. • Season with salt and pepper.

Croutons: Sauté the bread in the butter over medium heat until golden, 3–4 minutes. Season with salt and pepper. • Ladle the soup into bowls and top with the croutons. Garnish with parsley.

Soup

- 1 tablespoon extra-virgin olive oil
- 1 medium onion, coarsely chopped
- 2 cloves garlic, finely chopped
- 2 carrots, cut into $1/2$-inch (1-cm) cubes
- 2 stalks celery, cut into small pieces
- 1 teaspoon salt
- $1/2$ teaspoon smoked paprika (pimentòn)
- $1 1/2$ pounds (750 g) potatoes, peeled and cut into small cubes
- 5 cups (1.25 liters) water
- 1 pound (500 g) kale or white cabbage, finely sliced
- Salt and freshly ground black pepper

Croutons

- 2 slices bread, cut into $1/2$-inch (1-cm) cubes
- $1/4$ cup (60 g) butter
- 2 tablespoons finely chopped fresh parsley

Nutritional Facts
Amount per serving
Percentage of Daily Values
based on 2,000 calories

CALORIES	PROTEIN	FAT	FIBER	SALT
254	6g	11g	6g	1.1g

Serves: 6
Preparation: 15 minutes
Cooking: 35–40 minutes
Level: 1

LENTIL SOUP WITH CUMIN AND SWISS CHARD

Wash the lentils and transfer to a large soup pot with the water. Bring to a boil, add the Parmesan rind, if using, and bay leaf, and simmer until tender, 30–40 minutes. • While the lentils are cooking, heat 3 tablespoons of the oil in a frying pan over medium heat. Add the onion and a pinch of salt and sauté until golden, 6–8 minutes. Stir in the cumin and set aside. • Separate the chard leaves from the stems and cut the stems into ½-inch (1-cm) pieces. • Bring a large pan of salted water to a boil and add the chard stems and leaves. Bring back to a boil quickly and simmer until tender, 2–3 minutes. Refresh in cold running water. Drain and squeeze gently to remove excess water. • Chop coarsely. • Heat the remaining 3 tablespoons of oil

2	cups (200 g) small brown or dark green lentils
5	cups (1.25 liters) water, + more if needed
	Parmesan rind (optional)
1	bay leaf
6	tablespoons (90 ml) extra-virgin olive oil
1	medium onion, thinly sliced
	Salt
1	teaspoon cumin seeds, coarsely ground
2	pounds (1 kg) Swiss chard (silverbeet)
3	cloves garlic, sliced
	Freshly ground black pepper
	Freshly squeezed juice of 1 lemon
	Pita bread, toasted and cut into squares, to serve

■ ■ ■ *You can make this Lebanese soup with spinach instead of chard. There is no need to blanch spinach, because the leaves are tender enough.*

in a large pan over medium heat. Add the garlic and sauté until golden, 3–4 minutes. • Add the chard and toss briefly in the oil. Season with salt and pepper and remove from the heat. • Remove the bay leaf and Parmesan rind from the cooked lentils. Add the fried onion to the pot and stir. • Purée the lentil mixture with a handheld blender or in a food processor until almost smooth. • Return to the soup pot, stir in the braised chard, and reheat over low heat. If the soup is too thick, add more hot water. • Stir in the lemon juice and season with salt and pepper. • Serve hot with the pita bread.

(See photograph on the following page.)

Nutritional Facts
Amount per serving
Percentage of Daily Values
based on 2,000 calories

CALORIES	PROTEIN	FAT	FIBER	SALT
390	17g	22g	5g	1.3g
9%			20	23%

CREAMY CHESTNUT SOUP

Preheat the oven to 400°F (200°C/gas 6).
• Combine the parsnips, onion, and apple
in a large roasting pan with the garlic,
peppercorns, fennel seeds, salt, and oil.
Mix, spread out in the pan, and dot with
butter. Roast for 30 minutes, until tender
but not browned. • If using fresh chestnuts,
score each one with a little cross. Place in
a separate baking pan and roast for 20
minutes. • Shell the chestnuts, cover to
keep moist, and set aside. • Stir $^3/_4$ cup
(200 ml) of the broth into the roasting
pan. Scrape the vegetables and juices into
a large soup pot. Add the chestnuts. Pour
in the remaining broth, bring to a boil, and
simmer for 10 minutes. • Purée in a food
processor, adding half the cream little by
little. Pass through a sieve set over the
rinsed-out pan. • Reheat gently with the
remaining cream. Season with salt and
pepper. • Top with parsley and lemon zest.

$1^1/_2$	pounds (750 g) parsnips, cut into small cubes
1	onion, cut into wedges
1	apple, peeled, cored, and cut into wedges
2	small cloves garlic
6	peppercorns, crushed
1	teaspoon fennel seeds, lightly crushed
1	teaspoon salt
1	tablespoon sunflower oil
2	tablespoons butter
26	chestnuts or 1 (7-ounce/200-g) package vacuum-packed peeled and cooked chestnuts
$2^1/_2$	cups (600 ml) vegetable broth
1	cup (250 ml) light (single) cream
	Salt and freshly ground black pepper
1	tablespoon finely chopped fresh parsley
1	teaspoon finely grated lemon zest

Serves: 4
Preparation: 30 minutes
Cooking: 45 minutes
Level: 2

Nutritional Facts
*Amount per serving
Percentage of Daily Values
based on 2,000 calories*

 CALORIES 411 30

 PROTEIN 7g 5

 FAT 29g 38

 FIBER 13.7g 55

 SALT 1.9g 34

FARMER'S CABBAGE SOUP WITH CARAWAY CROUTONS

110

Soup: Heat the oil in a large soup pot over medium heat, add the shallots, and sauté for 2 minutes. Stir in the caraway, chile, and garlic, and sauté for 1 minute. • Add the cabbage and stir until just wilted, 2–3 minutes. • Cover with the water, add the potato and salt, and simmer until tender, 10–15 minutes. Remove from the heat, then blend briefly with a handheld blender. • Return to the pot, stir in the cream, and simmer for 5 minutes over low heat. Add a little water if too thick. • Season with salt and pepper.

Croutons: Preheat the oven to 400°F (200°C/gas 6). Put the bread on a baking sheet. Drizzle with oil and sprinkle with caraway seeds, salt, and pepper. • Bake for 10–15 minutes, until golden and crisp. Turn halfway through the cooking time. Drain on paper towels. • Ladle the hot soup into bowls and top with croutons.

Soup

1/4	cup (60 ml) extra-virgin olive oil
2	shallots, sliced
1	teaspoon caraway seeds
1/2	mild fresh red chile, seeded and thinly sliced
1	clove garlic, sliced
1	small green or white cabbage, shredded
4	cups (1 liter) water, + more if needed
3	potatoes, peeled and cut into small cubes
1	teaspoon salt
1	cup (250 ml) light (single) cream
	Salt and freshly ground black pepper

Croutons

3	slices bread, cut into small cubes
3	tablespoons extra-virgin olive oil
1	tablespoon caraway seeds

Serves: 6
Preparation: 30 minutes
Cooking: 25–30 minutes
Level: 1

Nutritional Facts
Amount per serving
Percentage of Daily Values
based on 2,000 calories

CALORIES	PROTEIN	FAT	FIBER	SALT
326	7g	23g	4.9g	1g
16%				

TURKISH LEEK AND YOGURT SOUP

Flavored Butter: Beat the butter in a small bowl until light and fluffy. Mix in the garlic, paprika, red pepper flakes, mint, and lemon zest. Press into a log, wrap in plastic wrap (cling film), and chill until needed.

Soup: Heat the butter and oil in a large soup pot over medium heat. When the butter starts to bubble, stir in the leeks and sauté over low heat for 10 minutes. • Add the chiles and mint and simmer, stirring frequently, until the leeks are soft and sweet, 10–15 minutes. Remove from the heat. • Whisk the egg yolk into the cornstarch in a large bowl. Stir in the yogurt and add the lemon zest, half the lemon juice, water, and salt. Whisk until all the ingredients are combined (it should be the consistency of light cream). Thin with a little more water, if needed. • Add this mixture to the leeks in the soup pot. • Stir in the cooked rice,

Flavored Butter

2　tablespoons unsalted butter, softened

1/2　small clove garlic, crushed

1/2　teaspoon sweet paprika

1/4　teaspoon crushed red pepper flakes

2　teaspoons finely chopped fresh mint

1/2　teaspoon finely grated lemon zest

Soup

2　tablespoons butter

3　tablespoons extra-virgin olive oil

4　leeks, trimmed, cut in half lengthwise, and thinly sliced

2　green chiles, seeded and finely sliced, or 1 teaspoon crushed red pepper flakes

1　tablespoon finely chopped fresh mint, or 1 teaspoon dried mint

1　large egg yolk

1 1/2　teaspoons cornstarch (cornflour)

1¹/₃ cups (350 g) plain Greek-style yogurt

1 teaspoon finely grated lemon zest

2 tablespoons freshly squeezed lemon juice

2 cups (500 ml) water, + more if needed

¹/₂ teaspoon salt, + more if needed

¹/₂ cup (60–75 g) cooked white rice (optional, for a thicker soup)

Freshly ground black pepper

if using. Gently heat the soup over medium-low heat, stirring every now and then. Don't let the mixture boil. • Check the seasoning and add salt, pepper, and more lemon juice to taste. • To finish, melt the flavored butter in a small pan over low heat. • Drizzle the butter over the soup just before serving.

113

Serves: 4
Preparation: 15–20 minutes
Cooking: 25–30 minutes
Level: 1

(See photograph on the following page.)

Nutritional Facts
Amount per serving
Percentage of Daily Values
based on 2,000 calories

 CALORIES 310 — 5

 PROTEIN 3g — 7%

 FAT 30g — 7

 FIBER 3g — 2%

 SALT 0.3g — 5%

VIENNESE POTATO SOUP

Put the porcini in a small bowl with enough warm water to cover. Soak for 20 minutes. • Combine the potato, celery, and carrot in a large soup pot and add the remaining water and salt. • Chop the porcini and add to the pot with their soaking liquid. Bring to a boil and simmer until tender, about 20 minutes. • Melt the butter in a frying pan over medium heat. Add the onion and sauté until softened, 3–4 minutes. • Stir in the flour until a light brown paste forms, about 2 minutes. • Mix in the lemon zest, garlic, marjoram, and caraway seeds. Pour in a ladleful of the vegetable liquid, stirring until thickened. • Scrape the contents from the frying pan into the soup pot and mix in well. Simmer for 5 minutes. Season with salt and pepper. • Serve hot with sour cream and parsley.

1/2 ounce (15 g) dried porcini or ceps

5 cups (1.25 liters) hot water

1 teaspoon salt, + more if needed

4 large potatoes, peeled and cut into small cubes

2 celery stalks, sliced

1 carrot, diced

2 tablespoons butter

1 onion, finely chopped

1 tablespoon all-purpose (plain) flour

1 teaspoon finely grated lemon zest

1 clove garlic, sliced

1/4 teaspoon dried marjoram

1/2 teaspoon caraway seeds

Freshly ground black pepper

4 tablespoons sour cream

2 tablespoons finely chopped fresh parsley

Serves: 4
Preparation: 15–20 minutes + 20 minutes to soak
Cooking: 30–40 minutes
Level: 1

Nutritional Facts
Amount per serving
Percentage of Daily Values
based on 2,000 calories

CALORIES	PROTEIN	FAT	FIBER	SALT
374	7g	15g	5g	1.5g
8	5	9	20	27

SWEET BUTTERNUT SQUASH SOUP

Caramelized Squash Seeds: Preheat the oven to 375°F (190°C /gas 5). Cut the squash in half and scoop out the seeds, discarding the fibers. Rinse the seeds and dry on a clean cloth. • Mix all the seed ingredients in a small bowl. • Line a baking sheet with parchment paper and brush with sunflower oil. Spread the seeds out on the baking sheet and bake for 10–15 minutes, until golden. Let cool. **Soup:** Using about 1 tablespoon of butter, dot the insides of the squash halves. Season with salt and pepper, and place a sprig of marjoram in each. Place in a roasting pan, skin side up, and add ½ cup (125 ml) of water. Roast for 35–40 minutes, or until tender when pierced with a sharp knife. • Let cool slightly in the cooking juices. • Put the saffron in a small bowl, add 2 tablespoons of water, and set aside. • Heat the remaining butter in a

■ ■ ■ *The caramelized seeds add an extra sweet touch to this soup. Use butternut squash if buttercup or kuri is not available.*

Caramelized Squash Seeds

- ½ cup (60 g) butternut squash seeds (from squash below)
- 1 tablespoon maple syrup
- 1 teaspoon brown sugar
- ¼ teaspoon salt
- 1 tablespoon sunflower oil

  Pinch cayenne pepper

Soup

- 1 butternut squash or pumpkin (about 1½ pounds/750 g)
- 1 small buttercup or red kuri squash
- 3 tablespoons unsalted butter

  Salt and freshly ground black pepper
- 4 sprigs of marjoram
- ¾ cup (200 ml) boiling water

  Pinch of saffron
- 1 large leek, white part only, cut into thin rounds
- 1 teaspoon salt

2 medium sweet potatoes, peeled and cut into ³/₄-inch (2-cm) cubes

¹/₂ teaspoon ground cinnamon

¹/₄ teaspoon ground cloves

¹/₂ teaspoon ground cumin or cumin seeds, roasted and lightly ground

¹/₂ teaspoon ground ginger or 2¹/₂ inches (8 cm) fresh ginger, peeled and finely grated

4 cups (1 liter) vegetable broth, warmed

³/₄ cup (200 ml) milk

¹/₄ teaspoon freshly grated nutmeg

2 tablespoons finely chopped fresh cilantro (coriander)

Serves: 6
Preparation: 10–15 minutes
Cooking: 75 minutes
Level: 2

large soup pot over medium-low heat until beginning to bubble then add the leek, salt, and remaining 2 tablespoons of water. Cover the pan and simmer for 10 minutes, stirring frequently. • Mix in the sweet potatoes, cinnamon, cloves, cumin, ginger, and saffron mixture. Stir well. • Pour in the broth, cover, and simmer for 10 minutes. • Meanwhile, scoop the flesh out of the squash and add to the soup, along with the liquid from the roasting pan. • Bring back to a boil and simmer for 10 minutes. Purée the soup in a food processor. • Return to the pan and add the milk, nutmeg, and a little more water if too thick. Taste, add salt if necessary, and gently reheat. • Serve hot, sprinkled with cilantro, coarsely ground black pepper, and the caramelized seeds.

(See photograph on the following page.)

Nutritional Facts
Amount per serving
Percentage of Daily Values
based on 2,000 calories

CALORIES	PROTEIN	FAT	FIBER	SALT
247	4g	14g	4.6g	1.1g
2%	9%	7%	18%	19%

MIDDLE EASTERN SPLIT PEA SOUP

Combine the water and split peas in a large soup pot. Bring to a boil and skim off any foam from the top. Simmer until the peas are soft, 40–60 minutes. • Heat the oil in a large frying pan over low heat and sauté the onion until soft and translucent, 3–4 minutes. Add the garlic, cumin, turmeric, and coriander and sauté for a few minutes. • Stir the onion mixture into the soup pot and add the salt and red pepper flakes. Simmer for 4–5 minutes, then remove from the heat. • Leave to cool a little before puréeing in batches with a handheld blender or in a food processor. Return to the pot and heat gently. Add lemon juice to taste. • If the soup is too thick—it should be quite creamy—add a little more water and adjust the seasoning. • Stir in the cilantro and drizzle with the extra oil.

- **8** cups (2 liters) cold water, + more as needed
- **3** cups (350 g) dried split green peas
- **1/4** cup (60 ml) extra-virgin olive oil + 2 tablespoons to serve
- **1** large onion, chopped
- **3** large garlic cloves, chopped
- **2** teaspoons cumin seeds, toasted and coarsely ground
- **1/2** teaspoon ground turmeric
- **1/2** teaspoon ground coriander
- **1** teaspoon salt
- **1/2** teaspoon crushed red pepper flakes
- Freshly squeezed juice of 1 lemon or lime
- **2** tablespoons fresh cilantro (coriander) leaves

Serves: 6
Preparation: 10 minutes
Cooking: 50–70 minutes
Level: 2

Nutritional Facts
Amount per serving
Percentage of Daily Values
based on 2,000 calories

 CALORIES **280**

 PROTEIN **14g** 30

 FAT **11g** 14

 FIBER **6.6g**

 SALT **0.8g** 15

FRENCH BEAN AND ALMOND SOUP

124

Melt half the butter in a medium soup pot over low heat. Add the onion and garlic and sauté until soft but not browned, about 5 minutes. • Stir in the flour and mix well. Add about half the broth, little by little, stirring all the time. Bring to a simmer and add the beans and herbs. • Cook until the beans are just tender, 5–8 minutes. Set aside to cool then purée the soup in a food processor. • Return to the pot and use the remaining broth, plus extra water, to dilute the soup to a creamy consistency. • Reheat and taste for seasoning, adding lemon juice, salt, and pepper. Don't let the soup boil. • Fry the almonds in the remaining butter in a small frying pan, stirring until golden brown. Mix into the soup and serve hot garnished with parsley.

1/4 cup (60 g) butter

1 medium onion, finely chopped

1 large clove garlic, finely chopped

1 tablespoon all-purpose (plain) flour

3 cups (750 ml) vegetable broth or water

12 ounces (350 g) fresh thin green beans, trimmed

1 tablespoon coarsely chopped fresh parsley + extra to garnish

1 teaspoon coarsely chopped fresh chervil

2 fresh sage leaves, coarsely chopped (optional)

2 teaspoons freshly squeezed lemon juice

Salt and freshly ground black pepper

2/3 cup (60 g) blanched almonds, coarsely chopped

Serves: 4
Preparation: 10 minutes
Cooking: 15–20 minutes
Level: 1

Nutritional Facts
Amount per serving
Percentage of Daily Values
based on 2,000 calories

 CALORIES **267** 13

 PROTEIN **6g** 13

 FAT **22g** 27

 FIBER **4g** 8

 SALT **0.6g** 1

HUNGARIAN CABBAGE AND APPLE SOUP

Put the currants in a small bowl, cover with hot water, and leave to soak for 10 minutes. Drain and set aside. • Heat the oil in a medium soup pot or deep frying pan over medium-low heat. Add the onion and sauté for 3 minutes. • Add the apple, cabbage, thyme, and $1/2$ teaspoon salt. Stir thoroughly and sauté for 5 more minutes. • Pour in the broth, cover, and simmer until the cabbage is tender but still retains a little bite, 6–8 minutes. • Stir in the caraway seeds, nutmeg, and lemon juice, and season with salt and pepper. • Remove the soup from the heat. Whip the cream until stiff and mix with the mustard, pinch of salt, and ground pepper. • Fold the cream into the soup. Ladle into small bowls and serve immediately, sprinkled with parsley and currants.

2	tablespoons currants
2	tablespoons sunflower oil
1	onion, cut in thin rings
2	tart apples, peeled, cored, and finely chopped
1	small white or green cabbage, cored and finely shredded
$1/2$	teaspoon dried thyme
	Salt
$2^{1}/3$	cups (600 ml) vegetable broth
$1/2$	teaspoon caraway seeds, ground
	Pinch of nutmeg
1	tablespoon freshly squeezed lemon juice
	Freshly ground black pepper
$1/3$	cup (90 ml) heavy (double) cream
1	heaped tablespoon coarse-grain mustard
1	tablespoon finely chopped fresh parsley

Serves: 4
Preparation: 15 minutes
+ 10 minutes to soak
Cooking: 14–16 minutes
Level: 1

Nutritional Facts
Amount per serving
Percentage of Daily Values
based on 2,000 calories

 CALORIES **267** 13%
 PROTEIN **4g** 9%
 FAT **19g** 23%
 FIBER **5.9g** 24%
 SALT **0.6g** 10%

ROASTED TOMATO GAZPACHO

Preheat the oven to 400°F (200°C/gas 6).
• Place the tomatoes, onions, and bell pepper, skin up, in a large roasting pan. Add the garlic. Drizzle with 2 tablespoons of oil, season with salt and pepper, and sprinkle with half the basil. Toss to coat, and spread out in a single layer. • Bake for 20–30 minutes, until the tomatoes and pepper are soft and their skin is charred in places. • Remove from the oven and place the pan over low heat, stir in half the broth, and bring briefly to a boil. • Add the remaining basil, chile, and vinegar, and let cool. • Chop in a food processor. • Dilute with enough of the remaining broth and iced water to make it into a thick, creamy mixture. Season with salt and pepper and chill thoroughly. • Serve with a few ice cubes, mint leaves, and cucumber, bell pepper, and croutons.

$1^{1}/_{2}$ **pounds (750 g) ripe tomatoes**

2 **small red onions, quartered**

1 **large red bell pepper (capsicum), quartered**

2 **cloves garlic, coarsely chopped**

4 **tablespoons (60 ml) extra-virgin olive oil**

Salt and freshly ground black pepper

1 **large handful basil leaves, torn**

$1^{1}/_{4}$ **cups (300 ml) vegetable broth**

1 **small fresh red chile, seeded and chopped**

3 **tablespoons red wine vinegar**

Iced water, optional

Mint leaves, to garnish

Finely diced peeled cucumber, to garnish

Finely diced red, green, and yellow bell peppers, to garnish

Fried croutons

Serves: 4
Preparation: 15 minutes
Cooking: 20–30 minutes
Level: 1

Nutritional Facts
Amount per serving
Percentage of Daily Values
based on 2,000 calories

 CALORIES **521** 25

 PROTEIN **14g** 26

 FAT **8g**

 FIBER **4.4g**

 SALT **1g** 19

JERUSALEM ARTICHOKE SOUP

Soup: Melt the butter in a large soup pot over medium heat. Add the onions and sauté until softened, 3–4 minutes. • Stir in the carrots, celery, artichokes, and salt. Cover and simmer over low heat for 10 minutes. • Pour in the broth and bring to a boil. Lower the heat and simmer until the tubers are soft, 20–25 minutes. • Add the parsley, reserving some to garnish.

Artichoke Crisps: Peel the tubers and place in a bowl of salted water. Pat dry and slice thinly. • Pour the oil into a large frying pan to a depth of ¹/₂ inch (1 cm), and heat to almost sizzling. Add the tuber slices and fry until golden. Drain on paper towels and sprinkle with salt. • Blend the soup in a food processor. • Return to the pot, stir in the crème fraîche and lemon juice, and reheat gently without letting it boil. • Serve hot with the crisps and remaining parsley.

Soup

- ¹/₃ cup (75 g) butter
- 2 onions, sliced
- 2 carrots, sliced
- 1 stalk celery, chopped
- 1¹/₄ pounds (600 g) Jerusalem artichokes, scrubbed and peeled (if skins are thick)
- ¹/₂ teaspoon salt
- 4 cups (1 liter) vegetable broth or water, heated
- ¹/₂ cup (25 g) flat-leaf parsley leaves
- 2 tablespoons freshly squeezed lemon juice
- 3 tablespoons crème fraîche, to garnish

Artichoke Crisps

- 8 ounces (250 g) large Jerusalem artichokes, scrubbed
- Sunflower oil, to fry
- Salt

Serves: 6
Preparation: 20–25 minutes
Cooking: 25–30 minutes
Level: 1

Nutritional Facts
Amount per serving
Percentage of Daily Values
based on 2,000 calories

 CALORIES 246 | 2%

 PROTEIN 6g | 3%

 FAT 21g | 26%

 FIBER 1.6g | 5%

 SALT 0.6g | 2%

CREAMY CZECH MUSHROOM SOUP

132

Heat 2 tablespoons of the oil in a soup pot over medium heat. Add the mushrooms and caraway seeds and sauté until the mushrooms soften, 5–7 minutes. • Remove from the heat, stir in half the dill, and season with salt and pepper. Transfer to a bowl. • In the same pot, melt the butter with the remaining oil over medium heat and add the flour, stirring until the mixture turns into a pale paste. • Gradually pour in the hot water and $1/2$ teaspoon salt and stir until smooth. Simmer for 10–15 minutes. • Mix in the mushrooms and bring back to a boil. Stir in the sugar, vinegar, and remaining dill. Add salt and pepper and simmer for 1–2 minutes. • Stir in the sour cream. Gently reheat without boiling. • Put the eggs in individual dishes and ladle the soup over the top. Garnish with chives.

■ ■ ■ *This Czech soup, called* kulajda, *is traditionally served with hard-boiled eggs.*

3	tablespoons corn oil
8	ounces (50 g) fresh chestnut or white button mushrooms, thinly sliced
$1/2$	teaspoon caraway seeds
3	tablespoons finely chopped fresh dill
	Salt and freshly ground black pepper
2	tablespoons unsalted butter
$1/3$	cup (50 g) all-purpose (plain) flour
$2^{1}/_{2}$	cups (700 ml) hot water
1	teaspoon sugar
1	tablespoon white wine vinegar
$3/4$	cup (200 ml) sour cream
4	hard-boiled eggs, shelled and halved (optional)
1	tablespoon snipped fresh chives, to garnish

Serves: 4
Preparation: 20–25 minutes
Cooking: 20–25 minutes
Level: 1

Nutritional Facts
Amount per serving
Percentage of Daily Values
based on 2,000 calories

CALORIES
412
20%

PROTEIN
10g
22%

FAT
36g

FIBER
0.7g

SALT
0.4g

SPICED TOMATO SOUP

Plunge the tomatoes into boiling water, leave for 1 minute, drain, then peel. Reserve the skins. Coarsely chop the tomatoes.
• Heat the olive oil in a large soup pot over low heat. Add the onion and leek and sauté until softened, 3–4 minutes. • Add the garlic, chile, carrot, potato, and 1 teaspoon salt. Cover and simmer over low heat for 10 minutes. • Stir in the tomatoes, sugar, and wine. Increase the heat and stir for 2 minutes. • Add enough water to just cover the vegetables and bring to a boil. Simmer uncovered for 10–15 minutes, until the vegetables are soft. • Purée in a food processor and return to the pot. • Stir in the sun-dried tomato purée, cumin, Tabasco, thyme, and lemon juice. • Heat the sunflower oil in a small pan over medium heat. Add the tomato skins and fry for 10–15 seconds. Drain on paper towels.
• Serve the soup topped with tomato skins.

2	pounds (1 kg) ripe tomatoes
2	tablespoons extra-virgin olive oil
1	red onion, coarsely chopped
1	small leek, sliced
2	cloves garlic, chopped
1	small fresh red chile, seeded and finely chopped
1	carrot, sliced
1	potato, diced
	Salt and freshly ground black pepper
1/2	teaspoon sugar
1/3	cup (90 ml) dry white wine
1²/3	cups (400 ml) water
1	tablespoon puréed sun-dried tomato
1/4	teaspoon ground cumin
	Dash of Tabasco
1	tablespoon fresh thyme, chopped
1	tablespoon freshly squeezed lemon juice
3	tablespoons sunflower oil

Nutritional Facts
Amount per serving
Percentage of Daily Values
based on 2,000 calories

CALORIES	PROTEIN	FAT	FIBER	SALT
165	3g	10g	3.4g	0.1g

Serves: 6
Preparation: 15–20 minutes
Cooking: 25–35 minutes
Level: 1

QUICK THREE-BEAN SOUP WITH BASIL BUTTER AND CROUTONS

Basil-Butter Garnish: Combine all the ingredients and chill until needed.

Soup: Heat the oil in a large soup pot over medium heat, add the onion and garlic, and sauté until softened, about 5 minutes. Season with salt and pepper. • Add the potato, beans, broth, paprika, and bay leaf. Stir and bring to a boil. Simmer gently, uncovered, until the potato is tender, 20–25 minutes. Remove the bay leaf and stir in the parsley and basil. Set aside to cool, then purée in a blender. • Return to the pot and add the lemon juice—you may have to thin the soup down with some boiling water.
• Season with salt and pepper to taste.
• Reheat the soup gently and ladle into individual dishes. • Float a disk of basil butter on top of each one and serve with croutons.

Basil-Butter Garnish
- 1/4 cup (60 g) butter
- 3 tablespoons finely chopped fresh basil
- 1/2 teaspoon finely grated lemon zest
- 1 teaspoon lemon juice

Soup
- 2 tablespoons extra-virgin olive oil
- 1 onion, chopped
- 2 cloves garlic, sliced
- Salt and freshly ground black pepper
- 1 large potato, diced
- 1 (14-ounce/400-g) can butter or lima beans, drained
- 1 (14-ounce/400-g) can cannellini beans, drained
- 1 (14-ounce/400-g) can kidney beans, drained
- 5 cups (1.25 liters) vegetable broth
- 1 teaspoon sweet paprika
- 1 bay leaf
- 1 tablespoon finely chopped fresh basil
- 2 tablespoons freshly squeezed lemon juice

Nutritional Facts
*Amount per serving
Percentage of Daily Values
based on 2,000 calories*

 CALORIES 264 13%
 PROTEIN 10g 22%
 FAT 12g
 FIBER 8g
 SALT 1.8g

Serves: 6
Preparation: 10 minutes
Cooking: 30–35 minutes
Level: 1

CHILLED ZUCCHINI SOUP

Preheat the oven to 400°F (200°C/gas 6).
• Season the zucchini with salt and pepper
and brush with oil. Place in a roasting pan
and bake for 20 minutes. • Baste the garlic
with oil, wrap in aluminum foil, and roast
in the oven at the same time, until very
soft. Set the zucchini and garlic aside to
cool. • Cut the zucchini into chunks. •
Squeeze out the soft flesh of the garlic
head onto a small plate. Mix the garlic with
the zucchini. • Combine both types of
cream, yogurt, 1 tablespoon lemon juice,
vinegar, mustard, and 2 tablespoons mint
in a food processor and purée until
smooth. • Put in a bowl and season with
salt and pepper. • Heat the remaining oil in
a small frying pan, add the walnuts,
remaining 1 teaspoon lemon juice, and a
pinch of salt and sauté for 2 minutes.
Sprinkle over the soup. • Serve chilled,
garnished with the remaining mint.

12 **ounces (350 g) small zucchini, trimmed**

Salt and freshly ground black pepper

2 **tablespoons extra-virgin olive oil**

1 **head garlic**

2/3 **cup (150 ml) light (single) cream**

2/3 **cup (150 ml) low-fat sour cream**

1 1/3 **cups (300 ml) plain low-fat yogurt**

1 **tablespoon + 1 teaspoon freshly squeezed lemon juice**

1 **tablespoon balsamic vinegar**

1 **tablespoon whole-grain mustard**

3 **tablespoons fresh mint leaves**

2 **tablespoons crushed walnuts, + extra to garnish**

Serves: 4
Preparation: 10 minutes
Cooking: 25 minutes
Level: 1

Nutritional Facts
Amount per serving
Percentage of Daily Values
based on 2,000 calories

CALORIES	PROTEIN	FAT	FIBER	SALT
323	10g	30g	1.5g	0.4g

ROASTED SUMMER VEGETABLE SOUP

140

Preheat the oven to 400°F (200°C/gas 6).
• Combine the zucchini, onion, shallots,
bell peppers, eggplant, fennel, celery root,
and tomatoes in a large roasting pan.
Sprinkle with thyme, garlic, 1 tablespoon
salt, and $1/2$ teaspoon pepper. Drizzle with
$1/3$ cup (90 ml) of oil and mix well to coat.
Roast for 30 minutes, stirring 2 or 3 times,
until all the vegetables are soft. • Pour half
the broth into the roasting pan and bring
to a boil over medium heat. • Chop the
mixture in a food processor—it should still
be grainy. • Transfer to a large soup pot
and stir in the remaining broth. Adjust the
seasoning and simmer for 5 minutes. •
Heat the remaining oil in a large frying
pan. Stir in the cabbage and cook with the
chile and salt until the cabbage softens but
retains some bite, 3–4 minutes. • Serve
hot, topped with the cabbage.

3	zucchini (courgettes), sliced
1	large red onion, sliced
3	shallots, peeled
1	red bell pepper (capsicum), seeded and cut into chunks
1	yellow bell pepper (capsicum), seeded and cut into chunks
2	small eggplant (aubergines), chopped
1	fennel bulb, cut into thick slices
1	celery root (celeriac), peeled and cut into wedges
8	tomatoes, quartered
2	tablespoons fresh thyme leaves
4	cloves garlic, chopped
	Salt and freshly ground black pepper
$1/2$	cup (125 ml) extra-virgin olive oil
6	cups (1.5 liters) vegetable broth
	Cabbage leaves cut into thin strips
	Fresh red chile, thinly sliced

Nutritional Facts
Amount per serving
Percentage of Daily Values
based on 2,000 calories

 CALORIES 272
 PROTEIN 6g
 FAT 21g
 FIBER 6.8g
 SALT 0.6g

Serves: 6
Preparation: 20 minutes
Cooking: 40 minutes
Level: 1

SUMMER PEA SOUP

Combine the peas, potato, onion, and lettuce in a medium soup pot over medium heat and pour in half the broth. Simmer uncovered until the lettuce and potato are tender, 10–15 minutes. • Purée in a blender or press through a fine sieve. • Return to the pot, add the remaining broth and lemon zest, bring to a boil, and simmer for 5 minutes. • Remove from the heat and stir in the cream, lemon juice, salt, and pepper. Chill thoroughly, about 2 hours. • Serve sprinkled with parsley or chives.

2 cups (250 g) shelled fresh peas

1 medium potato, peeled and cut into small cubes

1 onion, coarsely chopped

1 large head green lettuce, leaves separated and washed

$2^{1}/_{3}$ cups (600 ml) vegetable broth

$^{1}/_{2}$ teaspoon finely grated lemon zest

$1^{1}/_{3}$ cups (300 ml) half fat crème fraîche or light (single) cream

1 tablespoon freshly squeezed lemon juice

Salt and freshly ground black pepper

1 tablespoon finely chopped fresh parsley or chives

Serves: 4
Preparation: 10 minutes + 2 hours to chill
Cooking: 20 minutes
Level: 1

Nutritional Facts
Amount per serving
Percentage of Daily Values
based on 2,000 calories

 CALORIES 244

 PROTEIN 9g

 FAT 13g

 FIBER 4.7g

 SALT 0.8g

COOL CANTALOUPE SOUP

144

Cut the melons in half. Scoop out the seeds and fibers and discard. Scoop out the flesh, leaving a ¹/₂-inch (1-cm) border. Place the flesh in a bowl. Reserve the shells. • Chop the cardamom, basil, chile, garlic, and dill in a food processor until they form a smooth pesto (sauce). • Combine the melon flesh, pesto, oil, and salt in a food processor or blender and process until smooth. • Add the lemon juice and stir until well blended. • Spoon the soup into the melon shells and chill in the refrigerator for 1 hour before serving.

2 small cantaloupe (rock) melons, weighing about 2 pounds (1 kg) each
Seeds of 6 cardamom pods
2 leaves fresh basil, torn
1 small fresh green chile, seeded and finely chopped
¹/₂ clove garlic
1 bunch fresh dill or chervil, finely chopped
1 tablespoon extra-virgin olive oil
¹/₂ teaspoon salt
1 tablespoon freshly squeezed lemon juice

Serves: 4
Preparation: 20 minutes + 1 hour to chill
Level: 1

Nutritional Facts
Amount per serving
Percentage of Daily Values
based on 2,000 calories

 CALORIES 88
 PROTEIN 2g
 FAT 3g
 FIBER 3.3g
 SALT 0.8g 4%

MIXED BEAN AND SPELT SOUP IN BREAD ROLLS

Heat the oil in a large soup pot over medium heat. Add the onion, carrot, and celery and sauté until the onion is lightly browned, about 5 minutes. • Add the farro, garlic, rosemary, sage, and tomatoes and pour in the vegetable broth. Cover and simmer over low heat until the farro is tender, 30–40 minutes. • Cut the tops off the bread rolls and remove the bread interior. Cut the interior into small cubes. • Toast the bread cubes in a nonstick frying pan until lightly browned, about 5 minutes. • Add the beans and toasted bread cubes to the soup and return to a gentle simmer. • Spoon the soup into the rolls, place the rolls on serving plates, and serve hot.

1	tablespoon extra-virgin olive oil
1	onion, finely chopped
1	carrot, finely chopped
1	stalk celery, finely chopped
3/4	cup (100 g) farro
2	cloves garlic, finely chopped
1	teaspoon finely chopped fresh rosemary
1	teaspoon finely chopped fresh sage
4	cherry tomatoes
4	cups (1 liter) vegetable broth
6	large round whole-wheat (wholemeal or 5-cereal) crusty bread rolls
1	(14-ounce/400-g) can mixed beans, or cannellini

Serves: 6
Preparation: 40 minutes
Cooking: 55–65 minutes
Level: 1

Nutritional Facts
Amount per serving
Percentage of Daily Values
based on 2,000 calories

 CALORIES **260** 2%
 PROTEIN **10g** 22%
 FAT **4g** 5%
 FIBER **5.7g** 23%
 SALT **1.5g** 27%

MINESTRONE

Heat the oil in a large, heavy saucepan over medium-high heat. Add the onion, celery, and garlic and cook until golden, about 5 minutes. • Add the carrot and potato, and cook for 3–4 minutes, until they begin to color. Add the tomatoes, tomato paste, and beans and stir to combine. Pour in the broth and bring to a boil. • Add the pasta, zucchini, and cabbage, decrease the heat to medium-low, and gently simmer until the pasta and vegetables are cooked, 20–25 minutes. Stir in the parsley. Season with salt and pepper. • Serve hot with the Parmesan.

2	tablespoons extra-virgin olive oil
1	red onion, diced
2	stalks celery, diced
2	cloves garlic, finely chopped
1	large carrot, diced
2	medium potatoes, peeled and diced
1	(14-ounce/400-g) can tomatoes, with juice
2	tablespoons tomato paste
1	(14-ounce/400-g) can borlotti or red kidney beans, drained
5	cups (1.25 liters) vegetable broth
3/4	cup (130 g) small pasta shapes
2	medium zucchini (courgettes), diced
1/4	Savoy or green cabbage, coarsely chopped
1/4	cup finely chopped fresh flat-leaf parsley
	Salt and freshly ground black pepper
1/3	cup (50 g) freshly grated Parmesan

Nutritional Facts
Amount per serving
Percentage of Daily Values
based on 2,000 calories

CALORIES	PROTEIN	FAT	FIBER	SALT
238	10g	7g	4.1g	0.8g

Serves: 6
Preparation: 25 minutes
Cooking 30–35 minutes
Level: 2

CORN CHOWDER WITH POTATOES AND BELL PEPPERS

Heat the oil in a large soup pot over medium heat. Add the onions, garlic, chile, celery, and carrot and sauté until softened, about 5 minutes. • Add the salt. Cover and cook until the vegetables are tender, 5–10 minutes. • Add the cornstarch mixture and stir until blended. • Add the potatoes and corn. • Dissolve the tomato paste in 4 cups (1 liter) of the broth. Whisk the mixture into the vegetables. • Bring to a boil and simmer until the potatoes are just tender but not mushy, 8–10 minutes. • Add the bell peppers and pour in the remaining 4 cups (1 liter) of broth. Return to a gentle boil. Stir in the basil and parsley and serve hot.

3 tablespoons extra-virgin olive oil
2 onions, chopped
2 cloves garlic, finely chopped
1 mild fresh green chile, seeded and finely chopped
1 stalk celery, sliced
1 carrot, thinly sliced
1 teaspoon salt
1 tablespoon cornstarch (cornflour), dissolved in $1/4$ cup (60 ml) water
1 pound (500 g) new potatoes, thinly sliced
1 pound (500 g) frozen corn (sweet corn)
1 teaspoon tomato paste (concentrate)
8 cups (2 liters) vegetable broth
2 red bell peppers (capsicums), seeded and diced
2 tablespoons finely chopped fresh basil
1 tablespoon finely chopped fresh parsley

Serves: 6–8
Preparation: 25 minutes
Cooking 25–35 minutes
Level: 2

Nutritional Facts
Amount per serving
Percentage of Daily Values
based on 2,000 calories

 CALORIES 236 11%
 PROTEIN 6g 13%
 FAT 8g 10%
 FIBER 5.6g 23%
 SALT 1.5g 28%

TOMATO SOUP WITH NOODLES

152

Heat the oil in a large saucepan over medium-high heat. Add the onion, garlic, and cumin, if using, and sauté until the onion is softened, about 5 minutes. • Add the tomatoes and 2 cups (500 ml) of the broth. Reduce the heat to low, partially cover the pot, and simmer for 30 minutes. • To prepare the noodles, open the packages and discard the flavoring. Soak in boiling water for 10 minutes, or according to the instructions on the package. Drain well. • Add the remaining broth to the soup pot and the soaked noodles. Raise the heat to medium and bring to a boil. • Remove from the heat, garnish with the basil, if using, and serve hot.

2 tablespoons extra-virgin olive oil

1 large white onion, finely chopped

4 cloves garlic, finely chopped

1/2 teaspoon cumin seeds, freshly ground (optional)

2 (14-ounce/400-g) cans tomatoes, chopped, with juice

3 cups (750 ml) vegetable broth

Salt and freshly ground white pepper

4 (3-ounce/90-g) packages ramen noodles (350 g instant noodles)

1–2 tablespoons finely chopped fresh basil, to garnish (optional)

Serves: 4
Preparation: 15 minutes
Cooking: 40 minutes
Level: 1

Nutritional Facts
Amount per serving
Percentage of Daily Values
based on 2,000 calories

CALORIES	PROTEIN	FAT	FIBER	SALT
422	12g	11g	5.3g	0.5g
20%	26%	14%	21%	9%

VEGETABLE SOUP WITH PASTA AND PESTO

Pesto: Combine the basil, pine nuts, and garlic in a food processor and purée until smooth. • Add the cheese and oil and mix well.

Soup: Bring the broth to a boil in a large soup pot over medium heat. Add the green beans and potatoes. Season with salt and pepper and simmer for 15 minutes. • Add the pasta and cook until al dente and the vegetables are very tender, 5–7 minutes. • Add the pesto and mix well. Ladle into serving bowls. Serve hot.

Pesto

1 cup (50 g) fresh basil leaves

¹/₄ cup (45 g) pine nuts

2 cloves garlic, peeled

¹/₂ cup (60 g) freshly grated Parmesan cheese

¹/₃ cup (90 ml) extra-virgin olive oil

Soup

8 cups (2 liters) vegetable broth

12 ounces (350 g) green beans, topped, tailed, and cut in short lengths

2 large waxy (boiling) potatoes, peeled and cut into small cubes

 Salt and freshly ground black pepper

8 ounces (250 g) small bowties or other small soup pasta

Serves: 6
Preparation: 10 minutes
Cooking: 30 minutes
Level: 1

Nutritional Facts
Amount per serving
Percentage of Daily Values
based on 2,000 calories

CALORIES **440**   PROTEIN **13g**   FAT **23g**   FIBER **3.8g**   SALT **1.2g**

KASHA SOUP WITH WILD MUSHROOMS

Heat the oil in a large saucepan over medium heat. Add the onion and sauté until softened, about 5 minutes. • Stir in the mushrooms and garlic. Sauté until the mushrooms have softened slightly, about 5 minutes. • Add the kasha and bay leaf. Pour in the water. • Bring to a boil, lower the heat, and simmer until the kasha is tender and the mushrooms are cooked, about 20 minutes. • Season with salt and pepper. Swirl in the sour cream and garnish with the thyme. Remove the bay leaf. • Serve hot.

1/4 cup (60 ml) extra-virgin olive oil

1 medium onion, finely chopped

6 ounces (180 g) mixed wild mushrooms, thinly sliced

2 cloves garlic, finely chopped

1 cup (150 g) kasha (buckwheat groats)

1 bay leaf

4 cups (1 liter) water

Salt and freshly ground black pepper

1/4 cup (60 ml) sour cream, to garnish

1 tablespoon finely chopped fresh thyme, to garnish

Serves: 4
Preparation: 20 minutes
Cooking: 35 minutes
Level: 1

Nutritional Facts
Amount per serving
Percentage of Daily Values
based on 2,000 calories

CALORIES	PROTEIN	FAT	FIBER	SALT
310	5g	17g	1.8g	0.7g

BEAN SOUP WITH PESTO

Heat the oil in a large saucepan over medium heat. Add the onion and sauté until softened, about 5 minutes. • Add the butter beans, potatoes, and broth and bring to a boil. • Simmer over low heat for 20 minutes, or until the beans and potatoes are tender. • Remove the pan from the heat and blend with a handheld blender until smooth. • Return the pan to the heat and reheat gently. Season with salt and pepper. Stir in the pesto and serve hot.

2 tablespoons extra-virgin olive oil

1 onion, finely chopped

1 pound (500 g) frozen butter beans or lima beans

8 ounces (250 g) potatoes, peeled and cut into small cubes

4 cups (1 liter) vegetable broth

1 cup (250 ml) pesto (see page 154)

Salt and freshly ground black pepper

Serves: 4
Preparation: 15 minutes
Cooking: 30 minutes
Level: 1

Nutritional Facts
Amount per serving
Percentage of Daily Values
based on 2,000 calories

CALORIES	PROTEIN	FAT	FIBER	SALT
533	22g	36g	7.1g	2.9g
26	8	4	28	52

TUSCAN BREAD SOUP WITH TOMATO AND BELL PEPPERS

Preheat the broiler (grill) on a high setting. Grill the bell peppers, turning them from time to time, until they are charred all over. Remove from the grill and transfer to a plastic bag. Seal the bag and let rest for 10 minutes. Remove the peppers from the bag. Peel and discard the seeds. Thinly slice the bell peppers. • Heat the oil in a large saucepan over medium heat. Add the garlic and sauté until pale golden brown, 3–4 minutes. • Add the tomatoes and half the bell peppers. Bring to a boil. • Add the bread and mix well. Add the broth and mix well. Season with black pepper and bring to a boil. Simmer until the bread has broken down, about 15 minutes. Season with salt and add the basil and marjoram. • Ladle into serving bowls and top with the remaining peppers. Garnish with basil. Serve hot.

3 large red bell peppers (capsicums)

1/4 cup (60 ml) extra-virgin olive oil

2 cloves garlic, finely chopped

1 1/2 pounds (750 g) ripe tomatoes, chopped

8 ounces (250 g) firm-textured white bread, crusts removed and crumbled

3 cups (750 ml) vegetable broth

Freshly ground black pepper and salt

2 tablespoons finely chopped fresh basil, + extra leaves to garnish

2 tablespoons finely chopped fresh marjoram or oregano

Serves: 6
Preparation: 30 minutes
Cooking: 40 minutes
Level: 2

Nutritional Facts
Amount per serving
Percentage of Daily Values
based on 2,000 calories

CALORIES	PROTEIN	FAT	FIBER	SALT
228	5g	11g	3.2g	1.3g

BROCCOLI SOUP WITH CHEESE TOASTS

Separate the broccoli into florets. Finely chop the stalk and coarsely chop the leaves. • Heat 2 tablespoons of the oil in a large soup pot over high heat. Add the garlic and sauté until soft, 2–3 minutes. • Add the broccoli, (leaves, florets, and stalks), potato, and broth. Season with salt and white pepper. Partially cover and simmer over low heat until the broccoli is tender, about 15 minutes. • Remove from the heat, let cool slightly, and purée in a food processor until smooth. • Reheat the soup, then ladle into soup bowls. • Preheat the broiler (grill). • Sprinkle the sliced bread with the cheese and bell pepper and broil until the cheese has melted, 3–5 minutes. • Float the toast on the soup. Serve hot.

1	large head broccoli (about 2 pounds/ 1 kg)
4	tablespoons (60 ml) extra-virgin olive oil
2	cloves garlic, finely chopped
1	large potato, peeled and diced
6	cups (1.5 liters) vegetable broth
	Salt and freshly ground white pepper
4	slices bread, cut in fingers or small squares
1/2	cup (60 g) freshly grated cheddar or Emmental cheese
2	tablespoons diced red bell pepper (capsicum)

Serves: 4
Preparation: 20 minutes
Cooking: 25 minutes
Level: 1

Nutritional Facts
Amount per serving
Percentage of Daily Values
based on 2,000 calories

CALORIES	PROTEIN	FAT	FIBER	SALT
420	21g	22g	10.5g	1.2g

GRAINS
AND RICE

BULGUR WITH WALNUTS

Soak the bulgur in 2^1/$_2$ cups (600 ml) boiling water for 15 minutes. • Line a colander with a clean kitchen towel. Drain the bulgur, using the towel to squeeze out as much moisture as possible. • Chop the walnuts coarsely with the salt on a chopping board. • Mix the bulgur, walnuts, onion, tomatoes, and mint in a large bowl. Drizzle with the oil. • Refrigerate for 15 minutes. • Mix the yogurt and garlic in a small bowl. Chill in the refrigerator until you are ready to serve. Serve the bulgur with the garlic-flavored yogurt.

■ ■ ■ *Bulgur is made by soaking and cooking whole-wheat kernels, drying them, removing part of the bran, and then cracking the kernels into smaller pieces. Rich in dietary fiber, vitamins, and minerals, bulgur is more nutritious than white rice or couscous.*

1^1/$_3$ cups (200 g) fine or medium bulgur

1^1/$_2$ cups (150 g) shelled walnuts

^{1}/$_2$ teaspoon salt

1 onion, finely chopped

20 cherry tomatoes, halved

2 tablespoons finely chopped fresh mint

2 tablespoons extra-virgin olive oil

1 cup (250 ml) plain yogurt

1 clove garlic, finely chopped

Serves: 4
Preparation: 20 minutes
+ 15 minutes to soak
+ 15 minutes to chill
Level: 1

Nutritional Facts
Amount per serving
Percentage of Daily Values
based on 2,000 calories

CALORIES
547
26%

PROTEIN
15g
33%

FAT
33g
41%

FIBER
11g
44%

SALT
0.9g
16%

VEGETARIAN KIBBE WITH YOGURT

Soak the bulgur in 2 cups (500 ml) boiling water for 15 minutes. • Line a colander with a clean kitchen towel. Drain the bulgur, using the towel to squeeze out as much moisture as possible. • Season with salt and pepper. Stir in the flour, adding water if the mixture is too dry to stick together. • Shape the dough into balls the size of walnuts. • Steam the bulgur balls over a large pot of salted simmering water for 10 minutes. Drain well and let cool completely. • Put the yogurt in a serving bowl and stir in the garlic and mint. Add the bulgur balls. Season with salt and pepper. • Refrigerate for 30 minutes before serving. Garnish with mint leaves.

1 cup (180 g) fine or medium bulgur

Salt and freshly ground black pepper

1/2 cup (75 g) all-purpose (plain) flour

6 cups (1.25 liters) plain yogurt

2 cloves garlic, finely chopped

2 tablespoons finely chopped fresh mint, + extra to garnish

Serves: 4
Preparation: 45 minutes + 45 minutes to soak and chill
Cooking: 10 minutes
Level: 2

■ ■ ■ *Kibbe is the Middle Eastern version of the Western meatball. In vegetarian recipes, well-seasoned bulgur usually replaces the meat.*

Nutritional Facts
Amount per serving
Percentage of Daily Values
based on 2,000 calories

 CALORIES 400

 PROTEIN 22g

 FAT 3g

 FIBER 10g

 SALT 0.9g

FALAFEL WITH TABBOULEH

Tabbouleh: Soak the bulgur in 1 cup (250 ml) of boiling water for 15 minutes. • Line a colander with a clean kitchen towel. Drain the bulgur, using the towel to squeeze out as much moisture as possible. • Transfer the bulgur to a medium bowl and add the tomatoes, cucumber, onion, parsley, and mint.

Dressing: Whisk the lemon juice, oil, lemon zest, and garlic in a small bowl. Pour over the salad and toss to combine. Season with salt and pepper.

Falafel: Dry-fry the coriander and cumin seeds in a small frying pan over medium heat until fragrant, about 1 minute. Transfer to a mortar and pestle and grind to a fine powder. • Combine the garbanzo beans, onion, parsley, cilantro, garlic, chile, ground spices, and cayenne in a food processor. Blend until smooth. Season with salt and pepper. Shape into walnut-size balls and press lightly to flatten. • Heat the oil in a large frying

Tabbouleh

- 1/2 cup (100 g) fine or medium bulgur
- 2 medium tomatoes, diced
- 1 English (Lebanese) cucumber, halved lengthwise, seeded, and diced
- 1 small red onion, diced
- 1 cup (50 g) finely chopped fresh flat-leaf parsley
- 1/2 cup (25 g) finely chopped fresh mint

Dressing

- 1/4 cup (60 ml) freshly squeezed lemon juice
- 2 tablespoons extra-virgin olive oil
- 1 tablespoon finely grated lemon zest
- 1 garlic clove, finely chopped

  Salt and freshly ground black pepper

Falafel

1½ teaspoons coriander seeds

1½ teaspoons cumin seeds

1 (14-ounce/400-g) can garbanzo beans (chickpeas), drained

½ small onion, coarsely chopped

⅓ cup fresh flat-leaf parsley leaves

2 tablespoons fresh cilantro (coriander)

1 clove garlic, coarsely chopped

1 large green chile, seeded and chopped

 Pinch of cayenne pepper

 Salt and freshly ground black pepper

1 cup (250 ml) vegetable oil, for frying

½ cup (125 ml) plain yogurt, to serve

Serves: 4
Preparation: 45 minutes + 15 minutes to soak
Cooking: 20–25 minutes
Level: 2

pan over medium-high heat, until hot enough to brown a piece of bread when tested. • Cook the falafel in batches, until crisp and golden brown, 3–5 minutes on each side. Remove using a slotted spoon and place on paper towels to drain.
• Serve with the tabbouleh and yogurt.

■ ■ ■ *Serve these two classic Lebanese dishes as a starter or light lunch. They go beautifully together. You may also like to try them stuffed into pita bread.*

(See photograph on the following page.)

171

Nutritional Facts

Amount per serving
Percentage of Daily Values
based on 2,000 calories

 CALORIES 397 19%
 PROTEIN 14g 30%
 FAT 18g 22%
 FIBER 8g 32%
 SALT 0.6g 10%

PEARL BARLEY WITH BEANS

In separate bowls, soak the garbanzo beans, white beans, and barley overnight in cold water. • Drain well. Simmer the garbanzo beans, white beans, and barley in separate pots of salted water over low heat until each one is tender. This will take 35–45 minutes for the pearl barley, about 1 hour for the white beans, and up to 2 hours for the garbanzo beans. Cover the barley and beans with about an inch (2.5 cm) of water and keep them covered throughout the cooking times. • Drain the garbanzo beans, barley, and white beans. • Drizzle the oil over the mixture and season with salt and pepper. • Serve hot or at room temperature.

1¹/2 cups (250 g) dried garbanzo beans (chickpeas)

¹/2 cups (250 g) dried white beans, such as navy or Great Northern

1 cup (100 g) pearl barley

¹/4 cup (60 ml) extra-virgin olive oil

Salt and freshly ground black pepper

Serves: 6
Preparation: 10 minutes + 12 hours to soak
Cooking: 2 hours
Level: 1

Nutritional Facts
Amount per serving
Percentage of Daily Values
based on 2,000 calories

CALORIES	PROTEIN	FAT	FIBER	SALT
400	19g	12g	12g	0.1g

WHEAT BERRIES WITH ZUCCHINI AND PARMESAN

Soak the wheat berries in cold water for 12 hours. • Drain and transfer to a large saucepan. Pour in enough hot water to cover the wheat and double the volume. • Bring to a boil and simmer until tender, about 1 hour. • Grill the zucchini in a hot grill pan until tender. • Transfer to a bowl, season with salt and pepper, and drizzle with 2 tablespoons of oil. Sprinkle with the parsley and mint. • Drain the wheat berries thoroughly and set aside. Let cool. • Place the zucchini on a large serving dish and spoon the wheat over the top. Drizzle with the remaining oil and the lemon juice. • Add the toasted walnuts, Parmesan, and a few more leaves of fresh mint to garnish.

2 cups (350 g) wheat berries

4 zucchini (courgettes), thinly sliced lengthwise

Salt and freshly ground black pepper

6 tablespoons (90 ml) extra-virgin olive oil

2 tablespoons finely chopped fresh parsley

1 tablespoon finely chopped fresh mint, + extra leaves to garnish

1 tablespoon freshly squeezed lemon juice

20 walnuts, toasted and chopped

3 ounces (100 g) Parmesan cheese, shaved

Serves: 4–6
Preparation: 20 minutes
+ 12 hours to soak
Cooking: 1 hour
Level: 1

Nutritional Facts
Amount per serving
Percentage of Daily Values
based on 2,000 calories

 CALORIES 562 27

 PROTEIN 19g

 FAT 36g

 FIBER 7g 28

SALT 0.4g 8

COUSCOUS WITH SEVEN VEGETABLES

Bring the water to a boil in a large saucepan over medium heat. • Add 1 tablespoon of oil and salt to taste (about $^1/_2$ teaspoon). Stir in the couscous and saffron and mix well. • Remove from the heat, cover, and keep warm. • Heat the remaining 3 tablespoons of oil and the butter in a large frying pan over medium heat. Add the onions and sauté until softened, 3–4 minutes. • Add the carrots, squash, zucchini, fava beans, tomatoes, and cabbage and simmer over medium-low heat until the vegetables are tender, 15–20 minutes. • Stir in the garbanzo beans and raisins and cook until heated through, about 5 minutes. • Spoon over the couscous and serve hot, garnished with cilantro.

$1^1/_3$ cups (350 ml) water

4 tablespoons extra-virgin olive oil

Salt

2 cups (350 g) couscous

$^1/_8$ teaspoon saffron threads

2 tablespoons butter

2 large onions, finely chopped

3 carrots, thinly sliced

1 yellow summer squash, thinly sliced

3 zucchini, thinly sliced

1 cup (60 g) fresh fava (broad) beans

3 large tomatoes, peeled and chopped

$^1/_2$ medium green or white cabbage, finely shredded

1 (14-ounce/400-g) can garbanzo beans (chickpeas), drained

$^1/_4$ cup (45 g) raisins

Fresh cilantro (coriander), to garnish

Nutritional Facts
Amount per serving
Percentage of Daily Values
based on 2,000 calories

 CALORIES 502 24%

 PROTEIN 15g 33%

 FAT 18g 22%

 FIBER 7g 28%

 SALT 0.5g 8%

Serves: 6
Preparation: 30 minutes
Cooking: 25–30 minutes
Level: 1

SPICED COUSCOUS WITH MUSHROOMS

Bring the water to a boil in a large saucepan over medium heat. • Add 1 tablespoon of oil and salt to taste (about $1/2$ teaspoon). Stir in the couscous and cumin and mix well. • Remove from the heat, cover, and let rest for 2 minutes. • Add the remaining 4 tablespoons of oil and return to the heat. Cook for 3 minutes, stirring constantly with a fork to separate the grains. • Remove from the heat and add the garlic, mushrooms, tomatoes, Parmesan, and marjoram. Season with salt and pepper. Sprinkle with the pine nuts. • Serve hot or at room temperature.

■ ■ ■ *Many types of couscous are served in Africa and the Middle East. In North America and Europe a quick-cooking version of the North African variety, made from semolina, is primarily served.*

$1^1/3$ cups (350 ml) water

5 tablespoons extra-virgin olive oil

Salt

2 cups (350 g) couscous

1 tablespoon cumin seeds

2 cloves garlic, finely chopped

8 ounces (250 g) mushrooms, thinly sliced

12 cherry tomatoes, halved

3 ounces (100 g) Parmesan cheese, shaved

2 tablespoons finely chopped fresh marjoram

Freshly ground black pepper

$1/4$ cup (50 g) pine nuts, toasted

Serves: 6
Preparation: 10 minutes
Cooking: 10 minutes
Level: 1

Nutritional Facts
Amount per serving
Percentage of Daily Values
based on 2,000 calories

CALORIES	PROTEIN	FAT	FIBER	SALT
435	16g	21g	3g	0.3g

COUSCOUS WITH ROASTED VEGETABLES

Preheat the oven to 400°F (200°C/gas 6).
• Heat 1 tablespoon of the oil in a small frying pan over medium heat. Add the shallot and sauté until softened, 3–4 minutes. • Arrange the eggplant, zucchini, bell peppers, and olives on a baking sheet. Add the shallot and drizzle with 3 tablespoons of oil. • Bake for 20–25 minutes, until the vegetables are tender and slightly charred. Season with salt.
• Bring the water to a boil in a large saucepan over medium heat. • Add 1 tablespoon of oil and salt to taste (about $1/2$ teaspoon). Stir in the couscous and mix well. • Remove from the heat, cover, and let rest for 2 minutes. • Add the remaining 1 tablespoon of oil and return to the heat. Cook for 3 minutes, stirring constantly with a fork to separate the grains. • Stir in the roasted vegetables, and garnish with the fennel, if using. • Serve warm.

6	tablespoons (90 ml) extra-virgin olive oil
1	shallot, finely chopped
1	eggplant (aubergine), cut into small squares
2	zucchini (courgettes), cut into small cubes
1	large red bell pepper (capsicum), seeded and cut into small squares
1	large yellow bell pepper (capsicum), seeded and cut into small squares
$3/4$	cup (75 g) pitted black olives
	Salt
$1^1/4$	cups (300 ml) water
$1^1/2$	cups (270 g) couscous
2	tablespoons finely chopped fresh fennel leaves, to garnish (optional)

Serves: 4
Preparation: 10 minutes
Cooking: 30–35 minutes
Level: 2

Nutritional Facts
Amount per serving
Percentage of Daily Values
based on 2,000 calories

 CALORIES **128**
 PROTEIN **2g**
 FAT **9g**
 FIBER **2.3g** SALT **0.5g**

RICE WITH TOMATO PESTO AND MOZZARELLA

184

Combine the sun-dried tomatoes, cheese, almonds, capers, oil, and lemon juice in a food processor. Process until smooth.
• Bring a large pot of salted water to a boil, add the rice, and boil until tender.
• Drain well and transfer to a large bowl. Stir in the tomato pesto and season with salt and pepper. • Arrange the arugula on four serving dishes and top with the rice. Place the mozzarella balls on top.
• Serve immediately.

12 **sun-dried tomatoes packed in oil, drained**

1/4 **cup (30 g) freshly grated pecorino or Parmesan cheese**

2 **tablespoons blanched almonds, toasted**

1 **tablespoon salt-cured capers, rinsed and drained**

4 **tablespoons (60 ml) extra-virgin olive oil**

Freshly squeezed juice of 1/2 lemon

1 1/2 **cups (300 g) long-grain rice**

Salt and freshly ground black pepper

2 **cups (100 g) arugula (rocket)**

6 **ounces (180 g) mini mozzarella balls**

Serves: 4
Preparation: 10 minutes
Cooking: 15 minutes
Level: 1

Nutritional Facts
Amount per serving
Percentage of Daily Values
based on 2,000 calories

 CALORIES **586** 28

 PROTEIN **21g**

 FAT **42g**

 FIBER **4.9g**

 SALT **1.2g**

RICE WITH HERBS AND FETA

Combine the herbs in a food processor with the pine nuts, walnuts, chile, and garlic. Process until just smooth, 10–15 seconds. • Transfer the mixture to a large bowl and stir in the oil. • Add the cherry tomatoes and season with salt. • Bring a large pot of salted water to a boil, add the rice, and boil until tender. • Drain and let cool under cold running water. • Drain very thoroughly and add to the bowl with the tomato-and-herb mixture. Add the feta. • Toss well and serve immediately.

1 cup (50 g) mixed fresh herbs (such as marjoram, parsley, cilantro/coriander, thyme, chives, basil)

2 tablespoons pine nuts

8 walnuts, blanched

1 fresh red chile, seeded and finely chopped

1 clove garlic, peeled

1/4 cup (60 ml) extra-virgin olive oil

1 pound (500 g) cherry tomatoes, quartered

Salt

1 1/2 cups (300 g) long-grain rice

3 1/2 ounces (100 g) feta cheese, cut into small cubes

Serves: 4
Preparation: 10 minutes
Cooking: 15 minutes
Level: 1

Nutritional Facts
*Amount per serving
Percentage of Daily Values
based on 2,000 calories*

CALORIES	PROTEIN	FAT	FIBER	SALT
494	10g	40g	3.4g	1.1g
24	22	5	4	20

CHAMPAGNE RISOTTO WITH CILANTRO

Melt 2 tablespoons of the butter in a large frying pan over medium heat. Add the onion and sauté until transparent, about 3 minutes. • Add the rice and sauté for 2 minutes. • Pour in the champagne and cook until it evaporates, about 5 minutes. • Begin adding the stock, 1/2 cup (125 ml) at a time, cooking and stirring until each addition has been absorbed and the rice is tender, 15–18 minutes. • Season with salt and pepper and mix well. Remove from the heat. Stir in the remaining 2 tablespoons butter. Cover and let rest for 1 minute. Sprinkle with cilantro and Parmesan. Serve hot.

4 tablespoons (60 g) butter

1 large onion, finely chopped

1 3/4 cups (350 g) risotto rice, such as Arborio

1 cup (250 ml) dry champagne

3 cups (750 ml) vegetable stock, boiling

Salt and freshly ground black pepper

2 tablespoons finely chopped fresh cilantro (coriander)

3 ounces (90 g) Parmesan cheese, shaved

Serves: 4
Preparation: 10 minutes
Cooking: 25 minutes
Level: 1

Nutritional Facts
Amount per serving
Percentage of Daily Values
based on 2,000 calories

 CALORIES 571 21%

 PROTEIN 16g 35%

 FAT 20g 25%

 FIBER 2g 3

 SALT 1.3g 24%

GORGONZOLA AND CILANTRO RISOTTO

Melt the butter in a large frying pan over medium heat. • Add the onion and sauté until softened, 3–4 minutes. • Add the rice and cook for 2 minutes, stirring constantly. • Stir in the wine and, when this has been absorbed, begin stirring in the stock, ¹/₂ cup (125 ml) at a time. Cook and stir until each addition has been absorbed and the rice is tender, 15–18 minutes. • Stir in the Gorgonzola. Sprinkle with the cilantro and serve hot.

2 tablespoons butter

1 large onion, finely chopped

1¹/₂ cups (300 g) risotto rice, such as Arborio

¹/₃ cup (90 ml) dry white wine

4 cups (1 liter) vegetable stock, boiling

4 ounces (125 g) Gorgonzola dolce cheese, cut into cubes

2 tablespoons finely chopped fresh cilantro (coriander)

Serves: 4
Preparation: 10 minutes
Cooking: 25 minutes
Level: 1

Nutritional Facts
Amount per serving
Percentage of Daily Values
based on 2,000 calories

CALORIES	PROTEIN	FAT	FIBER	SALT
514	12g	22g	1g	2.2g
26	26	27		39

191

GREEN PEPPERCORN RISOTTO

Melt 2 tablespoons of the butter in a large frying pan over medium heat. Add the onion and sauté until softened, 3–4 minutes. • Add the rice and cook for 2 minutes, stirring constantly. • Stir in the wine and, when this has been absorbed, begin stirring in the stock, 1/2 cup (125 ml) at a time. Cook and stir until each addition of stock has been absorbed and the rice is tender, 15–18 minutes. • Add the green peppercorns. Stir in the remaining 2 tablespoons butter and the Parmesan. Garnish with the chives and serve.

4 tablespoons (60 g) butter

1 medium onion, finely chopped

1 1/2 cups (300 g) risotto rice, such as Arborio

1/3 cup (90 ml) dry white wine

4 cups (1 liter) vegetable stock, boiling

1 tablespoon green peppercorns, in brine, drained

2 tablespoons freshly grated Parmesan cheese

3 tablespoons snipped fresh chives

Serves: 4
Preparation: 10 minutes
Cooking: 25 minutes
Level: 1

Nutritional Facts
Amount per serving
Percentage of Daily Values
based on 2,000 calories

 CALORIES **423**

PROTEIN **8g**

FAT **14g**

 FIBER **1g**

SALT **1g**

CUMIN RICE WITH TOMATOES

194

Heat the oil in a large saucepan over low heat. Add the onion, cumin seeds, and garlic and sauté until the garlic turns pale gold, 3–4 minutes. • Add the chopped tomatoes. • Stir in the rice and pour in the water. Bring to a boil. Cover and simmer, stirring occasionally, until the rice is tender and has absorbed all of the liquid, 10–15 minutes. • Add the parsley and season with salt and pepper. Garnish with slices of tomato and the sprigs of parsley. • Serve hot.

3 tablespoons extra-virgin olive oil

1 large onion, finely chopped

1 teaspoon cumin seeds

1 clove garlic, finely chopped

6 medium tomatoes, peeled and chopped

1¹/₂ cups (300 g) long-grain rice

4 cups (1 liter) boiling water

2 tablespoons finely chopped fresh parsley, + extra sprigs to garnish

Salt and freshly ground black pepper

1 tomato, thinly sliced, to garnish

Serves: 4
Preparation: 10 minutes
Cooking: 20 minutes
Level: 1

Nutritional Facts
Amount per serving
Percentage of Daily Values
based on 2,000 calories

 CALORIES 274 13%
 PROTEIN 3.4g 7%
 FAT 17g 21%
 FIBER 2.4g 10%
 SALT 0.2g 4%

ZUCCHINI AND APPLE RISOTTO

Put the apples in a bowl. Drizzle with the lemon juice. • Heat the oil in a large frying pan over medium heat. Add the onion and sauté until softened, 3–4 minutes. • Add the potatoes, zucchini, and carrot and sauté for 2 minutes. • Add the rice and pour in $1/2$ cup (125 ml) of the stock, stirring until it is absorbed. Add the apples and lemon juice and mix well. Keep adding the stock, $1/2$ cup (125 ml) at a time, cooking and stirring until each addition has been absorbed and the rice is tender, 15–18 minutes. • Remove from the heat and stir in the soy sauce, curry powder, and dill. Season with salt and pepper and mix gently. • Cover and let rest for 1 minute. Garnish with dill and serve hot.

2   green apples, peeled, cored, and cut into small cubes

Freshly squeezed juice of 1 lemon

2   tablespoons extra-virgin olive oil

1   large onion, finely chopped

4   potatoes, peeled and cut into small cubes

3   zucchini (courgettes), cut into small cubes

1   carrot, peeled and cut into small cubes

$1^{1}/2$ cups (350 g) risotto rice, such as Arborio

3   cups (750 ml) vegetable stock, boiling, with a pinch of saffron threads

1   teaspoon dark soy sauce

1   teaspoon curry powder

2   tablespoons finely chopped fresh dill, + extra to garnish

Salt and freshly ground black pepper

Nutritional Facts
Amount per serving
Percentage of Daily Values
based on 2,000 calories

CALORIES	PROTEIN	FAT	FIBER	SALT
487	11g	7g	4.1g	1g

Serves: 4
Preparation: 10 minutes
Cooking: 25 minutes
Level: 1

RISOTTO WITH PEARS

Melt the butter in a large frying pan over medium heat. Add the onion and sauté until softened, 3–4 minutes. • Stir in the rice and cook for 2 minutes. • Add the wine and cook until evaporated. • Add ½ cup (125 ml) of boiling stock and the pears. • Continue adding stock, ½ cup (125 ml) at a time, cooking and stirring until each addition has been absorbed and the rice is tender, 15–18 minutes. Season with salt and pepper. • Add the Fontina and liqueur just before serving. • Stir well and serve hot.

2   tablespoons butter
1   onion, finely chopped
2   cups (400 g) risotto rice, such as Arborio
1   cup (250 ml) dry white wine
6   cups (1.5 liters) vegetable stock, boiling
4   medium pears, peeled, cored, and cubed
    Salt and freshly ground black pepper
3   ounces (90 g) Fontina cheese, diced
¼   cup (60 ml) pear liqueur

Serves: 4
Preparation: 10 minutes
Cooking: 25 minutes
Level: 2

Nutritional Facts
Amount per serving
Percentage of Daily Values
based on 2,000 calories

 CALORIES 326 6
 PROTEIN 2g
 FAT 22g 27
 FIBER 2.2g
 SALT 0.8g 5%

RISOTTO WITH RED ROSES

Pull the petals off the roses, reserving 8 of the best to use as a garnish. (Keep in a bowl of cold water). Separate the brightly colored petals from the less brightly colored ones. • Melt half the butter in a large frying pan over medium heat and cook the less highly colored petals until wilted. • Add the rice and cook for 2 minutes, stirring constantly. • Season with nutmeg and pepper. Add the wine and cook until evaporated. • Stir in $^1/_2$ cup (125 ml) stock and cook, stirring often, until the stock is absorbed. • Continue adding the stock, $^1/_2$ cup (125 ml) at a time, stirring often until each addition is absorbed and the rice is tender, 15–18 minutes. • When the rice is cooked, add the brightly colored rose petals. Fold in the cream and remaining butter. Add the Emmental and rosewater. • Garnish with the 8 reserved petals. Serve hot.

4   red roses (freshly opened buds)

$^1/_2$ cup (125 g) butter

2   cups (400 g) risotto rice, such as Arborio

$^1/_8$ teaspoon freshly grated nutmeg

Freshly ground black pepper

$^1/_2$ cup (125 ml) dry white wine

4   cups (1 liter) vegetable stock, boiling

$^1/_3$ cup (90 ml) light (single) cream

4   ounces (125 g) Emmental cheese

Few drops rosewater

Serves: 4
Preparation: 20 minutes
Cooking: 25 minutes
Level: 2

Nutritional Facts
Amount per serving
Percentage of Daily Values
based on 2,000 calories

CALORIES	PROTEIN	FAT	FIBER	SALT
761	18g	40g	1.1g	1.5g

GRAPEFRUIT RISOTTO

Heat the oil in a large frying pan over medium heat. Add the onions and sauté until softened, 3–4 minutes. • Stir in the rice. Cook for 2 minutes, stirring constantly. • Stir in the grapefruit juice and, when this has been absorbed, begin stirring in the stock, ¹/₂ cup (125 ml) at a time. • After about 10 minutes, add the butter. • Add more stock and cook and stir until each addition has been absorbed and the rice is tender, 15–18 minutes. Season with salt and pepper. • Stir in the Parmesan and garnish with the parsley. Serve hot.

3	tablespoons extra-virgin olive oil
2	small onions, thinly sliced
2	cups (400 g) risotto rice, such as Arborio
	Freshly squeezed juice of 2 grapefruit
5	cups (1.25 liters) vegetable stock, boiling
2	tablespoons butter
	Salt and freshly ground black pepper
4	tablespoons freshly grated Parmesan cheese
2	tablespoons finely chopped fresh parsley

Serves: 4
Preparation: 20 minutes
Cooking: 25–30 minutes
Level: 1

Nutritional Facts
Amount per serving
Percentage of Daily Values
based on 2,000 calories

CALORIES 613
PROTEIN 13g
FAT 23g
FIBER 2.8g
SALT 1.1g

SPINACH AND BELL PEPPER PAELLA

204

Cook the spinach in a little salted water until wilted, 2–3 minutes. • Drain, squeezing out excess moisture. Coarsely chop. • Heat the oil in a large frying pan over medium heat. Add the onions and garlic and sauté until softened, 3–4 minutes. • Add the pine nuts and chile and cook for 2 minutes. • Lower the heat and add the tomatoes and bell pepper. Cook for 5 minutes, stirring often. • Add the rice and stir for 2 minutes. Season with salt and pepper. • Add the paprika, saffron and water, and enough stock to cover the rice by 1 inch (2.5 cm). Bring to a boil and simmer until the rice is tender and almost all the liquid has been absorbed, about 15 minutes, stirring often. • Add the spinach and peas. Cook until tender, about 5 minutes. • Remove from the heat, cover, and let rest for 5 minutes. Garnish with the peppers, and serve hot.

1	pound (500 g) spinach
$1/3$	cup (90 ml) extra-virgin olive oil
2	onions, sliced
3	cloves garlic, finely chopped
2	tablespoons pine nuts
1	dried red chile, crumbled
4	tomatoes, peeled and chopped
1	green bell pepper (capsicum), seeded, cored, and sliced
$1^{1}/4$	cups (250 g) medium-grain rice, such as Goya or Arborio
	Salt and freshly ground black pepper
1	teaspoon sweet paprika
$1/2$	teaspoon saffron threads
1	tablespoon boiling water
3	cups (750) vegetable stock
1	cup (150 g) peas
2	Spanish piquillo peppers, sliced

Nutritional Facts
Amount per serving
Percentage of Daily Values
based on 2,000 calories

 CALORIES 409 2

 PROTEIN 11g 24

 FAT 22g 27

 FIBER 4.5g 18

 SALT 0.8g

Serves: 6
Preparation: 30 minutes
Cooking: 35–40 minutes
Level: 2

VEGETARIAN PAELLA

Heat the oil in a large paella pan or skillet over medium-low heat. Add the onions and garlic and sauté until softened, 3–4 minutes. • Add the bell peppers and tomatoes and cook until softened, 5–7 minutes. • Add the rice, green beans, zucchini, saffron mixture, and paprika and stir to coat. Pour in the hot vegetable broth, decrease the heat to low, and gently simmer for 30 minutes, stirring occasionally to ensure even cooking of the rice. • Stir in the peas and spinach. Remove from the heat, cover, and set aside for 10 minutes to finish cooking. Add the parsley and season with salt and pepper. • Serve hot.

3 tablespoons extra-virgin olive oil

2 onions, sliced

3 garlic cloves, minced

2 red bell peppers (capsicums), seeded and sliced

6 tomatoes, quartered

2 cups (400 g) medium-grain rice, such as Goya or Arborio

5 ounces (150 g) green beans, chopped

2 zucchini (courgettes), sliced

1 teaspoon saffron threads mixed with 3 tablespoons hot water

1 tablespoon smoked paprika (pimentòn)

5 cups (1.25 liters) vegetable broth, hot

1/2 cup (75 g) frozen peas

1 cup (50 g) baby spinach leaves

1/4 cup (25 g) chopped fresh flat-leaf parsley

Salt and freshly ground black pepper

Nutritional Facts
Amount per serving
Percentage of Daily Values
based on 2,000 calories

 CALORIES 537 26%
 PROTEIN 14g 30%
 FAT 11g 14%
 FIBER 6.5g 26%
 SALT 0.8g 14%

Serves: 4–6
Preparation: 30 minutes
Cooking: 50–55 minutes
Level: 2

SPICED RICE WITH TOFU

208

Melt the butter in a large saucepan over medium heat. Add the rice and sauté for 2 minutes. • Add the saffron, cloves, and cinnamon. Pour in the water and season with salt. Cover and bring to a boil. Simmer over low heat until the rice has absorbed all the liquid, 15–20 minutes, stirring occasionally. • Heat the oil in a large frying pan over medium heat. Add the onion and sauté until softened, 3–4 minutes. • Add the cardamom, peppercorns, and cumin and sauté for 30 seconds. • Add the bell pepper. Sauté for 5 minutes. • Add the tofu, raisins, almonds, cashew nuts, and pistachios. Sauté for 5 minutes more. • Add this mixture to the rice and mix well. Cover and let rest for 5 minutes. • Serve hot.

1/2	cup (125 g) butter
2	cups (400 g) basmati rice
1/2	teaspoon saffron threads
3	cloves
1/2	stick cinnamon
3	cups (750 ml) water
	Salt
2	tablespoons Asian sesame oil
1	onion, chopped
	Seeds from 4 cardamom pods
3	black peppercorns
1/2	teaspoon cumin seeds
1/2	green bell pepper (capsicum), seeded, cored, and sliced
8	ounces (250 g) firm tofu, diced
2	tablespoons golden raisins (sultanas)
2	tablespoons chopped almonds
1	tablespoon cashew nuts, halved
1	tablespoon pistachios

Nutritional Facts
Amount per serving
Percentage of Daily Values
based on 2,000 calories

 CALORIES **620** 30%
 PROTEIN **14g** 30%
 FAT **33g** 41%
 FIBER **2.7g** 11%
 SALT **0.4g** 7%

Serves: 4–6
Preparation: 30 minutes
Cooking: 35–40 minutes
Level: 2

AROMATIC LEMON RICE

Combine the rice in a large saucepan with the water, turmeric, and salt. Bring to a boil, cover, and simmer over low heat for 10 minutes. • Remove from the heat and leave covered. • Combine the coconut and the coconut milk in a small bowl. • Melt the butter in a small saucepan over medium heat. Add the oil, chile, cardamom, peppercorns, almonds, cumin, and mustard seeds. Sauté until the mustard seeds begin to crackle, 3–4 minutes. • Add this mixture to the rice. • Add the lemon juice and coconut mixture and mix with a fork. Simmer over low heat until the rice is soft and fluffy, about 5 minutes. • Serve hot, garnished with the cilantro.

2 cups (400 g) basmati rice
3 cups (750 ml) water
1 teaspoon ground turmeric
Salt
4 tablespoons shredded (desiccated) coconut
¼ cup (60 ml) coconut milk
¼ cup (60 g) butter
¼ cup (60 ml) peanut oil
1 green chile, seeded and thinly sliced
Seeds from 6 cardamom pods
3 whole black peppercorns
4 tablespoons chopped almonds
1 teaspoon cumin seeds
1 teaspoon mustard seeds
Freshly squeezed juice of 1 lemon
Fresh cilantro (coriander), to garnish

Nutritional Facts
Amount per serving
Percentage of Daily Values
based on 2,000 calories

 CALORIES 533 26%
 PROTEIN 9g 20%
 FAT 31g 38%
 FIBER 2.3g 9
SALT 0.2g

Serves: 4–6
Preparation: 20 minutes
Cooking: 20 minutes
Level: 2

NASI GORENG

Put the rice in a bowl and cover with cold water. Let soak for 1 hour. Rinse under cold running water until the water runs clear. • Put the rice and water in a pot and bring to a boil. Cover and simmer over low heat until tender and the liquid has been absorbed, 20–25 minutes. Spread the rice onto two baking sheets and let cool for 2 hours. • Heat 2 tablespoons of oil in a large wok over medium heat. Add the egg and cook for 1–2 minutes on either side to make a thin omelet. Transfer to a cutting board, roll up, and cut into thin strips. • Heat the remaining oil in the wok over medium heat. Add the onion, garlic, ginger, and chile and stir-fry until softened, 3–4 minutes. • Add the tamarind and peppers and stir-fry until tender, 3–4 minutes. Add the cabbage, rice, bean sprouts, soy sauce, and kecap manis and stir-fry until hot, 2–3 minutes. • Serve with the omelet and scallions.

2	cups (400 g) long-grain rice
3	cups (750 ml) water
4	tablespoons (60 ml) peanut oil
2	large eggs, beaten
1	small onion, sliced
2	garlic cloves, minced
1	teaspoon finely chopped fresh ginger
1	green chile, seeded and finely chopped
1	tablespoon tamarind paste
1	red bell pepper (capsicum), seeded and thinly sliced
1/4	Chinese cabbage (wom bok), shredded
2	cups (100 g) bean sprouts
1	tablespoon soy sauce
1	tablespoon kecap manis
4	scallions (spring onions), thinly sliced

Serves: 4
Preparation: 20 minutes + 2 hours to cool
Cooking: 20 minutes
Level: 2

Nutritional Facts
Amount per serving
Percentage of Daily Values
based on 2,000 calories

CALORIES	PROTEIN	FAT	FIBER	SALT
386	10g	23g	3.3g	1.8g

BAKED POLENTA WITH TASTY TOMATO TOPPING

Basic Polenta: Bring the water to a boil in a large pot. • Gradually sprinkle in the polenta, stirring constantly. Continue cooking over low heat, stirring often, until the polenta comes away from the sides of the pan, 45–50 minutes. • Drizzle cold water over a large metal pan. Spread the polenta to ¹/₂ inch (1 cm) thick. Let cool.

Tomato Topping: Preheat the oven to 400°F (200°C/gas 6). • Lightly oil a large baking dish. • Heat the oil in a large frying pan over medium heat. Add the garlic and sauté until pale gold, 3–4 minutes. • Add the tomatoes and simmer until reduced, 15–20 minutes. Season with salt and pepper. • Use a glass or cookie cutter to cut out disks of polenta about 2 inches (5 cm) in diameter. Arrange in the baking dish, overlapping slightly. • Cover with sauce and sprinkle with the Parmesan. • Bake for 10–15 minutes, until the cheese has melted.

Basic Polenta

8　cups (2 liters) water

2　cups (300 g) coarse-grained polenta (yellow cornmeal)

Tomato Topping

¹/₄　cup (60 ml) extra-virgin olive oil

4　cloves garlic, finely chopped

2　(14-ounce/400-g) cans tomatoes, with juice

　　Salt and freshly ground black pepper

1　cup (125 g) freshly grated Parmesan cheese

Serves: 6
Preparation: 20 minutes
Cooking: 1 hour
Level: 2

Nutritional Facts
Amount per serving
Percentage of Daily Values
based on 2,000 calories

CALORIES
374

PROTEIN
13g
28%

FAT
19g

FIBER
3.6g
4%

SALT
0.4g

BAKED POLENTA IN CHEESE SAUCE

216

Prepare the polenta. When cooked, turn out onto a metal pan and spread to 1 inch (2.5 cm) thick. Let cool for 3 hours. • Melt the butter in a saucepan over low heat. When it stops bubbling, add the flour and cook over low heat for 1–2 minutes, stirring constantly. • Begin adding the milk, a little at a time, stirring until the sauce is smooth. Season with a little nutmeg. • Turn up the heat and add all three cheeses, a handful at a time, stirring until smooth. • Preheat the oven to 400°F (200°C/gas 6). Oil a baking dish large enough to hold the polenta and sauce in a double layer. • Cut the polenta into 1-inch (2.5-cm) cubes. • Cover the bottom of the dish with half the polenta and pour half the sauce over the top. Put the remaining polenta on top and cover with the remaining sauce. • Bake for 25–30 minutes, until the top is golden brown. Serve hot.

Basic Polenta (see page 214)
- 2 tablespoons butter
- 1 tablespoon all-purpose (plain) flour
- 1 cup (250 ml) milk
  Pinch of nutmeg
- 6 ounces (180 g) Gorgonzola cheese, chopped
- 6 ounces (180 g) Emmental (or Gruyère, or similar) cheese, thinly sliced
- 1/2 cup (60 g) freshly grated Parmesan cheese

Serves: 6
Preparation: 20 minutes
  + 3 hours to rest
Cooking: 45–50 minutes
  + time to cook the polenta
Level: 2

Nutritional Facts
Amount per serving
Percentage of Daily Values
based on 2,000 calories

 CALORIES 544 26

 PROTEIN 24g 52

 FAT 31g 36

 FIBER 3.6g 14

 SALT 1.9g 35

POLENTA WITH MUSHROOMS

Prepare the polenta.

Mushroom Sauce: While the polenta is cooking, chop the mushroom stems into cubes. Cut the largest ones in half, leaving the smaller ones whole. • Heat the oil in a large frying pan over medium heat. Add the garlic and onion and sauté until softened, 3–4 minutes. • Add the mushrooms and season with salt and pepper. Cover and simmer over low heat for 20 minutes, stirring often. • Add the parsley. • Spoon the hot polenta onto individual serving plates. Spoon the mushrooms with their cooking juices on top and garnish with the Parmesan. • Serve immediately.

Basic Polenta
(see page 214)

Mushroom Sauce

2 **pounds (1 kg) chanterelle or white mushrooms**

¹/₄ **cup (60 ml) extra-virgin olive oil**

2 **cloves garlic, finely chopped**

1 **large red onion, finely chopped**

Salt and freshly ground black pepper

2 **tablespoons finely chopped fresh parsley**

¹/₃ **cup (75 g) shaved Parmesan cheese**

Serves: 4
Preparation: 30 minutes
Cooking: 25 minutes
+ time to cook the polenta
Level: 2

Nutritional Facts
Amount per serving
Percentage of Daily Values
based on 2,000 calories

 CALORIES 519

 PROTEIN 18g

 FAT 23g

 FIBER 12g

 SALT 0.4g

BAKED SEMOLINA GNOCCHI WITH PARMESAN

220

Preheat the oven to 400°F (200°C/gas 6).
• Butter a large baking dish. • Bring the
milk to a boil with 4 tablespoons of butter,
salt, pepper, and nutmeg. Sprinkle in the
semolina and beat vigorously with a whisk
to prevent clumps from forming. • Simmer
over low heat for 20 minutes, stirring
constantly. Remove from the heat and let
cool. Add 2 tablespoons of the Parmesan
and the beaten egg yolks. • Grease a work
surface and pour out the semolina. Smooth
it out with a spatula and let cool. • Use a
smooth pastry cutter to cut the dough into
2½-inch (6-cm) rounds. • Arrange the
leftover dough scraps in the bottom of the
prepared baking dish. Top with the rounds,
overlapping slightly. • Sprinkle with the
remaining 2 tablespoons butter and 4
tablespoons Parmesan. • Bake for 12–15
minutes, or until golden brown. • Serve hot.

4 cups (1 liter) milk
6 tablespoons (90 g) butter
Salt and freshly ground white pepper
⅛ teaspoon freshly grated nutmeg
1⅔ cups (250 g) semolina flour
6 tablespoons freshly grated Parmesan cheese
3 large egg yolks, beaten with 1 tablespoon milk
1 cup (125 g) freshly grated Parmesan cheese

Serves: 4
Preparation: 40 minutes
Cooking: 45 minutes
Level: 2

Nutritional Facts
Amount per serving
Percentage of Daily Values
based on 2,000 calories

CALORIES 743 36%
PROTEIN 35g 76%
FAT 42g 52%
FIBER 2.2g 9%
SALT 1.5g 27%

PASTA AND GNOCCHI

DITALINI WITH EGGPLANT SAUCE AND PINE NUTS

Put the eggplant in a colander. Sprinkle with the sea salt and let drain for 1 hour. Shake off excess salt. • Heat the frying oil in a frying pan to very hot. Fry the eggplant in batches until golden brown, 3–4 minutes. Drain on paper towels. • Broil (grill) the bell peppers until the skins are blackened. Put in a plastic bag for 10 minutes. Discard the skins and seeds and cut the flesh into small squares. • Heat the extra-virgin oil in a small saucepan over low heat. Add the onion and garlic with a pinch of salt and sweat for 15 minutes. • Toast the pine nuts in a frying pan over medium heat until golden, 2–3 minutes. • Cook the pasta in a large pot of salted boiling water until al dente. • Drain and transfer to a large serving bowl. Toss with the eggplant, bell peppers, onion, pine nuts, capers, olives, basil, parsley, and oregano. Serve hot.

2 eggplants (aubergine), with skin, very thinly sliced

Coarse sea salt

2 cups (500 ml) olive oil, for frying

2 yellow bell peppers (capsicums)

3 tablespoons extra-virgin olive oil

1 onion, finely chopped

2 cloves garlic, minced

Salt

4 tablespoons pine nuts

1 pound (500 g) ditalini

2 tablespoons salt-cured capers, rinsed

1 cup (100 g) green olives, pitted and coarsely chopped

1 small bunch fresh basil, torn

2 tablespoons finely chopped fresh parsley

1 tablespoon chopped fresh oregano

Serves: 6
Preparation: 30 minutes + 1 hour to drain
Cooking: 45 minutes
Level: 2

Nutritional Facts
Amount per serving
Percentage of Daily Values
based on 2,000 calories

 CALORIES 607

 PROTEIN 15g

 FAT 31g

 FIBER 5.7g

SALT 1.4g 25%

RIGATONI WITH RICOTTA BALLS

Preheat the oven to 400°F (200°C/gas 6).
• Combine the ricotta, Parmesan, flour, and a pinch of salt, egg yolk, parsley, and lemon zest in a bowl and stir until smooth.
• Shape into marble-size balls. Place in a baking pan and drizzle with 2 tablespoons of the oil. • Bake for 10 minutes, or until firm. • Chop the celery leaves in a food processor with the stock, 3 tablespoons of oil, lemon juice, and salt. • Cut the celery stalks into small squares. • Heat 1 tablespoon oil in a medium frying pan over medium heat. Add the celery stalks and sauté until almost tender, 4–5 minutes. Season with salt and remove from the heat. • Meanwhile, cook the pasta in a large pot of salted boiling water until al dente. Drain well and transfer to a heated serving dish. • Add the celery leaf mixture, sautéed celery, and ricotta balls. • Toss gently and serve hot.

12 ounces (350 g) fresh ricotta cheese, drained

4 tablespoons freshly grated Parmesan cheese

1/2 cup (75 g) all-purpose (plain) flour
Salt

1 large egg yolk

1 tablespoon finely chopped fresh parsley

1 tablespoon finely grated lemon zest

6 tablespoons (90 ml) extra-virgin olive oil

1 celery heart, with leaves

1/4 cup (60 ml) vegetable stock

1 tablespoon freshly squeezed lemon juice

1 pound (500 g) rigatoni

Serves: 6
Preparation: 30 minutes
Cooking: 20 minutes
Level: 2

Nutritional Facts
Amount per serving
Percentage of Daily Values
based on 2,000 calories

CALORIES
516
25%

PROTEIN
19g
41%

FAT
25g
31%

FIBER
0.5g
2%

SALT
1g
17%

RIGATONI WITH ROASTED BELL PEPPER SAUCE

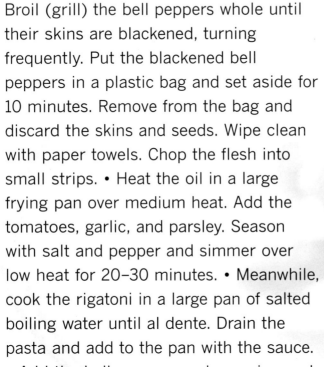

Broil (grill) the bell peppers whole until their skins are blackened, turning frequently. Put the blackened bell peppers in a plastic bag and set aside for 10 minutes. Remove from the bag and discard the skins and seeds. Wipe clean with paper towels. Chop the flesh into small strips. • Heat the oil in a large frying pan over medium heat. Add the tomatoes, garlic, and parsley. Season with salt and pepper and simmer over low heat for 20–30 minutes. • Meanwhile, cook the rigatoni in a large pan of salted boiling water until al dente. Drain the pasta and add to the pan with the sauce. • Add the bell peppers and pecorino and stir gently. • Serve hot.

2 large red bell peppers (capsicums)

1/4 cup (60 ml) extra-virgin olive oil

1 1/2 pounds (750 g) tomatoes, peeled and sliced

2 cloves garlic, finely chopped

2 tablespoons finely chopped fresh parsley

Salt and freshly ground black pepper

1 pound (500 g) rigatoni

6 tablespoons freshly grated pecorino cheese

Serves: 4
Preparation: 30 minutes
Cooking: 50–60 minutes
Level: 2

Nutritional Facts
Amount per serving
Percentage of Daily Values
based on 2,000 calories

 CALORIES 676 / 33
 PROTEIN 23g / 50
 FAT 21g / 8
 FIBER 7.2g / 29
 SALT 1.1g / 8

PENNE WITH RAW ARTICHOKES

Trim the artichoke stems, trim off the top third of the leaves, and discard the tough outer leaves by pulling them down and snapping them off. Cut in half lengthwise and scrape any fuzzy choke away with a knife. Cut into very thin slices. Place in a large serving bowl. • Whisk the oil and lemon juice in a small bowl and season with salt and pepper. Drizzle this mixture over the artichokes. • Meanwhile, cook the pasta in a large pot of salted boiling water until al dente. • Drain well and place in the bowl with the sauce. Toss well, sprinkle with the Parmesan, and serve hot.

6   fresh artichokes
1/2   cup (125 ml) extra-virgin olive oil
     Freshly squeezed juice of 1 large lemon
     Salt and freshly ground black pepper
1   pound (500 g) penne
5   ounces (150 g) Parmesan cheese, shaved

Serves: 4
Preparation: 20 minutes
Cooking: 15 minutes
Level: 1

Nutritional Facts
Amount per serving
Percentage of Daily Values
based on 2,000 calories

 CALORIES 578 28

 PROTEIN 21g

 FAT 28g 35

 FIBER 2.6g

SALT 1g 18

RIGATONI WITH CAULIFLOWER

Cook the cauliflower in a large pan of salted boiling water until crunchy tender, 2–3 minutes. • Remove the cauliflower with a slotted spoon, reserving the water. • Heat half the oil in a large saucepan over medium heat. Add the onion and sauté until pale gold, about 5 minutes. Season with salt and pepper. • Add the saffron and water and stir well. • Add the cauliflower, cover, and simmer over very low heat. • Heat the remaining oil in a small pot. Add the anchovies and stir until dissolved into the oil. • Add the anchovy mixture to the pan with the cauliflower together with the raisins and pine nuts. • Meanwhile, cook the rigatoni in the water used to cook the cauliflower, until al dente. • Drain the pasta and add to the pan with the sauce. Stir in the basil and cheese. Toss gently, garnish with extra basil, and serve hot.

1 small cauliflower, broken into florets
1/3 cup (90 ml) extra-virgin olive oil
1 large white onion, finely chopped
  Salt and freshly ground black pepper
1/4 teaspoon saffron threads
2 tablespoons water
6 anchovy fillets
1/3 cup (50 g) raisins
1/2 cup (60 g) pine nuts
1 pound (500 g) rigatoni
1 tablespoon finely chopped fresh basil + extra to garnish
1/2 cup (60 g) freshly grated pecorino cheese

Serves: 4
Preparation: 15 minutes
Cooking: 20 minutes
Level: 1

Nutritional Facts
Amount per serving
Percentage of Daily Values
based on 2,000 calories

 CALORIES 873
 PROTEIN 28g
 FAT 39g
 FIBER 6.7g
 SALT 1.5g

FUSILLI WITH MUSHROOMS

234

Heat 2 tablespoons of the oil in a large frying pan over medium heat. Add 3 cloves of garlic and sauté until pale gold, 2–3 minutes. • Add the mushrooms and half the parsley, season with salt and pepper, and simmer until the mushrooms are tender and their juices have reduced, 10–15 minutes. • Meanwhile, cook the pasta in a large pot of salted boiling water until al dente. Drain well and add to the pan with the sauce. • Sprinkle with the remaining garlic and parsley and drizzle with the remaining 2 tablespoons oil. Toss for 1–2 minutes and serve hot.

4 tablespoons extra-virgin olive oil

4 cloves garlic, finely chopped

1 1/2 pounds (750 g) white mushrooms, trimmed and thickly sliced

5 tablespoons finely chopped fresh parsley

Salt and freshly ground black pepper

1 pound (500 g) fusilli or rotini

Serves: 4
Preparation: 15 minutes
Cooking: 30 minutes
Level: 1

Nutritional Facts
Amount per serving
Percentage of Daily Values
based on 2,000 calories

CALORIES 582 28

PROTEIN 19g

FAT 17g

FIBER 6.2g

SALT 0.7g

FARFALLE WITH RADICCHIO AND GOAT CHEESE

Cook the pasta in a large pot of salted boiling water until it is al dente. • Meanwhile, heat 3 tablespoons of the oil in a large frying pan over medium heat. Add the onion and sauté until softened, about 3 minutes. • Add the radicchio and season with salt and pepper. Sauté for a few minutes, then add the beer. When the beer has evaporated, add the goat cheese and stir well, softening the mixture with the milk. • Drain the pasta well and add to the pan with the sauce. Toss for 1–2 minutes over medium heat. Drizzle with the remaining 1 tablespoon oil and serve hot.

1 pound (500 g) farfalle

4 tablespoons extra-virgin olive oil

1 large red onion, thinly sliced

2 heads red radicchio, cut into strips

Salt and freshly ground black pepper

1/4 cup (60 ml) beer

5 ounces (150 g) chèvre or other soft fresh goat cheese

2 tablespoons milk

Serves: 4
Preparation: 10 minutes
Cooking: 20 minutes
Level: 1

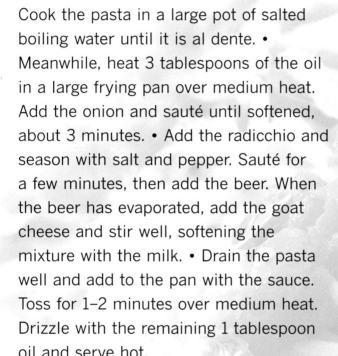

Nutritional Facts
Amount per serving
Percentage of Daily Values
based on 2,000 calories

 CALORIES 658 32

 PROTEIN 21 18

 FAT 22g 27

 FIBER 5.1g 20

 SALT 1.2g 21

PENNE WITH ZUCCHINI

238

Heat the oil in a large, deep frying pan until very hot. Fry the zucchini in batches until golden brown, 3–4 minutes per batch. Drain well on paper towels. Season with salt and cover with a plate to keep warm. • Cook the pasta in a large pot of salted boiling water until al dente. Drain and place in a heated serving dish. • Sprinkle with pecorino. Top with the fried zucchini, basil, and a drizzle of oil.

1 cup (250 ml) extra-virgin olive oil + extra to drizzle

1½ pounds (750 g) zucchini (courgettes), thinly sliced into rounds

Salt

1 pound (500 g) penne

½ cup (75 g) freshly grated pecorino cheese

½ cup (25 g) fresh basil leaves, torn

Serves: 4
Preparation: 10 minutes
Cooking: 30 minutes
Level: 1

Nutritional Facts
Amount per serving
Percentage of Daily Values
based on 2,000 calories

 CALORIES 751

 PROTEIN 29g

 FAT 24g

 FIBER 6g

 SALT 1.4g

FARFALLE WITH YOGURT AND AVOCADO

Heat 2 tablespoons of the oil in a large frying pan over medium heat. Add the onion and garlic and sauté until softened, 3–4 minutes. • Add the wine and simmer until evaporated. Set aside. • Cook the pasta in a large pot of salted boiling water until al dente. • Peel, pit, and dice the avocado. Drizzle with the lemon juice to keep it from turning brown. • Whisk the yogurt with the remaining 2 tablespoons of oil in a large bowl. Season with salt and pepper. Add the chile, celery, capers, and parsley. • Drain the pasta and toss in the yogurt sauce. Add the onion and avocado, toss again, and serve hot.

4	tablespoons (60 ml) extra-virgin olive oil
1	large onion, chopped
2	cloves garlic, finely chopped
1	tablespoon dry white wine
1	pound (500 g) farfalle
1	ripe avocado
	Freshly squeezed juice of 1 lemon
1	cup (250 ml) plain yogurt
	Salt and freshly ground black pepper
1	fresh red chile, thinly sliced
1	celery heart, thinly sliced
2	tablespoons salt-cured capers, rinsed
1	tablespoon finely chopped fresh parsley

Serves: 4
Preparation: 30 minutes
Cooking: 20 minutes
Level: 1

Nutritional Facts
Amount per serving
Percentage of Daily Values
based on 2,000 calories

 CALORIES **680** 35

 PROTEIN **20g**

 FAT **24g** 30

 FIBER **6g** 24

 SALT **0.9g**

SPICY FUSILLI WITH EGGPLANT

242

Heat the oil in a large frying pan over medium heat. Add the garlic and sauté until softened, 3–4 minutes. • Add the eggplant and chile and simmer for 10 minutes, stirring often. Season with salt and pepper. • Meanwhile, cook the pasta in a large pot of salted boiling water until al dente. • Drain the pasta thoroughly and place in the pan with the eggplant. Add the capers, oregano, and pine nuts. Toss well. • Serve hot.

1/3 cup (90 ml) extra-virgin olive oil

2 cloves garlic, finely chopped

1 large eggplant (aubergine), cut into small cubes

1 fresh chile, seeded and finely chopped

Salt and freshly ground black pepper

1 pound (500 g) fusilli, rotini, or other short pasta

2 tablespoons salted capers, rinsed

2 tablespoons finely chopped fresh oregano

4 tablespoons pine nuts

Serves: 4
Preparation: 15 minutes
Cooking: 20–24 minutes
Level: 1

Nutritional Facts
Amount per serving
Percentage of Daily Values
based on 2,000 calories

CALORIES
717
34%

PROTEIN
18g
39%

FAT
31g
38%

FIBER
5.4g
22%

SALT
0.7g
14%

CONCHIGLIE WITH YOGURT AND HERBS

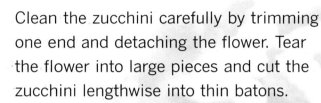

Clean the zucchini carefully by trimming one end and detaching the flower. Tear the flower into large pieces and cut the zucchini lengthwise into thin batons.
• Combine the yogurt, herbs, oil, garlic, nutmeg, salt, and pepper in a bowl and mix well. • Cook the pasta in a large pot of salted boiling water until al dente.
• Drain the pasta thoroughly and put in a large serving bowl. Add the zucchini and yogurt mixture and sprinkle with the Parmesan. • Toss well and serve.

6 small, very fresh zucchini (courgettes), with flowers, if possible

1 cup (250 ml) Greek-style yogurt

6 tablespoons finely chopped mixed fresh herbs, such as mint, marjoram, thyme, parsley, chives, etc.

2 tablespoons extra-virgin olive oil

2 cloves garlic, finely chopped

Pinch of freshly ground nutmeg

Salt and freshly ground black pepper

1 pound (500 g) conchiglie or medium shell pasta

1/2 cup (75 g) freshly grated Parmesan cheese

Serves: 4
Preparation: 15 minutes
Cooking: 10–15 minutes
Level: 1

Nutritional Facts
Amount per serving
Percentage of Daily Values
based on 2,000 calories

 CALORIES 648 31%
 PROTEIN 27g 59%
 FAT 19g 23%
 FIBER 4.8g 19%
 SALT 1.2g 21%

SPICY SPAGHETTI WITH GARLIC, PINE NUTS, AND RAISINS

Cook the pasta in a large pot of salted boiling water until al dente. • While the pasta is cooking, heat the oil in a large frying pan over medium heat. Add the garlic and chile and sauté until the garlic turns pale gold, 3–4 minutes. • Add the pine nuts and golden raisins. Season with salt and pepper. Sauté for 1 minute more. • Drain the pasta and add to the pan with the sauce. Add the parsley and toss over high heat for 1 minute. • Serve hot.

1	pound (500 g) spaghetti
1/3	cup (90 ml) extra-virgin olive oil
4	cloves garlic, finely chopped
1	fresh red chile, seeded and finely chopped
3/4	cup (100 g) pine nuts
1/2	cup (90 g) golden raisins (sultanas)
	Salt and freshly ground black pepper
5	tablespoons finely chopped fresh parsley

Serves: 4
Preparation: 10 minutes
Cooking: 15 minutes
Level: 1

Nutritional Facts
Amount per serving
Percentage of Daily Values
based on 2,000 calories

 CALORIES 765

 PROTEIN 19g

 FAT 31g

 FIBER 4.7g

 SALT 0.7g

SPAGHETTI WITH TOMATO SAUCE AND EGGPLANT

Eggplant: Put the eggplant slices in a colander and sprinkle with the coarse sea salt. Let drain for 1 hour. Shake off excess salt. • Heat the oil in a large, deep frying pan until very hot. • Fry the eggplant in small batches until golden brown, 5–7 minutes per batch. Drain on paper towels.

Tomato Sauce: Combine the tomatoes, onion, garlic, basil, oil, sugar, and salt in a medium saucepan. Cover and simmer over medium heat until the tomatoes have broken down, about 15 minutes. • Uncover and simmer over very low heat until the sauce has thickened, 15–20 minutes. • Transfer to a food processor and process until smooth. • Cook the spaghetti in a large pot of salted boiling water until al dente. Drain and add to the sauce. • Place the fried eggplant on a large heated serving dish and top with the spaghetti. Sprinkle with Parmesan and serve hot.

Eggplant

1   **pound (500 g) eggplant (aubergine), with skin, thinly sliced**

     Coarse sea salt

1   **cup (250 ml) olive oil, for frying**

Tomato Sauce

2   **pounds (1 kg) tomatoes, peeled and coarsely chopped**

1   **red onion, chopped**

2   **cloves garlic, finely chopped**

     Leaves from 1 small bunch fresh basil, torn

2   **tablespoons extra-virgin olive oil**

$^1/_8$ **teaspoon sugar**

     Salt

1   **pound (500 g) spaghetti**

1   **cup (125 g) freshly grated Parmesan cheese**

Serves: 4
Preparation: 30 minutes + 1 hour to drain
Cooking: 1 hour
Level: 2

Nutritional Facts
Amount per serving
Percentage of Daily Values
based on 2,000 calories

 CALORIES 800 39%
 PROTEIN 30g 65%
 FAT 32g 40%
 FIBER 9.4g 38%
 SALT 1.8g 33%

250

LINGUINE WITH MUSHROOMS

Clean the mushrooms very carefully and cut the larger ones into small pieces.
• Heat the oil in a frying pan over low heat. Add the onion, cover, and sweat for 20 minutes. Season with salt and add the garlic and chile. • Increase the heat and pour in the wine. Add the mushrooms and simmer over high heat until the wine has evaporated. • Stir in the tomatoes, basil, and parsley, and simmer until the mushrooms are tender, about 10 minutes. Season with salt. • Meanwhile, cook the pasta in a large pot of salted boiling water until al dente. • Drain and add to the sauce. Toss well and serve hot.

$1^1/2$ pounds (750 g) mixed mushrooms (porcini, white button mushrooms, chanterelle, enoki)

1 small onion, finely chopped

$1/4$ cup (60 ml) extra-virgin olive oil

Salt

2 cloves garlic, finely chopped

1 dried chile, crumbled

$1/4$ cup (60 ml) dry white wine

20 cherry tomatoes, quartered

Leaves from 1 bunch fresh basil, torn

1 tablespoon finely chopped fresh parsley

1 pound (500 g) linguine

Serves: 4
Preparation: 30 minutes
Cooking: 40 minutes
Level: 1

Nutritional Facts
Amount per serving
Percentage of Daily Values
based on 2,000 calories

CALORIES	PROTEIN	FAT	FIBER	SALT
615	20g	17g	7.3g	0.8g
30				

WHOLE-WHEAT SPAGHETTI WITH PESTO, POTATOES, AND BEANS

Pesto: Combine the basil, garlic, and pine nuts in a food processor and process until finely chopped, gradually adding the oil as you chop. • Transfer to a small bowl. Stir in the cheese, and season with salt and pepper.

Pasta: Cook the green beans in a large pot of salted boiling water until almost tender, 4–5 minutes. Drain and set aside. • Cook the pasta in a large pot of salted boiling water for 5 minutes. Add the potatoes and cook until the pasta is al dente and the potatoes are tender, 7–8 minutes more. • Drain well, reserving 2 tablespoons of the cooking liquid. Put the pasta and potatoes in a heated serving bowl. • Stir the reserved cooking liquid into the pesto. Pour the pesto into the pasta and potatoes, add the green beans, and toss well. • Season with pepper. Serve hot.

Pesto

- 1 **large bunch fresh basil leaves**
- 2 **cloves garlic**
- 2 **tablespoons pine nuts**
- 1/2 **cup (125 ml) extra-virgin olive oil**
- 4 **tablespoons freshly grated pecorino cheese**
- **Salt and freshly ground black pepper**

Pasta

- 12 **ounces (350 g) green beans, cut into short lengths**
- 1 **pound (500 g) whole-wheat (wholemeal) spaghetti**
- 8 **new potatoes, cut into small cubes**
- **Freshly ground black pepper**

Serves: 4
Preparation: 25 minutes
Cooking: 15 minutes
Level: 1

Nutritional Facts
Amount per serving
Percentage of Daily Values
based on 2,000 calories

CALORIES	PROTEIN	FAT	FIBER	SALT
950	28g	40	13.6g	1.4g
45	8	9	54	26

SPAGHETTI WITH FRESH TOMATO SAUCE AND LEMON

Blanch the tomatoes in boiling water for 2 minutes. Drain and peel them. Coarsely chop the flesh. • Cook the pasta in a large pot of salted boiling water until al dente. • Drain well and transfer to a large serving dish. • Add the tomatoes, basil, oil, lemon juice, and garlic. Season with salt and pepper. Toss well. • Garnish with basil and serve hot.

2 pounds (1 kg) ripe tomatoes

1 pound (500 g) spaghetti

4 tablespoons finely chopped fresh basil + extra leaves to garnish

1/3 cup (90 ml) extra-virgin olive oil

Freshly squeezed juice of 1 lemon

2 cloves garlic, finely chopped

Salt and freshly ground black pepper

Serves: 4
Preparation: 10 minutes
Cooking: 15 minutes
Level: 1

Nutritional Facts
Amount per serving
Percentage of Daily Values
based on 2,000 calories

 CALORIES 660 32%
 PROTEIN 17g 37%
 FAT 23g 28%
 FIBER 6.4g 26%
 SALT 0.8g 14%

LINGUINE WITH CHERRY TOMATOES AND PESTO

256

Preheat the oven to 350°F (180°C/gas 4).
• Place the cherry tomatoes on a baking sheet, sliced side up, and drizzle with 2 tablespoons of oil. Lightly dust with salt and white pepper. • Bake for 15 minutes.
• Combine the basil, Parmesan, garlic, almonds, and remaining oil in a food processor and process until smooth. Season with salt and white pepper.
• Meanwhile, cook the pasta in a large pot of salted boiling water until al dente.
• Drain well and place in a heated serving dish. • Add the pesto and baked tomatoes and toss gently. • Serve hot.

1^{1}/$_{2}$ pounds (750 g) cherry tomatoes, halved

6 tablespoons extra-virgin olive oil

Salt and freshly ground white pepper

2 cups (100 g) fresh basil

^{1}/$_{2}$ cup (60 g) freshly grated Parmesan cheese

2 cloves garlic, peeled

1^{1}/$_{2}$ ounces (45 g) blanched almonds

1 pound (500 g) linguine

Serves: 4
Preparation: 25 minutes
Cooking: 30 minutes
Level: 1

Nutritional Facts
Amount per serving
Percentage of Daily Values
based on 2,000 calories

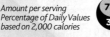

CALORIES	PROTEIN	FAT	FIBER	SALT
790	25g	34g	6.6g	1.1g
38%	54%	42%	26%	19%

BAKED PASTA WITH EGGPLANT

Put the eggplant in a colander and sprinkle with sea salt. Let drain for 1 hour. • Preheat the oven to 400°F (200°C/gas 6). • Butter a 13 x 9-inch (33 x 23-cm) baking dish and sprinkle with ¼ cup (30 g) of bread crumbs. • Heat the oil in a large frying pan until very hot. Fry the eggplant in small batches until golden brown, 3–4 minutes. Drain on paper towels. • Put the eggplant in a single layer on the bottom and sides of the baking dish. • Cook the pasta in a large pot of salted boiling water until al dente. • Drain and transfer to a large bowl. Mix in the tomato sauce, oregano, basil, and cheese. Season with pepper. • Spoon the pasta into the baking dish, taking care not to displace the eggplant. Top with the remaining eggplant. • Sprinkle with bread crumbs and dot with butter. • Bake for 25–30 minutes, until golden brown. • Let rest for 10 minutes before serving.

2	eggplants, each weighing about 1 pound (500 g), thinly sliced
	Coarse sea salt
³⁄4	cup (60 g) fine dry bread crumbs
1	cup (250 ml) olive oil, for frying
1	pound (500 g) bucatini or spaghetti
	Tomato Sauce (see Spaghetti with Tomato Sauce and Eggplant, page 248)
½	teaspoon dried oregano
	Leaves from 1 small bunch fresh basil, torn
1¹⁄4	cups (150 g) freshly grated Parmesan or pecorino cheese
	Freshly ground black pepper
¼	cup (60 g) chilled butter, shaved

Serves: 6
Preparation: 40 minutes
+ 70 minutes to drain and rest
Cooking: 45 minutes
Level: 2

Nutritional Facts
Amount per serving
Percentage of Daily Values
based on 2,000 calories

CALORIES	PROTEIN	FAT	FIBER	SALT
640	22g	30g	5.8g	1.2g

TAGLIATELLE WITH WALNUT SAUCE

Basic Fresh Pasta: Put the flour in a mound on a clean work surface. Make a well in the center and add the eggs. Use a fork to gradually incorporate the eggs into the flour. When almost all the flour has been absorbed, use your hands to gather the dough up into a ball. • Knead the dough by pushing down and forward on the ball of pasta with the palm of your hand. Fold the dough in half, give it a quarter-turn, and repeat. After 15–20 minutes, the dough should be smooth and silky, with tiny air bubbles visible near the surface. • Wrap in plastic wrap (cling film) and let rest at room temperature for 30 minutes. • Roll the dough through a pasta machine, reducing the thickness setting by one notch each time, until you reach the thinnest setting. • Put the pasta machine on the setting for tagliatelle and cut each sheet. Fold the tagliatelle into "nests" and set aside until you are ready to cook.

Basic Fresh Pasta
- 3 cups (450 g) all-purpose (plain) flour
- 4 large eggs, lightly beaten

Walnut Sauce
- 2 cups (100 g) fresh bread crumbs
- 1/2 cup (125 ml) milk
- 1 1/2 cups (175 g) shelled
- 4 cloves garlic, peeled
- Salt
- 2 tablespoons butter, cut up

Serves: 4
Preparation: 1 hour + 1 hour to rest
Cooking: 3–4 minutes
Level: 3

Walnut Sauce: Put the bread crumbs in a small bowl. Pour in the milk. • Shell the walnuts. Combine the walnuts and garlic in a food processor and chop briefly. Don't make the sauce too smooth—you should still be able to feel the texture of the walnuts. • Add the bread crumbs and milk (without squeezing the bread crumbs) and season with salt. Set aside to rest for 30 minutes. • Cook the tagliatelle in a large pot of salted boiling water until al dente, 3–4 minutes. • Drain the pasta and put in a bowl with the butter and walnut sauce. Toss gently and serve hot.

261

(See photograph on the following page.)

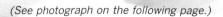

Nutritional Facts
Amount per serving
Percentage of Daily Values
based on 2,000 calories

CALORIES	PROTEIN	FAT	FIBER	SALT
920	27g	47g	6g	1.3g

FRESH PASTA WITH SCALLIONS AND TOMATOES

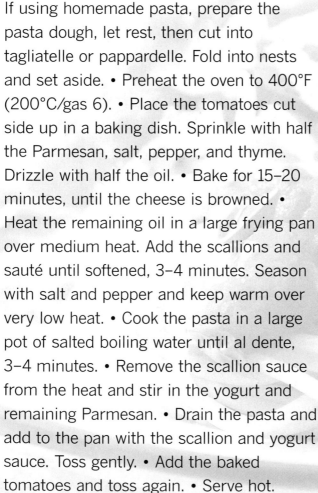

264

If using homemade pasta, prepare the pasta dough, let rest, then cut into tagliatelle or pappardelle. Fold into nests and set aside. • Preheat the oven to 400°F (200°C/gas 6). • Place the tomatoes cut side up in a baking dish. Sprinkle with half the Parmesan, salt, pepper, and thyme. Drizzle with half the oil. • Bake for 15–20 minutes, until the cheese is browned. • Heat the remaining oil in a large frying pan over medium heat. Add the scallions and sauté until softened, 3–4 minutes. Season with salt and pepper and keep warm over very low heat. • Cook the pasta in a large pot of salted boiling water until al dente, 3–4 minutes. • Remove the scallion sauce from the heat and stir in the yogurt and remaining Parmesan. • Drain the pasta and add to the pan with the scallion and yogurt sauce. Toss gently. • Add the baked tomatoes and toss again. • Serve hot.

14 ounces (400 g) store-bought pappardelle or tagliatelle or Basic Fresh Pasta (see page 260)

12 ounces (350 g) cherry tomatoes, halved

1/2 cup (75 g) freshly grated Parmesan cheese

Salt and freshly ground black pepper

2 tablespoons finely chopped fresh thyme

1/3 cup (90 ml) extra-virgin olive oil

8 scallions (spring onions), trimmed and thinly sliced

1 cup (250 ml) plain yogurt, at room temperature

Serves: 4
Preparation: 20 minutes + time to make and rest pasta
Cooking: 30 minutes
Level: 2

Nutritional Facts
Amount per serving
Percentage of Daily Values
based on 2,000 calories

CALORIES	PROTEIN	FAT	FIBER	SALT
593	22g	29g	1.8g	1.3g

WATERCRESS TAGLIOLINI WITH PESTO

Cook the watercress in salted boiling water until wilted, 2–3 minutes. Drain and finely chop in a food processor. • Put both flours and salt in a large bowl. Add the watercress and stir in the water until the dough is firm. • Transfer to a floured work surface and knead until smooth and elastic, about 10 minutes. Wrap in plastic wrap (cling film) and let rest for 1 hour. • Roll the dough through a pasta machine, reducing the thickness setting by one notch each time, until you reach the thinnest setting. • Put the pasta machine on the setting for tagliolini (thin ribbons) and cut each sheet. Fold into "nests." • Combine the basil, oil, cream cheese, pine nuts, and garlic in a food processor and process until smooth. • Cook the tagliolini in a large pot of salted boiling water until al dente, 2–3 minutes. • Drain and spoon the sauce over the top. Serve garnished with extra watercress.

8 ounces (250 g) watercress + extra to garnish

1¹/₂ cups (250 g) all-purpose (plain) flour

1¹/₂ cups (250 g) whole-wheat (wholemeal) flour

¹/₂ teaspoon salt

³/₄ cup (180 ml) water

1¹/₂ cups (75 g) fresh basil

¹/₄ cup (60 ml) extra-virgin olive oil

3 ounces (90 g) cream cheese

4 tablespoons pine nuts

3 cloves garlic

Serves: 4
Preparation: 1 hour + 1 hour to rest
Cooking: 4–6 minutes
Level: 3

Nutritional Facts
*Amount per serving
Percentage of Daily Values
based on 2,000 calories*

 CALORIES 750 36

 PROTEIN 19g

 FAT 35g

 FIBER 7.6g 30

 SALT 0.9g

MALTAGLIATI WITH ASPARAGUS AND PEAS

Pasta: If using homemade pasta, prepare the pasta dough. Shape into a ball, wrap in plastic wrap (cling film), and set aside to rest for 1 hour. • Roll the pasta out into thin sheets by hand or use a pasta machine. Cut the sheets into irregular diamond shapes.

Sauce: Melt the butter in a large frying pan over medium heat. Add the asparagus and sauté for 5 minutes.
• Add the peas and 2–3 tablespoons of water from the pasta pot. Cook until the peas are tender, about 5 minutes. • Cook the maltagliati in a large pot of salted boiling water until al dente, 3–4 minutes.
• Drain well and add to the pan with the asparagus sauce. Add the cream and parsley. Season with salt and pepper and toss well. • Serve hot.

Pasta

14 ounces (400 g) store-bought maltagliati or Basic Fresh Pasta (see page 260)

Sauce

1/4 cup (60 g) butter

1 pound (500 g) asparagus spears, cut into short pieces

1 cup (150 g) frozen peas

1/2 cup (125 ml) heavy (double) cream

2 tablespoons finely chopped fresh parsley

Salt and freshly ground black pepper

Serves: 4
Preparation: 45 minutes + time to make and rest pasta
Cooking: 15 minutes
Level: 3

Nutritional Facts
Amount per serving
Percentage of Daily Values
based on 2,000 calories

CALORIES 597 | PROTEIN 18g | FAT 33g | FIBER 5g | SALT 1g

TAGLIATELLE WITH PINE NUT AND WALNUT PESTO

If using homemade pasta, prepare the pasta dough, let rest, then cut into tagliatelle. Fold into nests and set aside. • Preheat the oven to 350°F (180°C/gas 4). • Roast the pine nuts in a baking dish until pale gold, about 5 minutes. • Shell the walnuts. Coarsely chop a few by hand to garnish. Finely chop the rest in a food processor with the pine nuts, garlic, parsley, and oil. Season with salt. • Cook the pasta in a large pot of salted boiling water until al dente, 3–4 minutes. • Drain and place in a heated serving dish. Cover with the sauce, toss carefully, garnish with the reserved walnuts, and serve.

14 ounces (400 g) store-bought tagliatelle or Basic Fresh Pasta (see page 260)

1/3 cup (45 g) pine nuts

1 pound (500 g) walnuts, in shell (or 1 cup/125 g shelled walnuts)

2 cloves garlic

1 cup (50 g) fresh parsley

1/4 cup (60 ml) extra-virgin olive oil

Salt

Serves: 4
Preparation: 30 minutes + time to make and rest pasta
Cooking: 15 minutes
Level: 2

Nutritional Facts
Amount per serving
Percentage of Daily Values
based on 2,000 calories

 CALORIES 645

 PROTEIN 18g 3%

 FAT 40g

 FIBER 2g

 SALT 1.3g 24%

BAKED SPINACH TAGLIATELLE

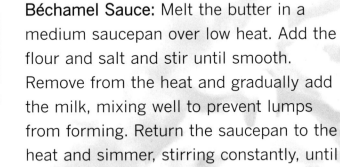

Béchamel Sauce: Melt the butter in a medium saucepan over low heat. Add the flour and salt and stir until smooth. Remove from the heat and gradually add the milk, mixing well to prevent lumps from forming. Return the saucepan to the heat and simmer, stirring constantly, until thickened and cooked. Set aside.

Pasta: Preheat the oven to 350°F (180°C/gas 4). • Cook the pasta in a large pot of salted boiling water until al dente, 3–4 minutes. Drain well. • Butter a large ovenproof baking dish and spread with a layer of Béchamel. Cover with pasta and top with pieces of butter. Sprinkle with Parmesan. Repeat this layering process until all the ingredients are in the dish, finishing with a layer of butter and cheese. • Bake for about 20 minutes, until golden brown. Serve hot.

Béchamel Sauce
- 1/4 cup (60 g) butter, cut into pieces
- 1/3 cup (50 g) all-purpose (plain) flour
- 1/4 teaspoon salt
- 2 cups (500 ml) milk

Pasta
- 1 pound (500 g) store-bought fresh spinach tagliatelle
- 1/4 cup (60 g) butter, cut into pieces
- 1 cup (120 g) freshly grated Parmesan cheese

Serves: 4
Preparation: 30 minutes
Cooking: 25 minutes
Level: 2

Nutritional Facts
Amount per serving
Percentage of Daily Values
based on 2,000 calories

CALORIES	PROTEIN	FAT	FIBER	SALT
774	24g	34g	2g	2.2g

POTATO GNOCCHI WITH TOMATO AND PARMESAN

Potato Gnocchi: Boil the potatoes in salted water until tender, 20–25 minutes. Slip off the skins, then mash with a potato masher until smooth (or run them through a potato ricer). • Add the flour, salt, egg, and Parmesan and knead until the dough is smooth. Shape into a ball. • Break off little bits of dough and roll them out into cylinders about as thick as your finger. Cut them into pieces about 3/4 inch (2 cm) long. • Preheat the oven to 400°F (200°C/gas 6).
Tomato Sauce: Melt the butter in a medium saucepan over medium heat. Add the tomatoes, garlic, onion, and salt. • Cover and simmer for about 10 minutes, until the tomatoes have broken down. Uncover and let reduce for 10 minutes. • Remove from the heat and process in a food processor until smooth. • Cook the gnocchi in small batches in a large pot of salted boiling water until they rise to the surface, about 2 minutes. Use

Potato Gnocchi

2 pounds (1 kg) boiling potatoes, with skins

1 2/3 cups (250 g) all-purpose (plain) flour

1/2 teaspoon salt

1 large egg

3 tablespoons freshly grated Parmesan cheese

Tomato Sauce

3 tablespoons butter

2 pounds (1 kg) firm-ripe tomatoes, peeled and coarsely chopped

2 cloves garlic, lightly crushed but whole

1 red onion, thinly sliced

Salt

3/4 cup (90 g) freshly grated Parmesan cheese

Serves: 4
Preparation: 20 minutes
Cooking: 1 hour
Level: 2

a slotted spoon to remove the gnocchi and transfer to a baking dish. • Cover with the some tomato sauce and sprinkle with some Parmesan. Repeat until all the gnocchi, sauce, and Parmesan are in the dish. • Bake for 12–15 minutes, or until bubbling and hot. • Serve hot.

■■■ *Potato gnocchi are not difficult to make, and they are very versatile. Serve them with this classic tomato sauce, or try them with melted butter and fresh herbs (sage is very good), melted Gorgonzola, fresh cream, and plenty of freshly ground black pepper, or any of your other favorite pasta sauces.*

(See photograph on the following page.)

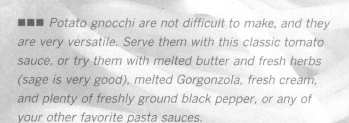

Nutritional Facts
Amount per serving
Percentage of Daily Values
based on 2,000 calories

CALORIES	PROTEIN	FAT	FIBER	SALT
729	26g	27g	8.2g	1.7g
35%				

278

POTATO GNOCCHI WITH HERBS AND SUN-DRIED TOMATOES

If using homemade potato gnocchi, prepare them first.

Sauce: Combine the pecorino with ½ cup (125 ml) of the milk in a small saucepan over low heat. • Put the cornstarch in a small bowl and stir in the remaining ¼ cup milk. Add to the pecorino, stirring constantly, and bring to a gentle simmer. Remove from the heat and stir in the herbs and sun-dried tomatoes. Season with salt and pepper. • Cook the gnocchi in small batches in a large pot of salted boiling water until they rise to the surface, about 2 minutes. • Use a slotted spoon to remove the gnocchi and transfer to a heated serving dish. • Pour the sauce over the top. Toss gently, and serve hot.

Potato Gnocchi (see page 274) or 1 pound (500 g) store-bought fresh potato gnocchi

Sauce

5 ounces (150 g) pecorino cheese, freshly grated

¾ cup (180 ml) milk

1 tablespoon cornstarch (cornflour)

4 tablespoons finely chopped fresh parsley

1 small bunch fresh chives, snipped

1 tablespoon finely chopped fresh thyme

1 tablespoon finely chopped fresh mint

Salt and freshly ground black pepper

16 sun-dried tomatoes packed in oil, drained and finely chopped

Nutritional Facts
*Amount per serving
Percentage of Daily Values
based on 2,000 calories*

 CALORIES 680

 PROTEIN 33g

 FAT 16g

 FIBER 8.3g

 SALT 2.4g

Serves: 4
Preparation: 20 minutes
Cooking: 30 minutes
Level: 2

SPINACH GNOCCHI WITH TOMATO SAUCE

Mix the ricotta and spinach in a large bowl. • Add the eggs, 1 cup (125 g) of Parmesan, and 1/2 cup (75 g) flour. Season with salt and pepper and add the lemon zest. • Dip your hands in the remaining 2 tablespoons of flour and form the spinach mixture into 2-inch (5-cm) balls. • Cook the gnocchi in a large pot of salted boiling water until they rise to the surface, 3–4 minutes per batch. • Remove with a slotted spoon and transfer to individual serving dishes. • Spoon the tomato sauce over the top of each serving and sprinkle with the extra Parmesan cheese. • Serve hot.

2 cups (500 g) fresh ricotta, strained through a fine-mesh sieve

1 1/2 cups (350 g) finely chopped cooked spinach, well drained

2 large eggs

1 cup (125 g) freshly grated Parmesan cheese + extra to serve

1/2 cup (75 g) + 2 tablespoons all-purpose (plain) flour

Salt and freshly ground black pepper

Finely grated zest of 1/2 lemon

Tomato Sauce (see page 274)

Serves: 6
Preparation: 30 minutes + time for the sauce
Cooking: 20 minutes
Level: 2

Nutritional Facts
Amount per serving
Percentage of Daily Values
based on 2,000 calories

 CALORIES 460
 PROTEIN 32g
 FAT 26g
 FIBER 3.7g
 SALT 1.9g

HERB GNOCCHI

Boil the herbs in salted water until tender, 2–3 minutes. Drain, squeezing out excess moisture. Chop finely. • Cook the potatoes in salted boiling water until tender, 20–25 minutes. Drain and peel. Mash and place in a bowl to cool. • Heat the oil in a frying pan over medium heat. Add the herbs and sauté for 2 minutes. • Season the potatoes with salt and pepper and work in half the herbs, the egg, and 1 cup (150 g) flour. • Break off walnut-size pieces of dough. Shape into balls. Coat with remaining flour. • Melt the butter in a frying pan over medium heat. Add the onion and sauté until softened, 3–4 minutes. • Pour in the wine and let evaporate. Add the garlic and remaining herbs and simmer for 10 minutes. • Cook the gnocchi in batches in salted boiling water until they rise to the surface, 3–4 minutes. • Use a slotted spoon to transfer to serving plates. Top with sauce and cheese.

12 ounces (350 g) mixed fresh herbs (mint, basil, fennel, sage, parsley, rosemary)

3 pounds (1.5 kg) boiling potatoes, with skins

1/4 cup (60 ml) extra-virgin olive oil

Salt and freshly ground white pepper

1 large egg, lightly beaten

1 1/3 cups (200 g) all-purpose (plain) flour

2 tablespoons butter

1/2 onion, finely chopped

1/4 cup (60 ml) dry white wine

1 clove garlic, finely chopped

6 tablespoons freshly grated Parmesan or pecorino cheese

Serves: 4
Preparation: 45 minutes
Cooking: 1 hour
Level: 2

Nutritional Facts
Amount per serving
Percentage of Daily Values
based on 2,000 calories

CALORIES	PROTEIN	FAT	FIBER	SALT
647	19g	32g	7.8g	1.3g
3	1	6	3	2

BAKED GNOCCHI WITH BUTTER AND SAGE

Preheat the oven to 400°F (200°C/gas 6).
• Cook the Swiss chard in a large pot of salted boiling water until tender, 7–10 minutes. Squeeze dry and finely chop.
• Butter a large baking dish. • Soak the bread in the milk for 15 minutes. Squeeze out excess milk and transfer to a food processor. Add the Swiss chard and egg yolks and process until smooth. • Mix in the fine dry bread crumbs, nutmeg, salt, and pepper. • Break off walnut-size pieces and form into elongated 1½-inch (4-cm) gnocchi. • Cook the gnocchi in batches in a large pot of salted boiling water until they rise to the surface, about 3 minutes. • Use a slotted spoon to scoop out and arrange in the dish. • Sprinkle with the Parmesan.
• Melt the butter with the sage in a small saucepan and drizzle over the gnocchi. Season with salt. • Bake for 10–15 minutes, until the cheese is bubbling. • Serve hot.

12 ounces (350 g) Swiss chard (silverbeet)

3½ cups (400 g) day-old bread crumbs

2 cups (500 ml) milk

2 large egg yolks

6 tablespoons fine dry bread crumbs

1/8 teaspoon freshly grated nutmeg

Salt and freshly ground black pepper

3/4 cup (90 g) freshly grated Parmesan cheese

1/2 cup (125 g) butter

Fresh sage leaves

Serves: 6
Preparation: 50 minutes
Cooking: 45 minutes
Level: 2

Nutritional Facts
Amount per serving
Percentage of Daily Values
based on 2,000 calories

CALORIES
660
3

PROTEIN
22g
8

FAT
38g
7

FIBER
7g
28

SALT
3.4g

CARROT AND POTATO GNOCCHI WITH ARUGULA SAUCE

Carrot and Potato Gnocchi: Cook the carrots and potatoes in a large pan of salted boiling water until tender, 15–20 minutes. Drain well. • Mash the carrots and potatoes together and let cool a little. • Stir in the egg, flour, salt, white pepper, and nutmeg, mixing well with a wooden spoon to obtain a firm dough. • Working quickly, scoop out pieces of dough and roll them on a lightly floured work surface into long sausage shapes about 3/4 inch (2 cm) in diameter. Cut the sausage shapes into pieces about 1 inch (2.5 cm) long. Set the gnocchi out on a floured clean cloth and leave for an hour or two to dry. • If preferred (this is optional, and slightly tricky, but gives the gnocchi their characteristic shape), press each piece with your thumb onto the tongs of a fork and twist. The gnocchi will have fork marks on one side.

Carrot and Potato Gnocchi

- 2 pounds (1 kg) carrots, cut into thick rounds
- 1 pound (500 g) potatoes, peeled and cut into chunks
- 1 large egg, lightly beaten
- 1 1/3 cups (200 g) all-purpose (plain) flour
  Salt and freshly ground white pepper
- 1/4 teaspoon freshly grated nutmeg

Sauce

- 2 cups (100 g) arugula (rocket)
- 2 cloves garlic
- 4 tablespoons pine nuts
- 2/3 cup (100 g) freshly grated pecorino cheese
  Salt and freshly ground black pepper
- 1/2 cup (125 ml) extra-virgin olive oil

Serves: 6
Preparation: 35 minutes
+ 1–2 hours to dry
Cooking: 45 minutes
Level: 2

Sauce: Combine the arugula, garlic, pine nuts, cheese, salt, and pepper in a blender or food processor and process until finely chopped. Transfer to a bowl and gradually stir in the oil. • Cook the gnocchi in batches in a large pan of salted boiling water until they rise to the surface, 3–4 minutes. • Scoop them out with a slotted spoon, drain well, and place in a warmed dish. Repeat until all the gnocchi are cooked. • Spoon the arugula sauce over the gnocchi. Toss gently and serve hot.

(See photograph on the following page.)

Nutritional Facts
Amount per serving
Percentage of Daily Values
based on 2,000 calories

CALORIES	PROTEIN	FAT	FIBER	SALT
563	15g	33g	6.3g	1.2g

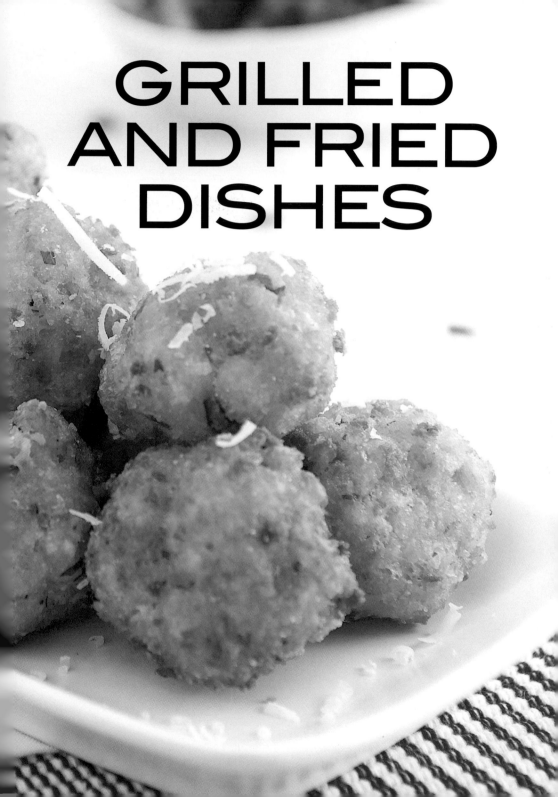

GRILLED AND FRIED DISHES

GRILLED SUMMER VEGETABLES

Prepare a medium-hot fire in a gas or charcoal grill or preheat an indoor grill pan over high heat. • Brush all the vegetables lightly with oil before placing them on the grill. • Place the zucchini on the grill and cook until tender, 3–4 minutes each side. Place on a serving plate and keep warm. • Place the bell pepper strips on the grill and cook until tender, about 5 minutes each side. Place on a serving plate and keep warm. • Place the eggplant slices on the grill and cook until tender, about 5 minutes each side. • Place the grilled vegetables on a large serving plate. Season with salt and pepper. Drizzle with the oil and serve hot or at room temperature.

4	medium zucchini (courgettes), thinly sliced lengthwise
1	red bell pepper (capsicum), seeded and cut in strips
1	yellow bell pepper (capsicum), seeded and cut in strips
1	large eggplant (aubergine) with skin, thinly sliced
	Salt and freshly ground black pepper
1/2	cup (125 ml) extra-virgin olive oil

Serves: 4
Preparation: 15 minutes
Cooking: 30 minutes
Level: 1

■ ■ ■ *These vegetables make a superb starter or can be served with soft, fresh cheeses and crusty bread for a healthy lunch or snack.*

Nutritional Facts
Amount per serving
Percentage of Daily Values
based on 2,000 calories

CALORIES	PROTEIN	FAT	FIBER	SALT
306	3g	30g	3.2g	0.1g

GRILLED ZUCCHINI

Prepare a medium-hot fire in a gas or charcoal grill, or preheat an indoor grill pan over high heat. • Mix the oil, garlic, basil, chile, and salt in a shallow dish. Add the zucchini and let marinate for 1 hour. • Drain the marinade from the zucchini slices. Arrange the zucchini in small batches on the grill. Cook until tender, 3–4 minutes, brushing with the marinade during cooking. • Transfer to a serving plate and serve hot or at room temperature.

$1/3$ cup (90 ml) extra-virgin olive oil

3 cloves garlic, finely chopped

1 small bunch fresh basil, torn

Dried chile, crumbled, or red pepper flakes, to taste

Salt

6 zucchini (courgettes), thinly sliced lengthwise

Serves: 4
Preparation: 10 minutes
  + 1 hour to marinate
Cooking: 20 minutes
Level: 1

Nutritional Facts
Amount per serving
Percentage of Daily Values
based on 2,000 calories

CALORIES	PROTEIN	FAT	FIBER	SALT
204	2g	21g	1.1g	0g
10	4	26	4	0

GRILLED EGGPLANT

296

Prepare a medium-hot fire in a gas or charcoal grill, or preheat an indoor grill pan over high heat. • Thinly slice the eggplants lengthwise. Brush lightly with a little oil, and season lightly to taste. • Cook the eggplant in batches on the grill until tender, turning often, about 10 minutes each batch. • Arrange in layers in a dish, placing slices of garlic and sage leaves between the layers. • Drizzle with vinegar to taste. • Cover and let marinate for 3–4 hours before serving.

4   medium large eggplants (aubergines)

1/2 cup (125 ml) extra-virgin olive oil

Salt and freshly ground black pepper

3   cloves garlic, thinly sliced

15 leaves fresh sage

Balsamic vinegar or red wine vinegar, to drizzle

Serves: 6
Preparation: 20 minutes
    + 1 hour to drain and
    3–4 hours to marinate
Cooking: 30–40 minutes
Level: 1

Nutritional Facts
Amount per serving
Percentage of Daily Values
based on 2,000 calories

 CALORIES 201 0%

 PROTEIN 2g

 FAT 20g 25%

 FIBER 3.8g 5%

 SALT 0.5g

GRILLED ONIONS

Prepare a medium-hot fire in a gas or charcoal grill or preheat an indoor grill pan over medium heat. • Blanch the onions in a pot of salted boiling water for 5 minutes. Drain and dry well. If the onions are large, cut them in half. Thread onto four skewers, alternating with a half bay leaf. Skewer the onions horizontally so that they will lie flat on the grill pan during cooking. • Brush generously with oil, and season to taste. Cook on the grill, turning often, until tender and golden brown, about 15 minutes. • Season and drizzle with more oil to taste. Serve hot or at room temperature.

20 small white onions, peeled

8 bay leaves, cut in half

1/2 cup (125 ml) extra-virgin olive oil

Salt and freshly ground black pepper

Serves: 4
Preparation: 10 minutes
Cooking: 15 minutes
Level: 1

Nutritional Facts
Amount per serving
Percentage of Daily Values
based on 2,000 calories

 CALORIES 348

 PROTEIN 3g

 FAT 29g

 FIBER 3.7g

 SALT 0.7g

VEGETABLE SKEWERS

Slice the zucchini into rounds $^1/_2$ inch (1 cm) thick. Cut the eggplant into slices of the same thickness, and cut into pieces the same size as the zucchini. Cut the bell peppers into 1-inch (2.5-cm) squares. • Thread the vegetables onto metal skewers. Set in a dish in a single layer. Prepare at least two skewers per person. • Combine the oil, paprika, lemon juice, and herbs in a small bowl. Season with salt and pepper and whisk well. Pour over the skewers, turning them to coat. Let marinate in the refrigerator for 2 hours. • Prepare a medium-hot fire in a gas or charcoal grill or preheat an indoor grill pan over high heat. • Drain the skewers, reserving the marinade to baste, and place half on the grill. Cook, turning so that they brown on all sides, until tender, about 10 minutes. Baste with the reserved marinade. Repeat with the remaining skewers. • Serve hot.

2   zucchini (courgettes)

1   eggplant (aubergine)

1   medium onion

1   small red bell pepper (capsicum)

1   small yellow bell pepper (capsicum)

1   small green bell pepper (capsicum)

$^1/_2$ cup (125 ml) extra-virgin olive oil

$^1/_2$ teaspoon hot paprika

Freshly squeezed juice of $^1/_2$ lemon

1   tablespoon finely chopped fresh herbs (oregano, mint, or thyme) + extra leaves to garnish

Salt and freshly ground black pepper

Serves: 4
Preparation: 25 minutes
  + 2 hours to marinate
Cooking: 20 minutes
Level: 1

Nutritional Facts
Amount per serving
Percentage of Daily Values
based on 2,000 calories

CALORIES	PROTEIN	FAT	FIBER	SALT
303	2g	30	3g	0.1g

VEGETABLE KEBABS WITH MOZZARELLA

Prepare a medium-hot fire in a gas or charcoal grill, or preheat an indoor grill pan over high heat. • Arrange the zucchini and eggplant on the grill and cook, turning often, until tender, 7–10 minutes. • Thread the vegetables onto metal skewers, alternating with the mozzarella, tomatoes, and basil leaves. Season with salt and pepper, and brush with the oil. • Cook on the grill until the cheese and tomatoes are heated through, about 5 minutes. • Serve hot.

2 zucchini (courgettes), thickly sliced

1 long, slender eggplant (aubergine), thickly sliced

8 baby mozzarella cheeses (bocconcini), cut in half

About 16 cherry tomatoes

Fresh basil leaves

Salt and freshly ground black pepper

1/2 cup (125 ml) extra-virgin olive oil

Serves: 4
Preparation: 20 minutes
Cooking: 15–20 minutes
Level: 1

 Nutritional Facts
Amount per serving
Percentage of Daily Values
based on 2,000 calories

 CALORIES 446 21%

 PROTEIN 13g 28%

 FAT 42g 52%

 FIBER 2.3g 9%

 SALT 1.3g 24%

ZUCCHINI WITH ARUGULA PESTO

Place the zucchini in a small, shallow dish. • Mix 3 tablespoons of oil, cider vinegar, balsamic vinegar, and garlic in a small bowl. Season with salt and pepper. Pour over the zucchini. Let marinate for 1 hour. • Put 1$^1/_2$ cups (75 g) of arugula in a blender with 4 tablespoons of pine nuts and the remaining oil and process until smooth. • Drain the zucchini, reserving the marinade. • Prepare a medium-hot fire in a gas or charcoal grill, or preheat an indoor grill pan over high heat. • Cook the zucchini in batches, turning often until tender, 4–5 minutes each batch. • Arrange the remaining arugula on a serving platter and place the zucchini on top. Sprinkle the remaining pine nuts and the raisins over the zucchini. Season with salt and pepper, and drizzle with the reserved marinade. • Serve hot or at room temperature.

4	zucchini (courgettes), thinly sliced lengthwise
8	tablespoons (125 ml) extra-virgin olive oil
2	tablespoons cider vinegar
1	tablespoon balsamic vinegar
1	clove garlic, thinly sliced
	Salt and freshly ground black pepper
2	cups (100 g) arugula (rocket)
6	tablespoons pine nuts
1–2	tablespoons hot water, optional
4	tablespoons raisins

Serves: 4
Preparation: 25 minutes
+ 1 hour to marinate
Cooking: 30 minutes
Level: 1

Nutritional Facts
Amount per serving
Percentage of Daily Values
based on 2,000 calories

CALORIES	PROTEIN	FAT	FIBER	SALT
430	5g	41g	1.3g	0.7g

PAN-FRIED POTATOES WITH SUN-DRIED TOMATOES

Bring a large pot of salted water to a boil, add the potatoes, and cook until almost tender, about 10 minutes (depending on their size). • Drain well and cut in half. • Heat the oil in a large frying pan over medium heat. Add the potatoes and sauté for 5 minutes. • Sprinkle with the paprika and season with salt. Add the sun-dried tomatoes and capers. Sauté until the potatoes are crisp, 3–5 minutes. • Sprinkle with the oregano and sauté for 1 minute more. • Serve hot.

- 1¹/₂ pounds (750 g) whole small new potatoes
- ¹/₂ cup (125 ml) extra-virgin olive oil
- ¹/₂ teaspoon sweet paprika
- Salt
- 6 sun-dried tomatoes packed in oil, drained and finely chopped
- 1 tablespoon capers, drained
- 1 teaspoon dried oregano

Serves: 4
Preparation: 10 minutes
Cooking: 20 minutes
Level: 1

Nutritional Facts
Amount per serving
Percentage of Daily Values
based on 2,000 calories

 CALORIES 429

 PROTEIN 5g

 FAT 29g

 FIBER 4.1g

 SALT 0.9g

BREADED ASPARAGUS WITH MINT DIP

308

Cook the asparagus in a large pot of salted boiling water until almost tender, about 5 minutes. Drain well and dry carefully on a clean towel. • Beat the eggs and Parmesan in a small bowl. • Heat the oil in a deep-fryer or deep saucepan. Test the oil temperature by dropping in a small piece of bread. If it immediately bubbles to the surface and begins to turn golden, the oil is ready. • Dip the asparagus in the beaten eggs and then in the bread crumbs, making sure they are well coated. • Fry the asparagus in small batches until golden brown, 3–4 minutes each batch. • Drain on paper towels. • Beat the yogurt, mayonnaise, and mint in a small bowl. • Season the asparagus with salt. • Serve hot with the mint dip on the side.

1	pound (500 g) asparagus, trimmed
2	large eggs
3	tablespoons freshly grated Parmesan cheese
4	cups (1 liter) vegetable oil, for frying
1	cup (150 g) fine, dry bread crumbs
1/2	cup (125 ml) plain yogurt
1/2	cup (125 ml) mayonnaise
1	tablespoon finely chopped fresh mint
	Salt

Serves: 6
Preparation: 10 minutes
Cooking: 20–30 minutes
Level: 1

Nutritional Facts
Amount per serving
Percentage of Daily Values
based on 2,000 calories

CALORIES	PROTEIN	FAT	FIBER	SALT
349	9g	30g	2.4g	1g

TOMATO AND BASIL RICE FRITTERS

Heat 2 tablespoons of the butter and oil in a large saucepan over medium heat. Add the onion and garlic and cook until softened, 3–4 minutes. Add the rice and cook, stirring to coat, for 2 minutes. Pour in the wine, tomatoes, and tomato paste and cook, stirring, until all the liquid has been absorbed. Decrease the heat to medium-low and gradually add the stock $^{1}/_{2}$ cup (125 ml) at a time, stirring until all the liquid is absorbed. Cook, stirring, for 20–25 minutes, or until all the rice is completely tender and cooked through (not al dente, as in traditional risotto). Stir in the Parmesan cheese, basil, and the remaining 1 tablespoon butter. Season with salt and pepper. • Spread the risotto onto a large tray and set aside to cool. • Form the cooled risotto into walnut-size balls. Place a piece of mozzarella in the center of each and

3   **tablespoons butter**

1   **tablespoon olive oil**

1   **medium onion, finely chopped**

2   **cloves garlic, finely chopped**

2   **cups (400 g) Arborio rice**

$^{1}/_{2}$ **cup (125 ml) dry white wine**

1   **(14-ounce/400-g) can tomatoes, with juice**

1   **tablespoon tomato paste (concentrate)**

3   **cups (750 ml) vegetable stock, boiling**

$^{1}/_{3}$ **cup (50 g) freshly grated Parmesan cheese**

1   **cup (50 g) finely chopped fresh basil leaves**

  Salt and freshly ground black pepper

4   **ounces (125 g) mozzarella cheese, cut into $^{3}/_{4}$-inch (2-cm) cubes**

¹/₂ cup (75 g) fine dry bread crumbs

4 cups (1 liter) vegetable oil, for deep frying

Serves: 6
Preparation: 30 minutes
+ 30 minutes to chill
Cooking: 45–50 minutes
Level: 2

reshape. Coat in bread crumbs, place on a tray, and refrigerate for 30 minutes, or until firm. • Heat the oil in a deep-fryer or deep saucepan. Test the temperature of the oil by dropping in a small piece of bread. If it immediately bubbles to the surface and begins to turn golden, the oil is ready. • Fry the fritters in batches in the hot oil until golden brown all over, 5–7 minutes per batch. Scoop out with a slotted spoon and drain on paper towels. • Serve hot.

311

(See photograph on the following page.)

Nutritional Facts
Amount per serving
Percentage of Daily Values
based on 2,000 calories

 CALORIES **602** 29%
 PROTEIN **14g** 30%
 FAT **31g** 38%
 FIBER **1.7g** 7%
 SALT **1.7g** 31%

STUFFED POTATO CROQUETTES

Cook the potatoes in a large pot of salted, boiling water for 10 minutes, or until tender. Drain and transfer to a large bowl. Mash until smooth. • Mix in the Parmesan, parsley, and 3 of the eggs. Season with salt and pepper. • Shape the mixture into 4-inch (10-cm) oblong croquettes. • Press pieces of mozzarella and sun-dried tomatoes into the center of each croquette. • Heat the oil in a deep-fryer or deep saucepan. Test the oil temperature by dropping in a small piece of bread. If it immediately bubbles to the surface and begins to turn golden, the oil is ready. • Dip the croquettes in the remaining beaten egg and then in the bread crumbs. • Fry until golden brown, turning with tongs in the oil. • Scoop out with a slotted spoon and drain on paper towels. • Serve hot.

2 pounds (1 kg) potatoes, peeled and cut into small chunks

1/2 cup (60 g) freshly grated Parmesan cheese

1 tablespoon finely chopped fresh parsley

4 large eggs, lightly beaten

Salt and freshly ground black pepper

4 ounces (125 g) mozzarella cheese, cut into cubes

6 sun-dried tomatoes packed in oil, drained and diced

4 cups (1 liter) vegetable oil, for frying

1 cup (150 g) fine, dry bread crumbs

Serves: 6
Preparation: 10 minutes
Cooking: 20 minutes
Level: 2

Nutritional Facts
Amount per serving
Percentage of Daily Values
based on 2,000 calories

 CALORIES 367 8%
 PROTEIN 20g 3%
 FAT 25g 1%
 FIBER 4.2g 7
 SALT 1.5g 27

ZUCCHINI FRITTERS

Bring a large pot of salted water to a boil. Add the zucchini and cook until almost tender, about 5 minutes. Drain and let cool slightly. • Pat dry and finely chop. • Transfer to a large bowl and mix in the pecorino, eggs, 1 cup (150 g) bread crumbs, parsley, and mint. Season with salt and pepper. • Dust your hands with flour and shape the mixture into balls about the size of walnuts. Roll in the remaining bread crumbs until well coated. • Heat the oil in a deep-fryer or deep saucepan. Test the oil temperature by dropping in a small piece of bread. If it immediately bubbles to the surface and begins to turn golden, the oil is ready. • Fry in small batches until golden and crisp, 4–5 minutes, turning once with tongs. • Scoop out with a slotted spoon and drain on paper towels. • Serve hot.

4	medium zucchini (courgettes)
1	cup (125 g) freshly grated pecorino cheese
2	large eggs
1¹/₂	cups (225 g) fine, dry bread crumbs
2	tablespoons finely chopped fresh parsley
2	tablespoons finely chopped fresh mint
	Salt and freshly ground black pepper
4	cups (1 liter) vegetable oil, for deep frying

Serves: 4
Preparation: 20 minutes
Cooking: 20 minutes
Level: 2

Nutritional Facts
*Amount per serving
Percentage of Daily Values
based on 2,000 calories*

 CALORIES **357**

 PROTEIN **17g**

 FAT **32g**

 FIBER **0.9g**

 SALT **1.4g**

PUMPKIN FRITTERS

Bring a large pot of salted water to a boil. Add the pumpkin and cook until tender, about 5 minutes, • Drain and process in a food processor until puréed. • Transfer to a large bowl and mix in the whole egg and 2 egg yolks, the flour, amaretto cookies, Parmesan, baking powder, nutmeg, and salt. • Beat the egg whites until stiff. Gently fold the whites into the pumpkin mixture. • Heat the oil in a deep-fryer or deep saucepan. Test the oil temperature by dropping in a small piece of bread. If it immediately bubbles to the surface and begins to turn golden, the oil is ready. • Fry tablespoons of the mixture in small batches, turning once or twice with tongs until golden brown and crisp, 5–7 minutes. • Remove with a slotted spoon and drain well on paper towels. • Serve hot.

2 cups (300 g) pumpkin or winter squash flesh, cut into 1-inch (2.5-cm) cubes

3 large eggs, 1 left whole and 2 separated

1 cup (150 g) all-purpose (plain) flour

1/2 cup (75 g) crumbled amaretto cookies or graham cracker crumbs

2 tablespoons freshly grated Parmesan cheese

1/2 teaspoon baking powder

1/4 teaspoon freshly grated nutmeg

1/2 teaspoon salt

4 cups (1 liter) vegetable oil, for deep frying

Serves: 6
Preparation: 20 minutes
Cooking: 30–35 minutes
Level: 2

Nutritional Facts
Amount per serving
Percentage of Daily Values
based on 2,000 calories

CALORIES	PROTEIN	FAT	FIBER	SALT
320	9g	20g	1.5g	0.7g

FRIED POTATO BALLS

Cook the potatoes in their skins in salted, boiling water for 20–25 minutes, until tender. Slip the skins off while hot and mash. • Transfer the mashed potato to a large bowl and mix in the butter, egg yolks, Parmesan, pine nuts, and parsley. Season with salt. • Beat the egg whites in a medium bowl until frothy. • Shape tablespoons of the potato mixture into balls the size of small marbles. • Dip in the egg white, then in the bread crumbs. • Heat the oil in a deep-fryer or deep saucepan. Test the oil temperature by dropping in a small piece of bread. If it immediately bubbles to the surface and begins to turn golden, the oil is ready. • Add the potato balls in small batches and fry, turning with tongs until golden, 5–7 minutes. • Scoop out with a slotted spoon and drain well on paper towels. • Serve hot.

2 pounds (1 kg) baking (floury) potatoes

1/4 cup (60 g) butter, cut up

3 large eggs, separated

1/2 cup (60 g) freshly grated Parmesan cheese

2 tablespoons pine nuts, finely chopped

1 tablespoon finely chopped fresh parsley

Salt

1 cup (150 g) fine, dry bread crumbs

4 cups (1 liter) vegetable oil, for deep frying

Serves: 6
Preparation: 25 minutes
Cooking: 45 minutes
Level: 2

Nutritional Facts
Amount per serving
Percentage of Daily Values
based on 2,000 calories

CALORIES
478

PROTEIN
14g

FAT
30g

FIBER
4g

SALT
1.2g

BREAD FRITTERS WITH SALSA

Salsa: Combine the tomatoes, onion, chiles, cilantro, and lime juice in a bowl. Season with pepper.

Fritters: Mix the bread, eggs, ¼ cup (30 g) of pecorino, and parsley in a large bowl. Season with salt and pepper.

• Shape the mixture into walnut-size fritters. • Heat the oil in a deep-fryer or deep saucepan. Test the oil temperature by dropping in a small piece of bread. If it immediately bubbles to the surface and begins to turn golden, the oil is ready. • Fry the fritters in small batches, turning with tongs, until browned, 5–7 minutes.• Remove with a slotted spoon and drain well on paper towels. • Arrange the fritters on a heated serving dish.

• Sprinkle the fritters with the remaining ¼ cup (30 g) pecorino and serve hot with the salsa passed separately.

Salsa

1	pound (500 g) firm ripe tomatoes, finely chopped
1	small sweet red onion, finely chopped
2	fresh chiles, finely chopped
2	tablespoons finely chopped fresh cilantro (coriander)
2	tablespoons freshly squeezed lime juice
	Freshly ground black pepper

Fritters

8	cups (400 g) day-old bread, crumbled
4	large eggs
½	cup (60 g) freshly grated pecorino cheese
2	tablespoons finely chopped fresh parsley
	Salt and freshly ground black pepper
4	cups (1 liter) vegetable oil, for deep frying

Nutritional Facts
Amount per serving
Percentage of Daily Values
based on 2,000 calories

CALORIES	PROTEIN	FAT	FIBER	SALT
568	23g	33g	5.7g	1.6g

Serves: 4
Preparation: 20 minutes
Cooking: 20–30 minutes
Level: 2

CORN FRITTERS

Mix the flour, eggs, milk, corn, and Parmesan in a large bowl until well blended. Season with pepper. • Heat the oil in a deep-fryer or deep saucepan. Test the oil temperature by dropping in a small piece of bread. If it immediately bubbles to the surface and begins to turn golden, the oil is ready. • Fry tablespoons of the corn mixture in small batches, turning with tongs until golden brown, 5–7 minutes. • Remove with a slotted spoon and drain well on paper towels. • Serve hot.

$2/3$ cup (100 g) all-purpose (plain) flour

2 large eggs, lightly beaten

$2/3$ cup (150 ml) milk

1 (14-ounce/400-g) can corn (sweet corn), drained

$3/4$ cup (90 g) freshly grated Parmesan cheese

Freshly ground black pepper

4 cups (1 liter) vegetable oil, for deep frying

Serves: 4
Preparation: 20 minutes
Cooking: 20–30 minutes
Level: 2

Nutritional Facts
Amount per serving
Percentage of Daily Values
based on 2,000 calories

 CALORIES 424
 PROTEIN 17g
 FAT 30g
 FIBER 1.7g
 SALT 2.3g

VEGETARIAN SPRING ROLLS

Soak the mushrooms in a bowl of boiling water for 20 minutes. Drain well. • Heat the peanut oil in a wok over medium-high heat. Add the celery and stir-fry for 3 minutes. • Add the bean sprouts, black mushrooms, carrot, and bamboo shoots and stir-fry for 2–3 minutes. • Add the soy sauce, sesame oil, salt, and sugar. • Divide the filling into 12 equal portions. Mix the flour and water to form a smooth paste. • Wrap one portion of filling in each of the spring-roll wrappers, using the paste to seal the spring rolls. • Heat the oil in a deep-fryer or deep saucepan. Test the oil temperature by dropping in a small piece of bread. If it immediately bubbles to the surface and begins to turn golden, the oil is ready. • Fry the spring rolls in batches until golden brown, 5–7 minutes. • Remove with a slotted spoon and drain well on paper towels. • Serve hot.

3 ounces (90 g) dried black Chinese mushrooms, cut into very thin strips

2 tablespoons peanut oil

1 stalk celery, finely chopped

2 cups (100 g) mung bean sprouts

1 medium carrot, cut into very thin strips

1/2 cup (60 g) bamboo shoots

1 teaspoon soy sauce

1 teaspoon Asian sesame oil

1/2 teaspoon salt

1/2 teaspoon sugar

12 spring roll wrappers

1 tablespoon all-purpose (plain) flour

1 tablespoon water

4 cups (1 liter) vegetable oil, for deep frying

Serves: 6
Preparation: 30 minutes
Cooking: 20 minutes
Level: 3

Nutritional Facts
Amount per serving
Percentage of Daily Values
based on 2,000 calories

CALORIES	PROTEIN	FAT	FIBER	SALT
270	5g	16g	1.5g	0.9g

SPICY PEANUT FRITTERS

Put the peanuts in a wok and dry-fry over low heat for 5 minutes. Rub to remove the skins and coarsely chop. • Combine the coriander seeds, ginger, garlic, red pepper flakes, salt, and turmeric in a food processor and process until finely chopped. • Sift both flours into a large bowl. Stir in the spice mixture and coconut milk, blending well. Add the peanuts. • Heat the oil in a deep-fryer or deep saucepan. Test the oil temperature by dropping in a small piece of bread. If it immediately bubbles to the surface and begins to turn golden, the oil is ready. • Add tablespoons of the batter in small batches. Fry, turning with tongs until golden brown, 3–5 minutes. • Remove with a slotted spoon and drain well on paper towels. Serve hot with the chili sauce.

1¼ cups (200 g) raw peanuts

1 teaspoon coriander seeds

2 teaspoons finely chopped fresh ginger

2 cloves garlic

1 teaspoon crushed red pepper flakes, or 2 small dried chiles, crumbled

1 teaspoon salt

½ teaspoon ground turmeric

1 cup (150 g) rice flour

⅔ cup (100 g) all-purpose (plain) flour

1 cup (250 ml) coconut milk

4 cups (1 liter) vegetable oil, for deep frying

½ cup (125 ml) Thai sweet chili sauce, to serve

Serves: 6
Preparation: 30 minutes
Cooking: 30 minutes
Level: 2

Nutritional Facts
Amount per serving
Percentage of Daily Values
based on 2,000 calories

 CALORIES 472 23

 PROTEIN 12g 16

 FAT 29g 36

 FIBER 3.3g

 SALT 2.2g

EGGPLANT FRITTERS

Preheat the oven to 400°F (200°C/gas 6).
• Cut the eggplants in half lengthwise and place them on a baking sheet cut side up.
• Bake for 15–20 minutes, until tender and golden brown. Let cool, and scoop out the flesh with a spoon, mashing it coarsely with a fork. • Mix the eggplant, parsley, basil, garlic, Parmesan, and eggs. Season with salt and pepper. Mix in enough bread crumbs to make a firm mixture. Shape into balls the size of walnuts. • Roll in the remaining bread crumbs. • Heat the oil in a deep-fryer or deep saucepan. Test the oil temperature by dropping in a small piece of bread. If it immediately bubbles to the surface and begins to turn golden, the oil is ready. • Fry in small batches, turning with tongs until golden brown, 5–7 minutes. • Remove with a slotted spoon and drain on paper towels. • Serve hot.

2	eggplants (aubergines)
1	tablespoon finely chopped fresh parsley
10	leaves fresh basil, torn
1	clove garlic, finely chopped
4	tablespoons freshly grated Parmesan cheese
2	large eggs, lightly beaten
	Salt and freshly ground black pepper
1	cup (150 g) fine, dry bread crumbs
4	cups (1 liter) vegetable oil, for deep frying

Serves: 4
Preparation: 15 minutes
Cooking: 40 minutes
Level: 2

Nutritional Facts
Amount per serving
Percentage of Daily Values
based on 2,000 calories

CALORIES
349
17

PROTEIN
12g
26%

FAT
26g
32%

FIBER
3.7g
15%

SALT
1.4g
25%

TOMATO CROQUETTES

Blanch the tomatoes in boiling water for 1 minute. • Drain and peel. Remove the seeds, chop coarsely, and let drain. • Mix the ricotta and egg yolks in a large bowl until smooth. • Add the tomatoes, parsley, and nutmeg. Season with salt and pepper and mix well. The mixture should be firm; if it is too runny, add 1–2 tablespoons of dry bread crumbs. • Form into oblong croquettes about 2 inches (4-cm) long and 1 inch (2.5-cm) thick. • Roll in the flour, dip in the beaten egg, and roll in the bread crumbs. • Heat the oil in a deep-fryer or deep saucepan. Test the oil temperature by dropping in a small piece of bread. If it immediately bubbles to the surface and begins to turn golden, the oil is ready. • Fry the croquettes in small batches, turning with tongs until golden brown, 5–7 minutes. • Remove with a slotted spoon and drain on paper towels. • Serve hot.

1 pound (500 g) ripe tomatoes

12 ounces (350 g) ricotta cheese, drained

2 large egg yolks + 2 large eggs, beaten until foamy

2 tablespoons finely chopped fresh parsley

1/4 teaspoon freshly grated nutmeg

Salt and freshly ground black pepper

1 cup (150 g) fine dry bread crumbs + 1–2 tablespoons as needed

1 cup (150 g) all-purpose (plain) flour

4 cups (1 liter) vegetable oil, for deep frying

Serves: 4
Preparation: 20 minutes
Cooking: 40 minutes
Level: 2

Nutritional Facts
Amount per serving
Percentage of Daily Values
based on 2,000 calories

 CALORIES 613

 PROTEIN 22g

 FAT 37g

 FIBER 4.1g

 SALT 1.5g

VEGETABLE SAMOSAS

Samosa Pastry: Sift the flour and salt into a medium bowl. Add the 2 tablespoons of oil and gradually add the water, kneading until a dough forms. Knead on a floured work surface until smooth and elastic, about 10 minutes. Shape into a ball and transfer to a lightly oiled bowl. Cover and let rest for 30 minutes.

Filling: Cook the potatoes in a pot of salted boiling water until tender. Drain and set aside to cool slightly. • Heat the 2 tablespoons of oil in a medium saucepan over medium-low heat. Add the mustard seeds, onion, garlic, curry leaves, garam masala, turmeric, coriander, cumin, and ground chile and sauté until the onion is soft and the spices are fragrant, 3–4 minutes. • Dice the potatoes and add to the pan. Add the peas and lemon juice and stir to combine. Remove from the heat and set aside to cool. • Knead the pastry for 2–3 minutes, then divide into eight balls. Roll

Samosa Pastry

2 cups (300 g) all-purpose (plain) flour

1 teaspoon salt

2 tablespoons (60 ml) vegetable oil

7 tablespoons warm water

Filling

8 ounces (250 g) potatoes, peeled

2 tablespoons Asian sesame oil

1 teaspoon brown mustard seeds

1 onion, finely diced

2 garlic cloves, minced

3 curry leaves (optional)

1/2 teaspoon garam masala

1/2 teaspoon ground turmeric

1/2 teaspoon ground coriander

1/2 teaspoon ground cumin

1/4 teaspoon ground chile

1 cup (150 g) frozen peas
1 tablespoon freshly squeezed lemon juice
  Vegetable oil, for frying
1 cup (250 ml) yogurt mixed with 2 tablespoons finely chopped fresh mint, to serve

Serves: 6
Preparation: 30 minutes + 30 minutes to rest
Cooking: 45 minutes
Level: 3

335

out one of the balls on a lightly floured work surface into a 7-inch (18 cm) disk. Cut the disk in half, moisten the edge with a little water, and form into a cone in your hand. Fill the cone three-quarters full with the filling. Moisten the inside edge of the opening and seal, pressing the edge with the prongs of a fork. Repeat the process with the remaining dough and filling. • Pour about 2 inches (5 cm) of oil into a wok. Test the oil temperature by dropping in a small piece of bread. If it immediately bubbles to the surface and begins to turn golden, the oil is ready. • Fry the samosas in batches, turning often with tongs until golden brown and crisp, 3–5 minutes. Remove with a slotted spoon and drain on paper towels. • Serve hot, with the minted yogurt on the side.

(See photograph on the following page.)

Nutritional Facts
Amount per serving
Percentage of Daily Values
based on 2,000 calories

 CALORIES 509

 PROTEIN 10g 9%

 FAT 30g

 FIBER 3.7g 15%

 SALT 0.9g 6

CAULIFLOWER AND PEA SAMOSAS

Prepare the samosa pastry and let rest. • Steam the potato for 5 minutes. Add the cauliflower and continue steaming until tender, 4–5 minutes more. • Heat the sesame oil in a pot over medium-low heat. Add the mustard seeds, onion, garlic, turmeric, coriander, cumin, garam masala, and ground chile and sauté until the onion is soft and the spices are fragrant, 3–4 minutes. Add the potato, cauliflower, peas, and lemon juice and stir to combine. Season with salt. • Assemble the samosas following the instructions on page 334. • Pour 2 inches (5 cm) of oil into a wok. Test by dropping in a small piece of bread. If it immediately bubbles to the surface and begins to turn golden, the oil is ready. • Fry the samosas in batches, turning with tongs until golden brown, 3–5 minutes. Remove with a slotted spoon and drain on paper towels. • Serve hot with mango chutney.

Samosa Pastry
(see page 334)

1 cup (170 g) potato, peeled and cut into ¹/₂ inch (1 cm) cubes

1¹/₂ cups (250 g) cauliflower, in florets

2 tablespoons sesame oil

1 teaspoon black mustard seeds

1 onion, finely diced

2 cloves garlic, minced

¹/₂ teaspoon ground turmeric

¹/₂ teaspoon ground coriander

¹/₂ teaspoon ground cumin

¹/₂ teaspoon garam masala

¹/₄ teaspoon ground chile

¹/₂ cup (75 g) frozen peas

1 tablespoon freshly squeezed lemon juice

Salt

Vegetable oil, for frying

Mango chutney, to serve

Serves: 4
Preparation: 45 minutes
     + 30 minutes to rest
Cooking: 30 minutes
Level: 2

Nutritional Facts
Amount per serving
Percentage of Daily Values
based on 2,000 calories

CALORIES	PROTEIN	FAT	FIBER	SALT
556	12g	26g	3.7g	1.2g

TEMPURA VEGETABLES

Dipping Sauce: Combine the soy sauce, vinegar, and ginger in a small bowl.

Tempura: Sift the flour and cornstarch into a medium bowl. Whisk the egg yolks and seltzer in a small bowl. Gradually add the yolk mixture to the flour, stirring with chopsticks or a fork until just combined. • Pour about 2 inches (5 cm) of oil into a wok. Test by dropping in a small piece of bread. If it immediately bubbles to the surface and begins to turn golden, the oil is ready. • Dip the vegetables into the prepared batter, add to the hot oil in small batches, and fry, turning occasionally until crisp, golden brown, and cooked through, 2–4 minutes. Remove with a slotted spoon and drain on paper towels. Keep warm in the oven while frying the remaining vegetables. • Serve hot with the dipping sauce.

Dipping Sauce

$3/4$ cup (180 ml) soy sauce

3 tablespoons rice wine vinegar

1 teaspoon finely grated fresh ginger

Tempura

$1^{1}/2$ cups (225 g) all-purpose (plain) flour

$1/2$ cup (75 g) cornstarch (cornflour)

3 large egg yolks

$1^{1}/2$ cups (375 ml) chilled seltzer (soda water)

Vegetable oil, for deep frying

1 small sweet potato, peeled and sliced $1/2$ inch (1 cm) thick

1 carrot, sliced $1/2$ inch (1 cm) thick

1 zucchini (courgette), sliced $1/2$ inch (1 cm) thick

1 small head broccoli, cut into florets

2 red bell peppers (capsicums), cut into small squares

Serves: 4
Preparation: 15 minutes
Cooking: 15 minutes
Level: 2

Nutritional Facts
*Amount per serving
Percentage of Daily Values
based on 2,000 calories*

 CALORIES 400

 PROTEIN 12g 26

 FAT 6g

 FIBER 5g

 SALT 4.1g 74

STEWS, CURRIES AND STIR-FRIES

VEGETABLE CURRY WITH COUSCOUS

Heat the oil in a saucepan over medium-high heat. Add the onions and garlic and sauté until softened, 3–4 minutes. • Add the bell peppers, eggplant, potatoes, zucchini, baby corn, and garbanzo beans. Stir well and sauté until the vegetables begin to soften, about 5 minutes. • Add the pepper, chiles, tomatoes, harissa, cumin, and stock. Stir well. Cover the pan and simmer over very low heat until the vegetables are tender, 30 minutes. • Garnish with the cilantro leaves and serve hot with the couscous.

■ ■ ■ *Harissa is a hot-chile-and-spice paste used in North African cuisines. It is available in Middle Eastern markets and food stores.*

$^1/4$ cup (60 ml) sesame oil

2 onions, chopped

2 cloves garlic, sliced

3 bell peppers (capsicums), sliced

2 eggplant (aubergines), chopped

4 potatoes, cubed

2 large zucchini (courgettes), sliced

8 ears baby corn

1 (14-ounce/400-g) can garbanzo beans (chickpeas), drained

$^1/2$ teaspoon freshly ground black pepper

1–2 fresh red chiles, finely chopped

1 (14-ounce/400-g) can tomatoes, with juice

1 tablespoon harissa

$^1/2$ teaspoon cumin seeds

2 cups (500 ml) vegetable stock

Fresh cilantro (coriander) leaves

Freshly cooked couscous, to serve

Nutritional Facts
Amount per serving
Percentage of Daily Values
based on 2,000 calories

 CALORIES 755 / 36

 PROTEIN 14

 FAT 19g

 FIBER 11.3g / 5%

 SALT 1.2 / 22%

Serves: 4
Preparation: 15 minutes
Cooking: 40 minutes
Level: 1

SPICY VEGETARIAN STEW

Heat the oil in a large saucepan over medium heat. Add the cumin seeds and sauté until fragrant, about 2 minutes. • Add the onion, celery, garlic, and curry paste and cook until the onions are softened, about 5 minutes. • Add the bell pepper, zucchini, eggplant, mushrooms, and tomatoes. Cover and simmer over medium heat until the vegetables begin to soften, about 5 minutes. • Add the chili sauce, chile powder, ground cumin, and coriander. Mix well, then add the kidney beans. Cover and cook until the vegetables are tender, about 25 minutes, stirring occasionally. • Stir in the lemon juice and cilantro. Serve hot over the rice.

2   tablespoons peanut oil

1   teaspoon cumin seeds

1   onion, thinly sliced

2   stalks celery, chopped

2   cloves garlic, sliced

1   teaspoon green curry paste

1   red bell pepper (capsicum), seeded and sliced

2   zucchini (courgettes), sliced

1   medium eggplant (aubergine), chopped

8   ounces (250 g) button mushrooms, quartered

2   (14-ounce/400-g) cans tomatoes, with juice

1   tablespoon Thai sweet chili sauce

1   teaspoon chile powder

2   teaspoons ground coriander

1   (14-ounce/400-g) can red kidney beans

Freshly squeezed juice of 1 lemon

Cilantro (coriander)

Freshly cooked basmati rice, to serve

Nutritional Facts

Amount per serving
Percentage of Daily Values
based on 2,000 calories

CALORIES	PROTEIN	FAT	FIBER	SALT
207	10g	8g	9.2g	1.2g

Serves: 4
Preparation: 30 minutes
Cooking: 40 minutes
Level: 1

VEGETARIAN CURRY WITH BROWN RICE

Peel and cube the squash. • Heat the oil in a large saucepan over medium heat. Add the mustard and cumin seeds and stir until fragrant, 2–3 minutes. • Add the chiles, garlic, ginger, and onions and sauté until softened, about 5 minutes. • Stir in the zucchini, potatoes, okra, winter squash, and mushrooms. Add the white pepper, Worcestershire sauce, and soy sauce. Pour in the stock, cover, and simmer until the vegetables are tender and the liquid is reduced a little, about 30 minutes. • Stir in the cream and simmer for 5 minutes more. • Garnish with the cilantro and serve hot over the brown rice.

1	cup (150 g) winter squash or pumpkin
2	tablespoons peanut oil
1/2	teaspoon mustard seeds
1/2	teaspoon cumin seeds
2	green chiles, sliced
2	cloves garlic, sliced
1	teaspoon minced ginger
2	onions, finely chopped
4	zucchini (courgettes) sliced
2	large potatoes, peeled and cubed
4	ounces (125 g) okra, sliced
4	ounces (125 g) button mushrooms, halved
1/2	teaspoon white pepper
1	tablespoon Worcestershire sauce
2	tablespoons soy sauce
2	cups (500 ml) vegetable stock
1/2	cup (125 ml) light (single) cream
	Cilantro (coriander)
	Freshly cooked brown rice, to serve

Serves: 4
Preparation: 15 minutes
Cooking: 45 minutes
Level: 1

Nutritional Facts
Amount per serving
Percentage of Daily Values
based on 2,000 calories

CALORIES	PROTEIN	FAT	FIBER	SALT
252	8g	13g	4.9g	1.6g

PINEAPPLE CURRY WITH COCONUT

Spice Paste: Grind the chile peppers, coriander seeds, garlic, shallots, turmeric, and ginger in a pestle and mortar.

Curry: Heat 2 tablespoons of the oil in a large wok or frying pan over medium-high heat. Add the spice paste and sauté until aromatic, 1–2 minutes. • Pour in the coconut milk and bring to a boil. • Add the pineapple, star anise, cinnamon, cloves, nutmeg, lemongrass, and lime juice. Season with salt and pepper. Cook over medium heat until the pineapple is heated through, 5–7 minutes. • Heat the remaining oil in a small frying pan over medium heat. Add the shallots and fry until golden brown, about 5 minutes. • Garnish the curry with the fried shallots and serve hot with the rice.

Spice Paste

6   dried red chile peppers
1   teaspoon coriander seeds
2   cloves garlic
6   shallots, chopped
1   teaspoon turmeric
1   tablespoon fresh ginger

Curry

3   tablespoons peanut oil
3   cups (750 ml) coconut milk
1   pineapple, cubed
2   star anise
1   stick cinnamon
1/4 teaspoon ground cloves
1/4 teaspoon ground nutmeg
1   stalk lemongrass, finely chopped
1   tablespoon freshly squeezed lime juice
    Salt and freshly ground black pepper
2   shallots, sliced
    Freshly cooked basmati rice, to serve

Serves: 4
Preparation: 25 minutes
Cooking: 20 minutes
Level: 1

Nutritional Facts
Amount per serving
Percentage of Daily Values
based on 2,000 calories

CALORIES	PROTEIN	FAT	FIBER	SALT
170	2g	9g	2g	1.2g

POTATO CURRY WITH COCONUT

Toast the cumin, fenugreek, and chiles in a medium saucepan over medium heat until fragrant, 2–3 minutes. • Add the onion and 1 tablespoon of ghee. Sauté over high heat until transparent, 2–3 minutes. • Remove from the heat and process in a food processor with 2 tablespoons of water until smooth. • Melt the remaining 2 tablespoons ghee in the same pan and sauté the curry leaves and mustard seeds for 30 seconds. • Stir in the spice paste, potatoes, turmeric, coconut, and remaining water. Season with salt. Cover and simmer over low heat until tender, 25–30 minutes, adding more water as needed. • Serve hot.

■■■*Ghee is a type of clarified butter that is widely used in Indian cooking. To make clarified butter, heat the butter in a saucepan over medium heat until it stops sizzling but before it turns brown. Skim the froth off the top and pour the butter through a fine sieve, leaving behind the milk solids on the bottom of the pan.*

1	teaspoon cumin seeds
1/2	teaspoon fenugreek seeds
2	dried red chiles, crumbled
1	onion, finely sliced
3	tablespoons ghee (clarified butter)
1	cup (250 ml) water + more, as required
8	curry leaves (optional)
1	teaspoon mustard seeds
1	pound (500 g) new potatoes, sliced
1/2	teaspoon ground turmeric
2	tablespoons shredded (desiccated) coconut
	Salt

Serves: 4
Preparation: 15 minutes
Cooking: 35–40 minutes
Level: 1

Nutritional Facts
Amount per serving
Percentage of Daily Values
based on 2,000 calories

CALORIES	PROTEIN	FAT	FIBER	SALT
302	4g	22g	3g	0.7g

SWEET-AND-SOUR BELL PEPPERS WITH OLIVES

Heat the oil in a large frying pan over medium heat. Add the onion, red and yellow bell peppers, and tomatoes. Season with salt. Sauté until the vegetables are almost tender, about 10 minutes. • Stir in the olives and capers and simmer for 5 more minutes. • Meanwhile, mix the vinegar and sugar in a cup until the sugar has dissolved. Add the mixture to the pan and let it evaporate over high heat for 2 minutes. • Add the bread crumbs, mix well and serve hot garnished with the basil.

1/4 cup (60 ml) extra-virgin olive oil

1 large onion, finely chopped

2 large red bell peppers (capsicums), seeded and thinly sliced

2 large yellow bell peppers (capsicums), seeded and thinly sliced

1 (14-ounce/400-g) can tomatoes, with juice

Salt

2/3 cup (60 g) green olives, pitted and coarsely chopped

2 tablespoons salt-cured capers, rinsed

1/3 cup (90 ml) white wine vinegar

1 tablespoon sugar

6 tablespoons fine, dry bread crumbs

Fresh basil leaves, to garnish

Serves: 4
Preparation: 10 minutes
Cooking: 15–20 minutes
Level: 1

Nutritional Facts
Amount per serving
Percentage of Daily Values
based on 2,000 calories

 CALORIES **288** 14·

 PROTEIN **7g** 5%

 FAT **17g** 21%

 FIBER **4.5g** 8·

 SALT **1.2g** 22%

MUSHROOMS WITH POTATOES AND HERBS

Heat 3 tablespoons of the oil in a large frying pan over medium heat. Add 1 tablespoon of parsley and 1 tablespoon of marjoram and sauté for 1 minute. • Add the potatoes and 1 clove of garlic. Sauté for 5 minutes. • Heat the remaining oil in another large frying pan over medium heat. Add 1 tablespoon of parsley and the remaining 1 tablespoon of marjoram and sauté for 1 minute. • Add the wild mushrooms and the remaining clove of garlic and sauté for 2 minutes. • Add the button mushrooms to the pan with the potatoes. Sauté until the mushrooms and potatoes are tender, 5–7 minutes. • Add the wild mushrooms to the pan with the potatoes and button mushrooms and stir over medium heat for 2 minutes. Season with salt and pepper. Sprinkle with the remaining 1 tablespoon parsley. • Serve hot.

6   **tablespoons (90 ml) extra-virgin olive oil**

3   **tablespoons finely chopped fresh parsley**

2   **tablespoons finely chopped fresh marjoram**

1   **pound (500 g) potatoes, peeled and cut into small chunks**

2   **cloves garlic, finely chopped**

1   **pound (500 g) wild mushrooms, trimmed and thinly sliced**

12   **ounces (350 g) button mushrooms, trimmed and thinly sliced**

    Salt and freshly ground black pepper

Serves: 4
Preparation: 10 minutes
Cooking: 20 minutes
Level: 1

Nutritional Facts
*Amount per serving
Percentage of Daily Values
based on 2,000 calories*

CALORIES	PROTEIN	FAT	FIBER	SALT
310	7g	22g	7.3g	0.7g

CAPONATA WITH RICE

Heat 3 tablespoons of the oil in a large frying pan over medium heat. Add the eggplants and onion and sauté until softened, about 10 minutes. • Add the celery, tomatoes, pear, olives, capers, and sugar. Season with salt and pepper. Add the water and vinegar. Simmer over low heat for about 15 minutes, or until all the vegetables have softened. • Meanwhile, bring a large pot of salted water to a boil. Add the rice and cook until tender, 12–15 minutes. • Drain and drizzle with the remaining 2 tablespoons of oil. Stir in the basil. • Oil four small $^3/_4$-cup (180-ml) molds with oil and fill with the seasoned rice, pressing down firmly with the back of a spoon. • Turn the rice out of the molds onto a serving dish and serve with the caponata.

5   tablespoons extra-virgin olive oil

2   eggplants (aubergines), diced

1   small onion, coarsely chopped

2   stalks celery, finely chopped

4   large tomatoes, coarsely chopped

1   firm-ripe pear, peeled and coarsely chopped

1   cup (100 g) black olives

1   tablespoon salt-cured capers, rinsed

1   tablespoon sugar

    Salt and freshly ground black pepper

$^1/_4$ cup (60 ml) water

2   tablespoons red wine vinegar

$1^1/_2$ cups (300 g) short-grain rice

1   tablespoon finely chopped fresh basil

Serves: 4
Preparation: 20 minutes
Cooking: 40–45 minutes
Level: 1

Nutritional Facts
Amount per serving
Percentage of Daily Values
based on 2,000 calories

 CALORIES 494 24

 PROTEIN 7g 15

 FAT 18g 2

 FIBER 4.9g 20

 SALT 2.1g 38

POTATO, GREEN BEAN, AND TOMATO STEW

Bring a pot of salted water to a boil. Add the potatoes and cook until almost tender, 15–20 minutes. • Drain and set aside. • Blanch the green beans in salted boiling water until almost tender, 5 minutes. • Drain and chop into short lengths. • Heat the oil in a large frying pan over medium heat. Add the onion, garlic, and parsley and sauté until the garlic is pale gold, 3–4 minutes. Season with salt and pepper. Add the tomatoes and simmer for 10 minutes. • Stir in the potatoes and green beans and simmer until tender, 10–15 more minutes.
• Serve hot.

12 ounces (350 g) potatoes, peeled and coarsely chopped

12 ounces (350 g) green beans, topped and tailed

¼ cup (60 ml) extra-virgin olive oil

1 onion, finely chopped

1 clove garlic, finely chopped

1 tablespoon finely chopped fresh parsley

Salt and freshly ground black pepper

3 large tomatoes, peeled and coarsely chopped

Serves: 4
Preparation: 20 minutes
Cooking: 40–50 minutes
Level: 2

Nutritional Facts
Amount per serving
Percentage of Daily Values
based on 2,000 calories

CALORIES 221 | PROTEIN 4g | FAT 14g | FIBER 3.9g | SALT 0.7g

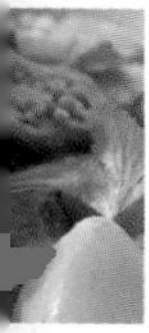

EGGPLANT STEW

362

Steam the eggplants over a large pot of boiling water until tender, about 20 minutes. • Cook the tomatoes with the oil, garlic, paprika, cumin, and pepper in a medium saucepan over medium heat until the tomatoes have broken down, about 20 minutes. Season with salt. • Add the eggplants and simmer over low heat until very tender and the tomatoes have flavored and colored the eggplant, about 15 minutes. • Drizzle with the lemon juice and a little extra oil. • Serve hot, garnished with the cilantro.

2 pounds (1 kg) eggplant (aubergines), cut into bite-sized chunks

1 pound (500 g) tomatoes, peeled and coarsely chopped

5 tablespoons extra-virgin olive oil + extra to drizzle

4 cloves garlic, finely chopped

1 tablespoon sweet paprika

1 teaspoon cumin seeds

1/2 teaspoon ground black pepper

Salt

Freshly squeezed juice of 1 lemon

Fresh cilantro (coriander) leaves, to garnish

Serves: 4
Preparation: 25 minutes
Cooking: 55 minutes
Level: 1

Nutritional Facts
Amount per serving
Percentage of Daily Values
based on 2,000 calories

CALORIES 213
PROTEIN 4g
FAT 18g
FIBER 6.2g
SALT 0.7g

SPICY POTATO CURRY

364

Bring a large pot of salted water to a boil. Add the potatoes and cook until almost tender, 15 minutes. Drain well. • Combine the white part of the scallions with the garlic, chile, salt, ginger, and cardamom seeds in a food processor and process to make a paste. • Heat the oil and butter in a large frying pan over low heat. Add the spice paste and sauté for 2 minutes. • Add the cinnamon, tomatoes, mustard seeds, and garam masala and simmer for 5 minutes, stirring constantly. • Stir in the yogurt and cook until the sauce has thickened slightly, 2 minutes. • Add the potatoes and cook until tender, 5–10 minutes. • Transfer to a serving dish. Garnish with the green part of the scallions and cilantro. • Serve hot.

■ ■ ■ *Garam marsala is a blend of spices used in Indian cooking. It is found in Asian markets and well-stocked supermarkets.*

2	pounds (1 kg) potatoes, peeled and cubed
2	scallions (spring onions), white and green parts separated, finely chopped
2	cloves garlic, finely chopped
1	fresh green chile, seeded and finely chopped
1	teaspoon salt
1	($2/3$ -inch/1.5-cm) piece fresh ginger, peeled and sliced
	Seeds from 2 cardamom pods
2	tablespoons peanut oil
1	tablespoon butter
1	stick cinnamon
2	large tomatoes, chopped
1	teaspoon mustard seeds
1	tablespoon garam masala
1/2	cup (125 ml) plain yogurt
	Fresh cilantro (coriander), to garnish

Serves: 4
Preparation: 20 minutes
Cooking: 35–40 minutes
Level: 2

Nutritional Facts
Amount per serving
Percentage of Daily Values
based on 2,000 calories

CALORIES	PROTEIN	FAT	FIBER	SALT
290	6g	11g	4.6g	1.5g
14				

BELL PEPPER AND POTATO STEW

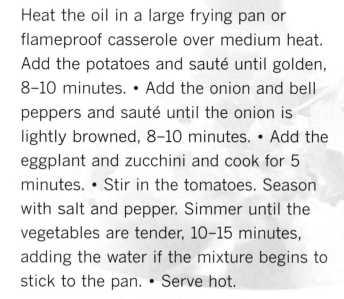

Heat the oil in a large frying pan or flameproof casserole over medium heat. Add the potatoes and sauté until golden, 8–10 minutes. • Add the onion and bell peppers and sauté until the onion is lightly browned, 8–10 minutes. • Add the eggplant and zucchini and cook for 5 minutes. • Stir in the tomatoes. Season with salt and pepper. Simmer until the vegetables are tender, 10–15 minutes, adding the water if the mixture begins to stick to the pan. • Serve hot.

¹/₄ cup (60 ml) extra-virgin olive oil

2 medium potatoes, peeled and cut into small cubes

1 large onion, finely chopped

1 red bell pepper (capsicum), seeded and cut into small chunks

1 green bell pepper (capsicum), seeded and cut into small chunks

1 eggplant (aubergine), cut into small cubes

1 large zucchini (courgette), cut into small cubes

4 large tomatoes, coarsely chopped

Salt and freshly ground black pepper

¹/₄ cup (60 ml) water, optional

Serves: 4
Preparation: 10 minutes
Cooking: 35–40 minutes
Level: 1

Nutritional Facts
Amount per serving
Percentage of Daily Values
based on 2,000 calories

CALORIES 266 • PROTEIN 5g • FAT 15g • FIBER 6.3g • SALT 0.8g

VEGETABLE STEW

Heat the oil in a large saucepan over medium heat. Add the onions and sauté until translucent, 5 minutes. • Add the eggplant, zucchini, yellow and green bell peppers, tomatoes, bay leaf, thyme, and garlic. Season with salt and pepper. • Cover and cook over low heat for 1 hour. • Stir in the olives and garnish with the basil. • Serve hot.

1/2 cup (125 ml) extra-virgin olive oil

2 onions, finely chopped

1 large eggplant (aubergine), cut into small cubes

4 zucchini (courgettes), cut into small cubes

1 yellow bell pepper (capsicum), seeded and cut into thin strips

1 green bell pepper (capsicum), seeded and cut into thin strips

2 pounds (1 kg) tomatoes, peeled, seeded, and chopped

1 bay leaf

1 tablespoon finely chopped fresh thyme

2 cloves garlic, finely chopped

Salt and freshly ground black pepper

1/2 cup (50 g) black olives

1 tablespoon fresh basil, torn

Nutritional Facts
Amount per serving
Percentage of Daily Values
based on 2,000 calories

 CALORIES 246

PROTEIN 3g

 FAT 21g 26

 FIBER 4.1g

 SALT 1g

Serves: 6
Preparation: 15 minutes
Cooking: 65 minutes
Level: 1

MUSHROOM STEW WITH PINE NUTS

Heat the oil in a large frying pan over medium heat. Add the potatoes and garlic and sauté until the garlic is pale gold, 3–4 minutes.• Add the mushrooms and season with salt and pepper. Cover and cook for 5 minutes. • Uncover and let the moisture evaporate. Stir in the pine nuts and almonds and cook for 10 minutes. • Sprinkle with the mint just before removing from heat. • Serve hot.

$1/4$ cup (60 ml) extra-virgin olive oil

2 large potatoes, diced

2 cloves garlic, finely chopped

$1^1/2$ pounds (750 g) fresh white mushrooms, trimmed and coarsely chopped

Salt and freshly ground black pepper

$2/3$ cup (120 g) pine nuts

$1/2$ cup (50 g) slivered almonds

1 tablespoon coarsely chopped fresh mint

Serves: 4
Preparation: 10 minutes
Cooking: 25 minutes
Level: 1

Nutritional Facts
Amount per serving
Percentage of Daily Values
based on 2,000 calories

CALORIES
514
25%

PROTEIN
13g
28%

FAT
42g
52%

FIBER
6.1g
24%

SALT
0.7g
14%

GREEN BEAN AND ZUCCHINI RATATOUILLE

372

Heat half the oil in a large frying pan or wide saucepan over medium heat. Add the whole garlic cloves and sauté for 1 minute. Add the zucchini and sauté until lightly browned, about 5 minutes. Lift out with a spatula and place on paper towels to drain. Sauté the bell pepper in the same oil until slightly browned, 3–5 minutes. Lift out the pepper and garlic and set aside with the zucchini. • Reduce the heat, pour in the remaining oil, and add the red and white onions. Sauté over low heat until soft but not browned, 8–10 minutes. Add the sliced garlic and coriander, and sauté for another 1 minute. • Add the tomatoes, thyme, and 2 tablespoons of the parsley. Season with a good pinch of salt. • Cover and cook until the tomatoes are meltingly soft, about 10 minutes. • Add the green beans and simmer, covered, for 4 minutes. Add the sugar snaps and fava beans, and mix in well. • Return the zucchini and

1/3 cup (90 ml) extra-virgin olive oil + extra to drizzle

5 cloves garlic, 2 unpeeled and whole, 3 peeled and sliced

3 medium zucchini (courgettes), halved lengthwise, and cut into 1-inch (2½-cm) pieces

1 large red bell pepper (capsicum), seeded and cut into ½-inch (1-cm) strips

1 red onion, halved and thinly sliced

1 white onion, halved and thinly sliced

1 tablespoon coriander seeds, coarsely crushed

1 pound (500 g) cherry tomatoes, halved

2 tablespoons thyme leaves, or 1 teaspoon dried thyme

3 tablespoons finely chopped fresh parsley

Salt

8 ounces (250 g) green beans, trimmed and halved widthwise

8 ounces (250 g) sugar snaps or snow peas (mangetout), trimmed and halved widthwise

5 ounces (150 g) shelled baby fava (broad) beans, thawed if frozen

Water, optional

Freshly squeezed juice of 1 lemon

Freshly ground black pepper

Serves: 4
Preparation: 15 minutes
Cooking: 40–45 minutes
Level: 1

373

peppers to the frying pan. Slip the peel off the fried garlic clove, mash, and stir into the mixture. Bring the vegetables back to the simmering point. • Simmer, uncovered, until all the vegetables are soft and the ratatouille is thick, 8–10 minutes. Stir frequently, adding a few tablespoons of water if the ratatouille is sticking to the bottom. • Taste and season with salt, pepper, and lemon juice. • Sprinkle with the remaining 1–2 tablespoons parsley and drizzle with olive oil. • Serve warm or at room temperature.

(See photograph on the following page.)

Nutritional Facts
Amount per serving
Percentage of Daily Values
based on 2,000 calories

 CALORIES 331 6 PROTEIN 9g 2 FAT 25g 3 FIBER 8.4g 34 SALT 0.7g 4%

STIR-FRIED VEGETABLES WITH NOODLES

Cook the noodles according to the instructions on the package. Drain well. • Heat the oil in a large wok over medium-high heat. Add the scallions, ginger, garlic, and peas and stir-fry for 2–3 minutes. • Add the tomatoes, herbs, soy sauce, and noodles and stir-fry for 2 more minutes. • Serve hot.

12 ounces (350 g) dried Chinese egg noodles

2 tablespoons Asian sesame oil

4 scallions (spring onions), coarsely chopped

2 teaspoons finely chopped fresh ginger

2 cloves garlic, finely chopped

2 cups (300 g) frozen peas

32 cherry tomatoes, halved

2 tablespoons finely chopped fresh parsley

2 tablespoons finely chopped fresh basil

2 tablespoons finely chopped fresh cilantro (coriander)

2 tablespoons finely chopped fresh chives

2 tablespoons light soy sauce

Serves: 4
Preparation: 15 minutes
Cooking: 10–15 minutes
Level: 1

Nutritional Facts
Amount per serving
Percentage of Daily Values
based on 2,000 calories

CALORIES	PROTEIN	FAT	FIBER	SALT
473	17g	14g	12g	1.4g

VEGETARIAN NOODLE STIR-FRY

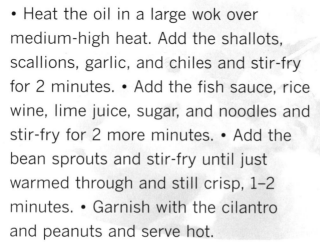

Cook the noodles according to the instructions on the package. Drain well. • Heat the oil in a large wok over medium-high heat. Add the shallots, scallions, garlic, and chiles and stir-fry for 2 minutes. • Add the fish sauce, rice wine, lime juice, sugar, and noodles and stir-fry for 2 more minutes. • Add the bean sprouts and stir-fry until just warmed through and still crisp, 1–2 minutes. • Garnish with the cilantro and peanuts and serve hot.

8   ounces (250 g) dried Chinese egg noodles

2   tablespoons peanut oil

4   shallots, coarsely chopped

6   scallions (spring onions), sliced

6   cloves garlic, sliced

2   fresh red chiles, seeded and sliced

2   tablespoons Thai fish sauce

1   tablespoon rice wine or dry sherry

2   tablespoons freshly squeezed lime juice

1   teaspoon sugar

    Salt and freshly ground black pepper

3   cups (150 g) mung bean sprouts

4   tablespoons coarsely chopped fresh cilantro (coriander)

4   tablespoons roasted peanuts, to garnish

Nutritional Facts
Amount per serving
Percentage of Daily Values
based on 2,000 calories

 CALORIES **358** 17%

 PROTEIN **11g** 24%

 FAT **15g** 19%

 FIBER **4g** 16%

 SALT **0.4g** 7%

Serves: 4
Preparation: 10 minutes
Cooking: 10 minutes
Level: 1

PUMPKIN AND LENTIL TAGINE

Put the lentils and water in a medium saucepan over high heat and bring to a boil. Decrease the heat to low, cover, and cook until just tender, 20–30 minutes.
• Cut the tomatoes in half crosswise and squeeze out the seeds. Coarsely grate the flesh into a small bowl and discard the skins. • Heat the oil in a large saucepan over medium heat. Add the onion and garlic and cook until softened, 3–4 minutes. Add the paprika, turmeric, cumin, and cayenne and cook until fragrant, 30 seconds. Add the tomato, tomato paste, and sugar and stir to combine. Add the squash and lentils with their cooking liquid and bring to a boil. Decrease the heat to low, cover, and cook until the squash is tender, 15–20 minutes.
• Stir in the parsley and cilantro and season with salt and pepper. Serve hot.

2 cups (200 g) Le Puy lentils
8 cups (2 liters) water
2 medium tomatoes
3 tablespoons extra-virgin olive oil
1 large onion, diced
4 garlic cloves, finely chopped
$1^{1}/_{2}$ teaspoons sweet paprika
1 teaspoon turmeric
1 teaspoon ground cumin
$^{1}/_{2}$ teaspoon ground cayenne pepper
1 tablespoon tomato paste
$^{1}/_{2}$ teaspoon sugar
$1^{1}/_{2}$ pounds (750 g) winter squash or pumpkin, peeled and cubed
3 tablespoons finely chopped fresh parsley
4 tablespoons chopped cilantro (coriander)
Salt and freshly ground black pepper

Serves: 4
Preparation: 30 minutes
Cooking: 30–40 minutes
Level: 1

Nutritional Facts
Amount per serving
Percentage of Daily Values
based on 2,000 calories

CALORIES
279
13%

PROTEIN
15g
33%

FAT
10g
12%

FIBER
7.7g
31%

SALT
0.8g
14%

TEMPEH STIR-FRY

Heat the vegetable oil in a large wok over medium-high heat. Add the tempeh and stir-fry until crisp, 2–3 minutes. Remove using a slotted spoon and set aside to drain on paper towels. Discard any remaining oil. • Heat the sesame oil in the wok over medium heat. Add the onion, garlic, ginger, and chile and stir-fry until softened, about 5 minutes. Add the broccoli and green beans and stir-fry for 2 minutes. Add the red and green bell peppers and stir-fry until vegetables are slightly tender but still crisp, 2–3 more minutes. Pour in the satay sauce and soy sauce and heat through. Toss to coat. • Serve with jasmine rice and topped with bean sprouts.

1/4 cup (60 ml) vegetable oil

10 ounces (300 g) tempeh, thinly sliced

2 tablespoons Asian sesame oil

1 onion, sliced

2 cloves garlic, sliced

1 (3/4-inch/2-cm) piece fresh ginger, peeled and finely chopped

2 fresh red chiles, seeded and finely chopped

1 small head broccoli, cut into florets

8 ounces (250 g) green beans, trimmed and cut into short lengths

1 red bell pepper (capsicum), seeded and thinly sliced

1 green bell pepper (capsicum), seeded and thinly sliced

1/2 cup (125 ml) Thai satay or peanut sauce

2 tablespoons soy sauce

1 cup (50 g) mung bean sprouts

Jasmine rice, to serve

Nutritional Facts
Amount per serving
Percentage of Daily Values
based on 2,000 calories

 CALORIES
520
25%

 PROTEIN
25g
54%

 FAT
38g
47%

 FIBER
8.7g
35%

 SALT
1.2g
21%

Serves: 4
Preparation: 30 minutes
Cooking: 10 minutes
Level: 1

RED BEAN CHILI

Put the bulgur wheat in a small bowl, pour in 1 cup (250 ml) of the boiling water, cover, and set aside. • Heat the oil in a medium saucepan over medium-low heat. Add the onion, celery, and garlic and sauté until softened, about 5 minutes. • Add the bell peppers, cumin, and cayenne and cook for 1 minute, or until fragrant. Add the kidney beans, tomatoes, tomato paste, chile, vinegar, and sugar. Stir in the bulgur and the remaining ¼ cup (60 ml) water and bring to a boil. Decrease the heat to low and cook until the stew has thickened and the flavors have developed, 15–20 minutes. Season with salt and pepper. • Serve hot with the rice and topped with sour cream and parsley.

½ cup bulgur wheat

1¼ cups (300 ml) water, boiling

2 tablespoons vegetable oil

1 large onion, diced

1 stalk celery, diced

2 garlic cloves, sliced

2 large red bell peppers (capsicums), seeded and diced

1 teaspoon ground cumin

1 teaspoon cayenne pepper

1 (14-ounce/400-g) can kidney beans, drained

1 (14-ounce/400-g) can tomatoes, with juice

2 tablespoons tomato paste (concentrate)

1 red chile, chopped

1 tablespoon red wine vinegar

2 teaspoons sugar

Salt and freshly ground black pepper

Jasmine rice, to serve

¾ cup (180 g) sour cream, to serve

Fresh parsley

Nutritional Facts
Amount per serving
Percentage of Daily Values
based on 2,000 calories

CALORIES	PROTEIN	FAT	FIBER	SALT
339	10g	16g	6.6g	1.5g

Serves: 4
Preparation: 30 minutes
Cooking: 30–40 minutes
Level: 1

PAD THAI

Put the noodles in a medium bowl, add boiling water to cover, and soak for 5 minutes, or until softened. Drain and set aside. • Heat the oil in a large wok over medium-high heat. Add the garlic and cook until softened, about 30 seconds. • Add the Chinese cabbage and tofu and stir-fry for 1 minute, or until the cabbage begins to soften. Push to the side, add the eggs, and cook, stirring to scramble for 1 minute. • Decrease the heat to medium. Add the noodles, jaggery, tamarind paste, soy sauce, and chili sauce and stir-fry for 1 minute. Add the bean sprouts and scallions and stir-fry for another 1 minute, tossing to combine. • Divide the pad Thai among 4–6 serving plates and top with cilantro and peanuts. • Serve hot with lime wedges to garnish.

14 ounces (400 g) dried rice stick noodles
2 tablespoons peanut oil
2 cloves garlic, sliced
1/4 Chinese cabbage (wom bok), chopped
8 ounces (250 g) firm tofu, cubed
4 large eggs, beaten
3 tablespoons finely grated jaggery (palm sugar) or brown sugar
1 1/2 tablespoons tamarind paste
1 1/2 tablespoons light soy sauce
1 1/2 tablespoons Thai sweet chili sauce
3 cups (150 g) mung bean sprouts
5 scallions (spring onions), cut into 2-inch (5 cm) lengths
1/2 cup cilantro (coriander) leaves
1/4 cup (40 g) roasted peanuts, chopped
1 lime, quartered

Serves: 4
Preparation: 15 minutes
Cooking: 10 minutes
Level: 1

Nutritional Facts
Amount per serving
Percentage of Daily Values
based on 2,000 calories

 CALORIES 728 / 35

PROTEIN 32g / 70

 FAT 30g / 37

 FIBER 6.2g / 25

 SALT 1.6g / 25

BAKED
VEGETABLES

BEET AND POTATO BAKE

Cook the beets in a pot of salted boiling until tender, 20–25 minutes. Drain, peel, and cut into ½-inch (1-cm) slices. • Cook the potatoes in a pot of salted boiling until just tender, 20–25 minutes. Drain, peel, and cut into ½-inch (1-cm) slices.
• Heat the oil in a large frying pan over medium heat. Add the garlic and sauté for 2 minutes. Add the beets, season with the salt, and stir in the lemon juice. Lower the heat and gradually stir in the sour cream. Simmer for 2–3 minutes. • Preheat the oven to 375°F (190°C/gas 5). • Butter a 2-inch (5-cm) deep ovenproof dish. • Put a layer of potatoes in the dish. Season with salt and pepper, dot with butter, and sprinkle with feta and dill. Top with a layer of beet mixture. Repeat, finishing with a layer of beets sprinkled with the remaining cheese and butter. • Bake for 20–25 minutes, until golden. • Serve hot.

4	beets (beetroots), about 1 pound (500 g), scrubbed
1	pound (500 g) thin-skinned waxy (salad) potatoes,
2	tablespoons extra-virgin olive oil
3	large cloves garlic, thinly sliced
1	teaspoon salt
1	tablespoon freshly squeezed lemon juice
1¼	cups (300 ml) sour cream or reduced-fat crème fraîche
1	tablespoons butter, cut into small pieces
5	ounces (150 g) feta cheese, crumbled
2	tablespoons fresh dill, finely chopped
2	tablespoons walnut pieces, toasted

Serves: 4
Preparation: 20 minutes
Cooking: 50–70 minutes
Level: 1

Nutritional Facts
Amount per serving
Percentage of Daily Values
based on 2,000 calories

 CALORIES 467 22%
 PROTEIN 14g 30%
 FAT 30g 32%
 FIBER 5.5g 22%
 SALT 1.7g 31%

SPICY BUTTERNUT GRATIN

Spice Mixture: Put the cumin, coriander, and cardamom in a small frying pan over medium heat and cook, stirring, until fragrant, about 2 minutes. • Transfer to a mortar, add the cloves, and pound with a pestle until broken up but not too fine. Discard the cardamom skins. • Put the sesame seeds into the same pan and dry-roast until golden, 2–3 minutes. Add to the mortar, with the hazelnuts, red pepper flakes, and salt. Pound until coarse.

Gratin: Preheat the oven to 350°F (180°C gas 4). • Put the squash in a large bowl, add the oil, and toss until coated. Sprinkle with 2 tablespoons of mint, paprika, and spice mixture, and mix well. Transfer to a roasting pan large enough to hold the wedges in one layer. • Bake for 30–40 minutes, until tender and fragrant. • Top with the remaining mint. Serve hot.

Spice Mixture

1	tablespoon cumin seeds
1	tablespoon coriander seeds
5	cardamom pods
3	cloves
2	tablespoons sesame seeds
2	tablespoons hazelnuts, toasted
1/2	teaspoon crushed red pepper flakes
1/2	teaspoon salt

Gratin

2	pounds (1 kg) butternut squash, peeled, fibers and seeds discarded, and cut into thick wedges
1/4	cup (60 ml) extra-virgin olive oil
3	tablespoons finely chopped fresh mint
1	teaspoon hot paprika

Serves: 4
Preparation: 15–20 minutes
Cooking: 35–45 minutes
Level: 2

Nutritional Facts
*Amount per serving
Percentage of Daily Values
based on 2,000 calories*

 CALORIES **280** TE

 PROTEIN **5g**

 FAT **21g**

 FIBER **4.8g**

 SALT **0.7g** TE

PROVENÇAL BAKE

Preheat the oven to 350°F (180°C/gas 4).
• Halve the scallion bulbs lengthwise and finely chop the green part. • Combine the scallions, tomatoes, eggplant, zucchini, bell peppers, and garlic in a large bowl. Stir in the oil and salt. • Mix well, then transfer to a large ovenproof dish. • Add the rosemary and bay leaf, and arrange the lemon quarters on top. Cover with aluminum foil and bake for 1½–2 hours, stirring every 20 minutes and adding more oil if the vegetables dry out.
• Serve hot or at room temperature.

■ ■ ■ *Serve this tasty mixed vegetable bake for lunch with plenty of freshly baked bread.*

10	scallions (spring onions)
5	large ripe tomatoes, blanched, peeled, and chopped
1	medium eggplant (aubergine), chopped into cubes
2	zucchini (courgettes), cut into rounds
1	red bell pepper (capsicum), seeded and coarsely chopped
1	yellow bell pepper (capsicum), seeded and coarsely chopped
1	green bell pepper (capsicum), seeded and coarsely chopped
6	cloves garlic, peeled and finely chopped
1/3	cup (90 ml) extra-virgin olive oil + extra if needed
1	teaspoon salt
1	sprig rosemary
1	bay leaf
1	lemon, halved and quartered

Nutritional Facts
Amount per serving
Percentage of Daily Values
based on 2,000 calories

| CALORIES | PROTEIN | FAT | FIBER | SALT |
| 258 | 3g | 22g | 4.8g | 1.2g |

Serves: 4
Preparation: 30 minutes
Cooking: 1½–2 hours
Level: 1

POTATO AND KOHLRABI GRATIN

Preheat the oven to 350°F (180°C/gas 4).
• Butter a shallow ovenproof dish. • Pat the vegetable slices dry with a kitchen towel. • Make a layer of kohlrabi and a few slices of onion in the dish. Season with salt and pepper. Cover with a layer of potatoes and slices of onion. Season with salt and pepper. Top with a layer of cheese. Repeat, finishing with a cheese layer. • Put the cream, milk, and garlic in a small bowl. Season with salt, pepper, and chile. • Pour over the vegetables and grate on some nutmeg. • Cover with aluminum foil and bake for 45–50 minutes. Remove the foil and bake for 20 minutes, until golden and tender. • Garnish with the marjoram. Serve hot with the salad greens.

■ ■ ■ *Kohlrabi is German for "cabbage turnip." It is not the root of the plant that is eaten, but the bulbous part of the stem. It is a popular vegetable in Central and Eastern Europe and is high in vitamin C.*

2 kohlrabies, peeled and thinly sliced

1 onion, very finely sliced

Salt and freshly ground pepper

1 pound (500 g), peeled waxy potatoes, sliced

8 ounces (250 g) Cheddar or other full-flavored cheese, grated

$2/3$ cup (150 ml) heavy (double) cream

$2/3$ cup (150 ml) milk

1 clove garlic, thinly sliced

Pinch of ground chile powder

Nutmeg

Fresh marjoram, to garnish

Salad greens, to serve

Serves: 4
Preparation: 20 minutes
Cooking: 65–70 minutes
Level: 1

Nutritional Facts
Amount per serving
Percentage of Daily Values
based on 2,000 calories

CALORIES	PROTEIN	FAT	FIBER	SALT
584	22g	43g	3.8g	1.1g
28	8	55	15	20%

BUBBLING BRUSSELS SPROUTS

Preheat the oven to 375°F (190°C/gas 5).• Lightly butter a shallow ovenproof dish. • Remove any unsightly outer leaves from the sprouts, trim the bottom of each one, and cut in half. • Bring a large pot of salted water to a boil. Add the sprouts and return to a boil. Cook for 3 minutes. • Drain the sprouts and transfer to the prepared dish. Sprinkle with the blue cheese and dot with teaspoons of the goat cheese. • Put the mustard and parsley in a small bowl and whisk in the cream and milk. Season with a salt and pepper and a grating of nutmeg. Pour over the sprouts and sprinkle the Parmesan on top. • Bake for 12–15 minutes, until a golden crust has formed and the cream is bubbling. • Serve hot.

1¹/₂ **pounds (750 g) Brussels sprouts**

5 **ounces (150 g) blue cheese, crumbled**

2 **ounces (60 g) chèvre or other fresh goat cheese**

1 **tablespoon coarse-grain mustard**

1 **tablespoon finely chopped fresh parsley**

1¹/₄ **cups (300 ml) heavy (double) cream or reduced-fat crème fraîche**

¹/₄ **cup (60 ml) milk**

Salt and freshly ground black pepper

Nutmeg

2 **tablespoons freshly grated Parmesan cheese**

Serves: 4
Preparation: 10 minutes
Cooking: 15–20 minutes
Level: 1

Nutritional Facts
Amount per serving
Percentage of Daily Values
based on 2,000 calories

CALORIES	PROTEIN	FAT	FIBER	SALT
417	22g	32g	7.1g	2g

BELL PEPPERS WITH MUSHROOM COUSCOUS

Preheat the oven to 400°F (200°C/gas 6).
• Cut the bell peppers in half horizontally and remove the seeds and core. • Prepare the couscous according to the instructions on the package. • Heat the oil in a large frying pan over medium heat. Add the mushrooms and sauté for 3 minutes.
• Add the garlic, tomatoes, scallions, mint, and cilantro. Cook over low heat for 5 minutes. • Add the couscous and cook for 3 minutes. • Drizzle with the lemon juice and season with salt and pepper. Mix well and spoon the mixture into the bell peppers. Place in a large, oiled baking dish. Cover with aluminum foil and bake for 30 minutes, or until the bell peppers are tender. • Remove the bell peppers from the oven and garnish with the cilantro. • Serve hot with the yogurt.

3   large red bell peppers (capsicums)

1   cup (150 g) couscous

1/4   cup (60 ml) extra-virgin olive oil

8   ounces (250 g) button mushrooms, trimmed and coarsely chopped

1   clove garlic, finely chopped

10   cherry tomatoes

6   scallions (spring onions), finely chopped

1   tablespoon finely chopped fresh mint

2   tablespoons finely chopped fresh cilantro (coriander) + extra, to garnish

Freshly squeezed juice of 1/2 lemon

Salt and freshly ground black pepper

3/4   cup (180 ml) plain yogurt

Serves: 4
Preparation: 15 minutes
Cooking: 40–45 minutes
Level: 1

Nutritional Facts
Amount per serving
Percentage of Daily Values
based on 2,000 calories

 CALORIES 344

 PROTEIN 10g 22%

 FAT 16g 20%

 FIBER 5.9g 24%

 SALT 0.8g 5%

BAKED ZUCCHINI WITH CHEESE AND HERBS

402

Preheat the oven to 400°F (200°C/gas 6). • Arrange the zucchini on a large oiled baking sheet in a single layer. Sprinkle with the garlic, oregano, and parsley. Drizzle with the water. Season with salt and pepper and drizzle with the oil. Sprinkle with the Parmesan. Cover with aluminum foil and bake for 15 minutes. • Remove the foil and bake for 5 more minutes, or until the zucchini are tender and the cheese has melted. • Serve hot.

1 pound (500 g) zucchini (courgettes), thinly sliced

2 cloves garlic, finely chopped

1 tablespoon finely chopped fresh oregano

2 tablespoons finely chopped fresh parsley

2 tablespoons water

Salt and freshly ground black pepper

1/4 cup (60 ml) extra-virgin olive oil

6 tablespoons freshly grated Parmesan cheese

Serves: 4
Preparation: 10 minutes
Cooking: 20 minutes
Level: 1

Nutritional Facts
Amount per serving
Percentage of Daily Values
based on 2,000 calories

CALORIES
213
0%

PROTEIN
8g
7

FAT
19g
23%

FIBER
1.2g
5

SALT
1g
8%

TOMATO AND ZUCCHINI GRATIN

Preheat the oven to 400°F (200°C/gas 6). • Put the bread in the bowl of a food processor and process for 30 seconds to make bread crumbs. • Add 2 tablespoons of oil, the cilantro, and thyme. Season with salt and pepper. Blend until well mixed. • Layer the tomatoes and zucchini in a large baking dish. Sprinkle with the bread crumb mixture and drizzle with the remaining oil. • Bake for about 20–25 minutes, or until lightly browned on top. • Serve hot.

6   slices white or whole-wheat (wholemeal) bread, crusts removed

1/3   cup (90 ml) extra-virgin olive oil

2   tablespoons finely chopped fresh cilantro (coriander)

1   tablespoon finely chopped fresh thyme

    Salt and freshly ground black pepper

1   pound (500 g) tomatoes, thinly sliced

1   pound (500 g) zucchini (courgettes), very thinly sliced lengthwise

Serves: 4
Preparation: 15 minutes
Cooking: 20–25 minutes
Level: 1

Nutritional Facts
Amount per serving
Percentage of Daily Values
based on 2,000 calories

 CALORIES 340 16%
 PROTEIN 8g 17%
 FAT 22g 27%
 FIBER 5g 20%
 SALT 1.3g 24%

STUFFED VEGETABLES

Preheat the oven to 450°F (225°C/gas 7). Lightly oil a large baking pan. • Heat a little water in the bottom of a steamer. • Cut the tomatoes, bell peppers, zucchini, onions, and eggplant in half horizontally. • Remove the seeds from the bell peppers and scoop or cut out the flesh from one half of each of the onions, zucchini, tomatoes, and eggplant. Chop the scooped-out flesh with the remaining halves of the vegetables.
• Steam the hollowed-out vegetables for 5 minutes. • Heat 1/4 cup (60 ml) of oil in a large frying pan over high heat. Add the chopped vegetables and sauté until softened, 5–6 minutes. • Add the vinegar and season with salt, pepper, and parsley. Place the steamed vegetable halves in the prepared baking dish. Fill with the cooked filling. Drizzle with the remaining 1/4 cup (60 ml) oil. • Bake for 10 minutes, or until the vegetables are tender. • Serve hot.

6   **large ripe tomatoes**

6   **small bell peppers (capsicums), mixed colors**

6   **zucchini (courgettes)**

6   **white onions, peeled**

3   **long thin eggplant (aubergines)**

1/2   **cup (125 ml) extra-virgin olive oil**

2   **tablespoons balsamic vinegar**

    Salt and freshly ground black pepper

2   **tablespoons finely chopped fresh parsley**

Serves: 6
Preparation: 10 minutes
Cooking: 20 minutes
Level: 2

Nutritional Facts
Amount per serving
Percentage of Daily Values
based on 2,000 calories

CALORIES	PROTEIN	FAT	FIBER	SALT
270	6g	21g	8.1g	1.6g

408

BAKED TOMATOES WITH HERB CRUST

Preheat the oven to 400°F (200°C/gas 6). • Grease a large baking dish with oil. • Combine the basil, cilantro, garlic, oil, and pine nuts in a food processor and process until smooth. Season with salt and pepper. • Arrange the tomatoes in the prepared dish cut-side up. Sprinkle lightly with salt. • Spoon the herb mixture on top of each of the tomatoes. • Bake for 15–20 minutes, until the tomatoes have softened and are lightly browned on top. • Sprinkle with the cheese flakes and serve hot or at room temperature.

1   small bunch fresh basil

1   small bunch fresh cilantro (coriander)

1   clove garlic, peeled

6   tablespoons extra-virgin olive oil

3   tablespoons pine nuts

Salt and freshly ground black pepper

4   large ripe tomatoes, halved horizontally

2   ounces (60 g) ricotta salata or aged pecorino cheese, shaved

Serves: 4
Preparation: 10 minutes
Cooking: 15–20 minutes
Level: 1

Nutritional Facts
Amount per serving
Percentage of Daily Values
based on 2,000 calories

CALORIES
 243
12

PROTEIN
 4g
1

FAT
 24g
30

FIBER
 1.4g
6

SALT
 0.8g
14

CHEESE AND POTATO BAKE

Boil the potatoes in their skins until tender but still firm, 15–20 minutes.
• Drain well and let cool for 15 minutes.
• Peel and let cool completely. • Preheat the oven to 400°F (200°C/gas 6). Butter a large baking dish. • Cut the potatoes into ½-inch (1-cm) slices and arrange in layers in the prepared baking dish, dotting each layer with the butter and the Parmesan. Season with salt and pepper. Pour in the milk. • Bake for 20–25 minutes, until golden brown.
• Serve hot.

1½ pounds (750 g) potatoes

¼ cup (60 g) butter, cut up

4 ounces (125 g) Parmesan cheese, thinly sliced

Salt and freshly ground black pepper

1 cup (250 ml) milk

Serves: 4
Preparation: 40 minutes
Cooking: 35–45 minutes
Level: 1

Nutritional Facts
Amount per serving
Percentage of Daily Values
based on 2,000 calories

 CALORIES 465 22%
 PROTEIN 23g 50%
 FAT 28g 35%
 FIBER 3.5g 14%
 SALT 1.9g 35%

SAVORY BAKE

Preheat the oven to 350°F (180°C/gas 4).
• Butter the bottom and sides of an 11-inch
(28-cm) springform pan. • Place the toast
in a food processor and chop to make fine
bread crumbs. • Set aside 1 tablespoon of
butter and melt the rest in a small frying
pan over low heat. Add the bread crumbs
and cook until the butter has been
absorbed. Add the water. • Firmly press the
bread crumb mixture into the bottom and
sides of the prepared springform pan.
• Combine the ricotta, cream cheese,
Parmesan, eggs, salt, and pepper in a large
bowl and beat until creamy. • Spoon over
the crumb base, smoothing the surface.
• Cut the tomatoes in half and arrange on
the top of the cheesecake, pressing them
in slightly. • Bake for 25–30 minutes, or
until browned on top. • Garnish with
parsley let cool before serving.

12 slices whole-wheat
    (wholemeal) toast

1/2 cup (125 g) butter,
    cut up

1/4 cup (60 ml) cold
    water

1 1/2 cups (400 g) ricotta
    cheese, drained

3   (3-ounce) packages
    (250 g) cream
    cheese, at room
    temperature

1/2 cup (60 g) freshly
    grated Parmesan
    cheese

3   large eggs

    Salt and freshly
    ground black pepper

12 cherry tomatoes,
    halved

    Fresh parlsey,
    to garnish

Serves: 8
Preparation: 40 minutes
    + 1 hour to cool
Cooking: 30–35 minutes
Level: 2

Nutritional Facts
Amount per serving
Percentage of Daily Values
based on 2,000 calories

CALORIES	PROTEIN	FAT	FIBER	SALT
512 25%	17g 37%	37g 39%	4.1g 16%	1.8g 32%

EGGPLANT BAKE

Layer the eggplant with salt in a colander. Let drain for 1 hour. • Preheat the oven to 350°F (180°C/gas 4). • Rinse the eggplants under cold running water and dry with paper towels. Dust with flour. • Heat the vegetable oil in a large frying pan over high heat. Add the eggplant in batches and fry, turning often, until golden brown. Drain on paper towels. • Heat the extra-virgin olive oil in a large frying pan over medium heat. Add the onion and sauté until softened, 3–4 minutes. • Add the tomatoes and basil, season with salt and pepper, and simmer over low heat for 20 minutes. Arrange a layer of eggplant in an ovenproof dish. Sprinkle with Parmesan, cover with a layer of mozzarella then tomato sauce. Repeat this layering process until all the ingredients are in the dish, finishing with a layer of cheese. • Bake until golden and bubbling, about 40 minutes. • Serve hot.

4 medium eggplants (aubergines), sliced 1/4-inch (5-mm) thick

1 tablespoon coarse sea salt

1/2 cup (75 g) all-purpose (plain) flour

1 cup (250 ml) vegetable oil, for frying

2 tablespoons extra-virgin olive oil

1 small onion, finely chopped

1 1/2 pounds (750 g) tomatoes, peeled and chopped

10 fresh basil leaves, torn

Salt and freshly ground black pepper

1 1/2 cups (180 g) freshly grated Parmesan cheese

8 ounces (250 g) fresh mozzarella cheese, thinly sliced

Serves: 6
Preparation: 30 minutes + 1 hour to drain
Cooking: 90 minutes
Level: 2

Nutritional Facts
Amount per serving
Percentage of Daily Values
based on 2,000 calories

 CALORIES 403 19%

 PROTEIN 25g 54%

 FAT 26g 32%

 FIBER 5.3g 22%

 SALT 2g 36%

ZUCCHINI LASAGNE

Preheat the oven to 400°F (200°C/gas 6).
• Heat 5 tablespoons of oil in a large frying pan over medium heat. Add the zucchini in batches and fry until browned, about 5 minutes. Drain on paper towels.
• Sauté the bread crumbs in the same pan with 2 tablespoons of oil, 1 tablespoon of butter, and the garlic, until golden, 3–4 minutes. • Sauté the shallots and carrots in the remaining oil over medium heat until browned, 3–4 minutes. • Add the asparagus and cream and simmer for 10 minutes. Season with the salt. • Line a baking dish with zucchini. Cover with a layer of asparagus mixture and sprinkle with the bread crumbs and Parmesan. Repeat until all the ingredients are in the dish, finishing with bread crumbs and Parmesan. • Dot with the remaining 1 tablespoon butter. • Bake for 15–20 minutes, until browned. • Serve hot.

1/2 cup (125 ml) extra-virgin olive oil

1 1/2 pounds (750 g) zucchini (courgettes), thinly sliced lengthwise

3 cups (100 g) fresh bread crumbs

1 tablespoon butter, cut up

1 clove garlic, finely chopped

5 shallots, coarsely chopped

2 carrots, cut into small cubes

8 ounces (250 g) asparagus spears, trimmed

3/4 cup (180 ml) light (single) cream

Salt

1/2 cup (60 g) freshly grated Parmesan cheese

Serves: 4
Preparation: 25 minutes
Cooking: 45 minutes
Level: 1

Nutritional Facts
Amount per serving
Percentage of Daily Values
based on 2,000 calories

CALORIES	PROTEIN	FAT	FIBER	SALT
607	21g	45g	6.9g	1g

VEGETABLES STUFFED WITH RICE

Preheat the oven to 350°F (180°C/gas 4).
• Oil a large baking dish. • Slice the tops off
the tomatoes. Use a teaspoon to hollow
them out, placing the flesh in a small bowl.
Place the tomatoes upside down in a
colander to drain. • Cut the tops off the bell
peppers and remove the seeds and cores.
• Bring a large pot of salted water to a boil.
Add the rice and cook for 10 minutes.
• Drain and let cool in a large bowl. • Heat
2 tablespoons of oil in a large frying pan
over medium heat. Add the onion, garlic,
and oregano and sauté until softened, 3–4
minutes. • Add the pine nuts and currants
and sauté for 2 minutes. Stir in the basil
and parsley. • Add this mixture and the
tomato flesh to the rice. Season with salt
and pepper. • Stuff the tomatoes and bell
peppers with the rice. • Put in the baking
dish and drizzle with the remaining oil. Bake
for 50 minutes, or until tender. • Serve hot.

2	large tomatoes
2	red or green bell peppers (capsicums)
1	cup (200 g) long-grain rice
1/3	cup (90 ml) extra-virgin olive oil
1	red onion, finely sliced
2	cloves garlic, thinly chopped
1	teaspoon dried oregano
3	tablespoons pine nuts
3	tablespoons currants
4	tablespoons finely chopped fresh basil
3	tablespoons finely chopped fresh parsley
	Salt and freshly ground black pepper

Serves: 4
Preparation: 40 minutes
Cooking: 70 minutes
Level: 2

Nutritional Facts
Amount per serving
Percentage of Daily Values
based on 2,000 calories

CALORIES	PROTEIN	FAT	FIBER	SALT
515 25%	7g 15%	27g 33%	4.5g 18%	0.7g 14%

420

POTATO CAKES WITH CHERRY TOMATOES

Preheat the oven to 350°F (180°C/gas 4). • Oil six 1-cup (250-ml) ramekins. • Bring a large pot of salted water to a boil. Add the potatoes and cook until tender, 15–20 minutes. • Drain and mash in a large bowl using a potato ricer. • Add the cheese and shallots. Season with salt and pepper and mix well. • Add the beaten eggs to the potato mixture and mix well. • Divide the potato mixture among the prepared ramekins, pressing it in with the back of a spoon. • Bake until lightly browned, about 20 minutes. • While the potato cakes are in the oven, heat the oil in a medium frying pan over medium heat. Add the tomatoes and thyme. Season with salt and pepper and sauté for 5 minutes. Remove from the heat. • Turn the potato cakes out onto a heated serving dish. • Spoon the tomato mixture over the top. • Serve hot.

1¹/2 pounds (750 g) baking (floury) potatoes, peeled and cut into chunks

¹/2 cup (60 g) freshly grated Parmesan cheese

2 shallots, finely chopped

Salt and freshly ground black pepper

4 large eggs, lightly beaten

¹/4 cup (60 ml) extra-virgin olive oil

1 pound (500 g) cherry tomatoes, halved

1 tablespoon finely chopped fresh thyme

Serves: 6
Preparation: 15 minutes
Cooking: 40–45 minutes
Level: 1

Nutritional Facts
Amount per serving
Percentage of Daily Values
based on 2,000 calories

 CALORIES 263

 PROTEIN 10g 22%

 FAT 15g 9%

 FIBER 3.1g 2%

 SALT 0.8g 4%

POTATO BAKE WITH TOMATO AND OREGANO

Preheat the oven to 400°F (200°C/gas 6). • Oil a large ovenproof dish. • Heat 2 tablespoons of the oil in a large frying pan over medium heat. Add the onion and sauté until softened, 4–5 minutes. • Add the potatoes and sauté for 5 minutes. Season with salt and pepper. • Transfer to the ovenproof dish. Arrange the tomatoes in a layer on top of the potatoes. Sprinkle with oregano and bread crumbs. Drizzle with the remaining oil. • Bake until the potatoes are tender, 35–40 minutes. • Serve hot.

1/3 cup (90 ml) extra-virgin olive oil

1 large onion, finely chopped

1 1/2 pounds (750 g) potatoes, peeled and thinly sliced

Salt and freshly ground black pepper

12 ounces (350 g) cherry tomatoes, halved

1/2 teaspoon dried oregano

1/2 cup (60 g) fine, dry bread crumbs

Serves: 4
Preparation: 15 minutes
Cooking: 45–50 minutes
Level: 1

Nutritional Facts
Amount per serving
Percentage of Daily Values
based on 2,000 calories

 CALORIES 367 18

 PROTEIN 5g 1

 FAT 22g 27%

 FIBER 5.7g 23

 SALT 0.3g 5

424

POTATO AND ZUCCHINI LOAF

Bring a large pot of salted water to a boil. Add the potatoes and cook until tender, 20–25 minutes. • Drain and mash in a large bowl using a potato ricer. • Preheat the oven to 350°F (180°C/gas 4). • Grease a 9 x 5-inch (12 x 23-cm) loaf pan. • Heat the oil in a large frying pan over medium heat. Add the onion and garlic and sauté until softened, 3–4 minutes. • Add the zucchini and season with salt and pepper. Sauté for 15 minutes, until the zucchini begin to break down. Remove and discard the garlic. • Add the eggs, Parmesan, pecorino, zucchini, and parsley to the potatoes. Season with salt and pepper and mix well. • Place in the prepared pan and sprinkle with the bread crumbs. • Bake for 45–50 minutes, until well browned. • Serve hot or warm.

1   pound (500 g) baking (floury) potatoes, peeled

1/4   cup (60 ml) extra-virgin olive oil

1   large onion, finely chopped

1   clove garlic, lightly crushed

1   pound (500 g) zucchini (courgettes), sliced

    Salt and freshly ground black pepper

3   large eggs, lightly beaten

1/2   cup (60 g) freshly grated Parmesan cheese

1/2   cup (60 g) freshly grated pecorino cheese

1   tablespoon finely chopped fresh parsley

1/4   cup (30 g) fine, dry bread crumbs

Serves: 4
Preparation: 15 minutes
Cooking: 1 hour 30 minutes
Level: 2

Nutritional Facts
Amount per serving
Percentage of Daily Values
based on 2,000 calories

CALORIES
460
22%

PROTEIN
23g
50%

FAT
28g

FIBER
3.7g

SALT
1.5g

BRIE AND VEGETABLE CLAFOUTIS

Preheat the oven to 350°F (180°C/gas 4). • Heat the oil in a large frying pan over medium heat. Add the shallot and sauté until softened, 2–3 minutes. • Add the zucchini, carrots, asparagus, and fava beans and sauté for 5 minutes. • Oil two baking sheets. Place the bread on the baking sheets and dust with paprika. Toast until lightly browned. • Mix the flour and milk in a small bowl. • Heat the cream and eggs in a medium saucepan over medium heat, stirring constantly. Do not boil. Add the milk mixture and stir until the sauce begins to thicken. • Line the bottom of a large baking dish with the toast and cover with the Brie. Spoon the vegetables over the top. • Pour the sauce over the top and sprinkle with the Parmesan. • Bake for 20–25 minutes, until the vegetables are tender and the topping is nicely browned. • Serve hot.

2 tablespoons extra-virgin olive oil

1 shallot, finely chopped

2 zucchini (courgettes), cut into small cubes

2 carrots, cut into small cubes

12 asparagus spears, trimmed

2/3 cup (100 g) frozen fava (broad) beans

8 slices whole-wheat (wholemeal) bread

1 teaspoon sweet paprika

1 tablespoon all-purpose (plain) flour

1/3 cup (90 ml) milk

1/3 cup (90 ml) light (single) cream

2 large eggs, beaten

5 ounces (150 g) Brie cheese, thinly sliced

1 cup (125 g) freshly grated Parmesan cheese

Serves: 4
Preparation: 20 minutes
Cooking: 45 minutes
Level: 2

Nutritional Facts
Amount per serving
Percentage of Daily Values
based on 2,000 calories

CALORIES	PROTEIN	FAT	FIBER	SALT
565	31g	31g	7.3g	1.8g

STUFFED EGGPLANTS

Preheat the oven to 350°F (180°C/gas 4).
• Cut the eggplants in half lengthwise.
Scoop out the centers and chop the flesh
into small cubes. • Mix the eggplant
flesh, mozzarella, and garlic in a medium
bowl. Stir in the oil and season with salt
and pepper. • Arrange the hollowed-out
eggplant halves in an oiled baking dish.
Spoon the filling mixture into the
eggplants. Sprinkle with the chopped
tomatoes. • Bake for 30–35 minutes,
or until the topping is bubbling and the
eggplants are well cooked. • Garnish
with the basil and serve hot or at
room temperature.

4   small eggplants
    (aubergines)

8   ounces (250 g)
    mozzarella cheese,
    cut into small cubes

1   clove garlic, finely
    chopped

2   tablespoons extra-
    virgin olive oil

    Salt and freshly
    ground black pepper

3   firm-ripe tomatoes,
    cut into small cubes

2   tablespoons finely
    chopped fresh basil,
    to garnish

Serves: 4
Preparation: 20 minutes
Cooking: 30–35 minutes
Level: 1

Nutritional Facts
Amount per serving
Percentage of Daily Values
based on 2,000 calories

 CALORIES 282 14%
 PROTEIN 19g 41%
 FAT 20g 25%
 FIBER 6g 24%
 SALT 0.9g 17%

EGGS, CHEESE AND TOFU

EGG QUESADILLAS

Preheat the oven to 325°F (170°C/gas 3). • Whisk the eggs and milk in a medium bowl. Season with salt and pepper. • Heat the butter in a medium frying pan over medium-low heat. Pour in the egg mixture and cook, stirring with a wooden spoon, until thick curds begin to form, 3–4 minutes. Stir in the scallions and chile and set aside. • Heat $1/2$ tablespoon of oil in a large frying pan over medium-high heat. Place a tortilla in the pan and cover with one quarter of the scrambled egg. Sprinkle with one quarter of the cheese and cover with another tortilla. Cook until crisp and golden brown, 1–2 minutes on each side. Slide onto a baking tray and place in the oven to keep warm. Repeat the process with the remaining tortillas, scrambled egg, and cheese. • Cut into quarters and serve with tomato salsa and cilantro.

8	large eggs, lightly beaten
3	tablespoons milk
	Salt and freshly ground black pepper
2	tablespoons butter
4	scallions (spring onions), thinly sliced
1	large red chile, seeded and thinly sliced
2	tablespoons extra-virgin olive oil
8	(8-inch/20-cm) flour tortillas
8	ounces (250 g) Cheddar or Monterey Jack cheese, grated
	Tomato salsa, to serve
	Fresh cilantro (coriander), leaves to garnish

Serves: 4
Preparation: 15 minutes
Cooking: 15 minutes
Level: 2

Nutritional Facts
Amount per serving
Percentage of Daily Values
based on 2,000 calories

 CALORIES 320 15

 PROTEIN 9g 20

 FAT 19g 23

 FIBER 1.7g 7

 SALT 0.6g 7

TOFU BURGERS

Heat 1 tablespoon of oil in a small frying pan over medium-low heat. Add the onion and garlic and sauté until softened, about 5 minutes. Add the soy sauce, lemon juice, and cumin and sauté until fragrant, 1 minute. Transfer to a medium bowl. • Add the tofu to the bowl along with the flour, sunflower seeds, sesame seeds, and parsley. Season with salt and pepper and stir to combine. • Shape the tofu mixture into eight evenly sized burgers. • Heat the remaining 3 tablespoons oil in a large frying pan over medium heat. Cook the burgers in batches until golden brown, 4–5 minutes on each side. • Serve hot with a garden salad and chutney.

1/4 cup (60 ml) vegetable oil

1 medium onion, finely chopped

2 cloves garlic, finely chopped

2 tablespoons soy sauce

1 tablespoon freshly squeezed lemon juice

1/2 teaspoon ground cumin

8 ounces (250 g) firm tofu, crumbled

1/4 cup (30 g) all-purpose (plain) flour

2 tablespoons sunflower seeds

2 tablespoons sesame seeds

2 tablespoons finely chopped fresh parsley

Salt and freshly ground black pepper

Mixed salad greens, to serve

Mango chutney, to serve

Nutritional Facts
Amount per serving
Percentage of Daily Values
based on 2,000 calories

 CALORIES **230**

 PROTEIN **11g**

 FAT **23g**

 FIBER **1.5g**

 SALT **1.7g** 30%

Serves: 4
Preparation: 15 minutes
Cooking: 8–10 minutes
Level: 1

TOFU AND BLACK BEAN STIR-FRY

Heat the oil in a large wok over medium-high heat. Add the onion, garlic, black beans, chiles, and ginger and stir-fry until softened, 2–3 minutes. • Add the tofu and stir-fry until golden brown, 2 minutes. • Pour in the soy sauce and kecap manis and toss to coat. Add the broccoli and cook for 1 minute. • Add the mushrooms and bell pepper and stir-fry until vegetables are slightly tender but still crisp, about 2 more minutes. • Stir in the Chinese cabbage and stir-fry until wilted, about 1 minute. • Serve hot with jasmine rice.

■ ■ ■ *Kecap manis is a dark brown, fairly sweet Indonesian soy sauce. It is available in Asian supermarkets; if you can't find it replace with sweet, dark soy sauce.*

2	tablespoons Asian sesame oil
1	medium onion, sliced
2	cloves garlic, sliced
2	tablespoons Chinese fermented black beans, chopped
2	large fresh red chiles, seeded and sliced
1	teaspoon finely chopped fresh ginger
12	ounces (350 g) firm tofu, sliced
2	tablespoons light soy sauce
2	tablespoons kecap manis or sweet soy sauce
1	bunch Chinese broccoli, or regular broccoli, in florets
5	ounces (150 g) oyster or shiitake mushrooms, halved
1	red bell pepper (capsicum), seeded and sliced
1/2	Chinese cabbage (wom bok), chopped
	Freshly cooked jasmine rice, to serve

Nutritional Facts
Amount per serving
Percentage of Daily Values
based on 2,000 calories

 CALORIES 213 10%
 PROTEIN 16g 35%
 FAT 12g 15%
 FIBER 3.9g 16%
 SALT 2.6g 48%

Serves: 4
Preparation: 15 minutes
Cooking: 10 minutes
Level: 1

438

AGEDASHI TOFU

Sauce: Combine the kombu dashi stock, soy sauce, and mirin in a small saucepan and bring to a boil. Decrease the heat to low and keep warm.

Tofu: Pour about 2 inches (5 cm) of oil into a wok over medium heat. Test the oil by dropping in a small piece of bread. If it immediately bubbles to the surface and begins to turn golden, the oil is ready.
• Pat the tofu dry on paper towels and toss in the cornstarch to coat. • Fry the tofu in batches until crisp and golden, about 2 minutes on each side. Remove using a slotted spoon and drain on paper towels.
• Divide the tofu among four serving bowls, drizzle with the sauce, and top with the radish, scallions, and ginger. • Serve hot.

■ ■ ■ *Kombu dashi is a seaweed stock that is widely used in Japanese cooking. It is very easy to prepare: Place 2 cups (500 ml) of cold water in a bowl with one 4-inch (10-cm) square of dried kombu (Japanese kelp). Leave in the refrigerator overnight.*

Sauce
1   cup (250 ml) kombu dashi stock

1/4   cup (60 ml) light soy sauce

2   tablespoons mirin

Tofu
    Vegetable oil, for deep frying

2   (7-ounce/200-g) blocks soft tofu, quartered

3/4   cup (125 g) cornstarch (cornflour)

1   daikon (white radish), peeled and sliced into very thin strips

4   scallions (spring onions), thinly sliced

1   (1½-inch/4-cm) piece fresh ginger, peeled and finely grated

Serves: 4
Preparation: 15 minutes
Cooking: 15 minutes
Level: 1

Nutritional Facts
Amount per serving
Percentage of Daily Values
based on 2,000 calories

CALORIES	PROTEIN	FAT	FIBER	SALT
186	7g	3g	1.6g	2.2g

BAKED TOMATO OMELET

Heat the oil in a medium frying pan over medium-low heat. Add the onion and garlic and sauté until softened, 3–4 minutes. • Add the paprika, coriander, cayenne, and sugar and sauté until fragrant, about 1 minute. • Add the tomatoes and cook until the sauce has thickened, about 10 minutes. Stir in the parsley and season with salt and pepper. • Smooth the sauce in pan to create an even surface. Pour the eggs over the top. Cover and cook over medium heat until set, 10–15 minutes. • Serve hot, topped with cilantro.

2	tablespoons extra-virgin olive oil
1	medium onion, sliced
1	clove garlic, finely chopped
1½	teaspoons sweet paprika
1½	teaspoons ground coriander
¼	teaspoon cayenne pepper
¼	teaspoon sugar
2	(14-ounce/400-g) cans plum tomatoes, coarsely chopped, with juice
4	tablespoons finely chopped fresh parsley
	Salt and freshly ground black pepper
8	large eggs, lightly beaten
	Fresh cilantro (coriander) leaves, to garnish

Serves: 4
Preparation: 15 minutes
Cooking: 25–30 minutes
Level: 1

Nutritional Facts
Amount per serving
Percentage of Daily Values
based on 2,000 calories

 CALORIES 262 13%
 PROTEIN 17g 37%
 FAT 20g 25%
 FIBER 1.2g 5%
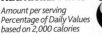 SALT 1.2g 22%

442

TOMATOES WITH EGGS AND BASIL

Preheat the oven to 400°F (200°C/gas 6). Oil a baking dish just large enough to hold the tomatoes in a single layer. • Cut the tops off the tomatoes and use a teaspoon to hollow out the centers. Place the flesh in a bowl with the basil. Season the insides of the tomatoes lightly with salt. • Break an egg into each tomato and top up with the tomato and basil mixture. Season with salt and pepper and sprinkle with the cheese. Drizzle with the oil. • Bake for 15–20 minutes, until the tomatoes have softened and the eggs have set. • Serve hot or at room temperature.

4   medium-large ripe tomatoes
    Salt and freshly ground black pepper
4   leaves basil, torn
4   large eggs
6   tablespoons freshly grated Parmesan cheese
2   tablespoons extra-virgin olive oil

Serves: 2
Preparation: 10 minutes
Cooking: 15–20 minutes
Level: 1

■ ■ ■ *This makes enough for four starters (one stuffed tomato each) or two light lunches (or brunches).*

Nutritional Facts
Amount per serving
Percentage of Daily Values
based on 2,000 calories

	CALORIES	PROTEIN	FAT	FIBER	SALT
	458	29g	35g	2.4g	1g
	22%	63%	43%	10%	19%

SPICY TOFU

Soak the dried mushrooms in $^1/_4$ cup (60 ml) warm water for 15 minutes.
• Sauté the celery and garlic in the vegetable oil in a large wok over medium heat for 3 minutes. • Add the mushrooms, tofu, and chile peppers and stir-fry for 3 minutes. • Stir in the vegetable stock, soy sauce, sesame oil, and sugar. Stir-fry for 5 minutes, or until the liquid has reduced slightly. • Mix the water and cornstarch in a small bowl. Stir into the wok to thicken the sauce.
• Season with pepper, garnish with the parsley, and serve hot.

2   teaspoons dried black mushrooms
2   stalks celery, finely chopped
2   cloves garlic, finely chopped
2   tablespoons vegetable oil
2   pounds (1 kg) firm tofu, cubed
2   fresh red chile peppers, chopped
$1^1/_2$ cups (375 ml) vegetable stock
1   tablespoon soy sauce
1   tablespoon Asian sesame oil
$^1/_2$ teaspoon sugar
1   tablespoon water
1   teaspoon cornstarch (cornflour)
    Freshly ground black pepper
1   tablespoon finely chopped fresh parsley

Serves: 6
Preparation: 20 minutes
    + 15 minutes to soak
Cooking: 10 minutes
Level: 1

Nutritional Facts
Amount per serving
Percentage of Daily Values
based on 2,000 calories

CALORIES	PROTEIN	FAT	FIBER	SALT
229	20g	15g	0.6g	0.5g
	3%	9%		

SWEET SPICY TOFU

Heat the oil in a large wok or frying pan over medium-high heat. • Add the tofu, half the scallions, half the garlic, and the ginger and stir-fry for 3 minutes. • Add the chiles and stir-fry for 1 minute. • Stir in the sherry, soy sauce, 1 cup (250 ml) water, and salt. Bring to a boil and simmer for 3 minutes. • Mix the remaining 1 tablespoon water and cornstarch in a small bowl. Stir into the wok and cook until the mixture thickens, 2–3 minutes. • Sprinkle with the remaining scallion and garlic. • Transfer to a heated plate and serve hot.

2   tablespoons Asian sesame oil

2   pounds (1 kg) firm tofu, cut into small cubes

2   scallions (spring onions), finely chopped

2   cloves garlic, finely chopped

1   teaspoon finely chopped fresh ginger

2   small fresh red chiles, seeded and finely chopped

1   tablespoon dry sherry

1¹/₂ tablespoons soy sauce

1   cup (250 ml) + 1 tablespoon water

¹/₂ teaspoon salt

1¹/₂ teaspoons cornstarch (cornflour)

Serves: 6
Preparation: 20 minutes
Cooking: 10 minutes
Level: 1

Nutritional Facts
Amount per serving
Percentage of Daily Values
based on 2,000 calories

CALORIES 217
PROTEIN 20g

FAT 14g

FIBER 0.6g

SALT 0.8g

OMELET WITH CHINESE VEGETABLES

Mix 1 tablespoon of water, 1 tablespoon of soy sauce, 1 teaspoon of cornstarch, and the white wine in a large bowl. Add the tofu and let marinate for 10 minutes. • Stir in 1 tablespoon of the oil. • Chop the soaked noodles into short lengths. • Chop the bok choy and spinach into short lengths. • Heat a large wok over medium heat and add 3 tablespoons of oil. • Add the tofu and marinade and stir-fry for 3 minutes. Remove from the wok and set aside. • Add the bok choy and spinach to the wok and stir-fry for 3 minutes, or until slightly wilted. • Remove from the wok and set aside. • Add 1 tablespoon of oil and sauté the scallions until lightly browned. Add the bean thread, vegetable stock, and remaining 1 tablespoon soy sauce. • Cook until the sauce has reduced, 2–3 minutes. • Stir in the bean sprouts. Cook for 3 more minutes. • Stir in the tofu and bok choy mixtures. Transfer to

2	tablespoons water
2	tablespoons soy sauce
2	teaspoons cornstarch (cornflour)
1	teaspoon white wine
4	ounces (125 g) firm tofu, coarsely chopped
1/3	cup (90 ml) peanut oil
2	ounces (60 g) dried bean thread or cellophane noodles, soaked in warm water for 10 minutes and drained
1	bok choy, coarsely chopped
4	ounces (125 g) fresh spinach leaves, stems removed
6	scallions (spring onions), sliced
1	cup (250 ml) vegetable stock
2	cups (100 g) mung bean sprouts
3	large eggs, lightly beaten

Serves: 4
Preparation: 40 minutes
+ 10 minutes to
marinate
Cooking: 20 minutes
Level: 1

a serving dish. • Beat the eggs with the remaining 1 tablespoon of water, and 1 teaspoon of cornstarch, in a medium bowl until frothy. • Heat the remaining 1 teaspoon of oil in a large frying pan over medium heat. • Pour in the beaten egg mixture, tilting the pan so that the batter thinly covers the bottom. • Cook until light golden brown on the underside, 3–5 minutes. Use a large spatula to flip the omelet and cook until golden, 2–3 minutes. • Serve the omelet hot with the tofu and vegetables.

(See photograph on the following page.)

Nutritional Facts
Amount per serving
Percentage of Daily Values
based on 2,000 calories

CALORIES	PROTEIN	FAT	FIBER	SALT
375	13g	27g	1.9g	1.5g

TOFU WITH MUSHROOMS

Place a wok over high heat. Pour in about 2 inches (5 cm) of oil. Test the oil temperature by dropping in a small piece of bread. If it immediately bubbles to the surface and begins to turn golden, the oil is ready. • Add the tofu in two batches and fry until golden brown all over, 5–7 minutes per batch. • Drain on paper towels. • Heat the peanut oil in a wok, add the scallions and ginger and stir-fry until softened, 2–3 minutes. • Add the mushrooms and stir-fry for 3 minutes. • Stir in the bamboo shoots, vegetable stock, soy sauce, sesame oil, and the fried tofu. Season with pepper. Bring to a boil and simmer for 3 minutes. • Add the bok choy and cook for 2 minutes more. • Mix the cornstarch and water in a small bowl. Stir into the wok and cook to thicken the mixture, 1–2 minutes. • Serve hot.

Vegetable oil, for frying

2 pounds (1 kg) firm tofu, cubed

3 tablespoons peanut oil

2 scallions (spring onions), thinly sliced

1 tablespoon finely chopped fresh ginger

1 pound (500 g) button mushrooms, sliced

$1/2$ cup (125 g) thinly sliced bamboo shoots

1 cup (250 ml) vegetable stock

$2^1/2$ tablespoons soy sauce

1 teaspoon Asian sesame oil

Freshly ground black pepper

4 baby bok choy, cut in half

2 teaspoons cornstarch (cornflour)

1 tablespoon water

Serves: 6
Preparation: 20 minutes
Cooking: 25 minutes
Level: 1

Nutritional Facts
Amount per serving
Percentage of Daily Values
based on 2,000 calories

 CALORIES 259

 PROTEIN 23g 50

FAT 17g 2

FIBER 2.5g

 SALT 1.3g

TOMATO AND BELL PEPPER FRITTATA

454

Heat the oil in a large frying pan over medium heat. Add the bell peppers and onion and sauté until tender, about 10 minutes. • Stir in the tomatoes and basil. Season with salt and pepper. • Beat the eggs in a medium bowl until frothy. • Pour the eggs into the frying pan. Stir well, then leave to cook until the eggs have set, 5–7 minutes. • Turn on the broiler (grill) and broil the frittata until the top is golden, 3–4 minutes. • Serve hot.

2 tablespoons extra-virgin olive oil

3 bell peppers (capsicums) of mixed colors, seeded, cored, and coarsely chopped

1 onion, thinly sliced

12 ounces (350 g) cherry tomatoes, coarsely chopped

4 leaves fresh basil, torn

Salt and freshly ground black pepper

6 large eggs

Serves: 4
Preparation: 20 minutes
Cooking: 18–21 minutes
Level: 1

Nutritional Facts
Amount per serving
Percentage of Daily Values
based on 2,000 calories

CALORIES	PROTEIN	FAT	FIBER	SALT
160	6g	10g	3.9g	0.8g

EGG CURRY

456

Heat the ghee in a large frying pan over medium heat. Add the onion and sauté until golden brown, about 10 minutes. • Add the ginger, garlic, garam masala, coriander seeds, and ground chile and sauté for 2 minutes. • Stir in the tomatoes and cook for 5 minutes. Add the cilantro. • Add the eggs and cook over low heat until the sauce thickens, 5 minutes. • Serve hot with the rice.

1 tablespoon ghee (clarified butter) or vegetable oil

1 onion, finely chopped

1 (^{1}/2-inch/1-cm) piece fresh ginger, thinly sliced

1 clove garlic, thinly sliced

1 teaspoon garam masala

1 teaspoon coriander seeds

^{1}/2 teaspoon ground chile powder

1 cup (250 g) chopped tomatoes

1 small bunch fresh cilantro (coriander), finely chopped

4 hard-cooked eggs, peeled and left whole

Freshly cooked basmati rice, to serve

Serves: 2
Preparation: 20 minutes
Cooking: 20–25 minutes
Level: 1

Nutritional Facts
Amount per serving
Percentage of Daily Values
based on 2,000 calories

 CALORIES 265 13%
 PROTEIN 17g 37%
 FAT 19g 23%
 FIBER 1.7g 7%
 SALT 0.5g 9%

BAKED POTATO FRITTATA

Preheat the oven to 375°F (190°C/gas 5). • Oil a 9-inch (23-cm) square baking pan. • Bring a large pot of salted water to a boil. Add the potato slices and cook until just tender, 5–7 minutes. • Drain well and set aside. • Heat the oil in a large frying pan over medium heat. Add the onion and sauté until softened, 3–4 minutes. Season with salt. • Beat the eggs in a medium bowl until frothy. Mix in the potatoes, onion, and Parmesan. • Pour the mixture into the prepared pan. • Bake for 12–15 minutes, until golden brown. • Serve hot or at room temperature.

12 ounces (350 g) potatoes, peeled and thinly sliced

1 large red onion, coarsely chopped

2 tablespoons extra-virgin olive oil

Salt

4 large eggs

4 tablespoons freshly grated Parmesan cheese

Serves: 4
Preparation: 20 minutes
Cooking: 30–35 minutes
Level: 1

Nutritional Facts
Amount per serving
Percentage of Daily Values
based on 2,000 calories

 CALORIES 369 18%
 PROTEIN 15g 33%
 FAT 27g 33%
 FIBER 2g 8%
 SALT 1g 19%

CREPES WITH TWO CHEESES

Crêpes: Mix the water and garbanzo bean flour in a small bowl. • Beat the eggs and milk in a bowl until frothy. • Mix in the all-purpose flour, butter, and garbanzo flour mixture. Season with salt. • Heat 1 teaspoon of butter in a small frying pan over medium heat. • Pour in 2 tablespoons of batter, tilting to cover the bottom. • Cook until pale gold on the underside, 2–3 minutes. Flip with a large spatula and cook until golden, 2–3 minutes. Repeat until all the batter has been used. Stack the crêpes on a plate. • Preheat the oven to 400°F (200°C/gas 6). • Butter a large baking dish.

Cheese Filling: Mix the ricotta, goat cheese, ½ cup of Parmesan, marjoram, parsley, garlic, salt, and pepper in a bowl. • Spread the crêpes with the filling and roll up. Place seam-side down in the dish. Sprinkle with the remaining cheese. • Bake for 15 minutes, until browned. • Serve hot.

Crêpes

- ⅔ cup (150 ml) water
- ⅔ cup (100 g) garbanzo bean (chickpea) flour
- 2 large eggs
- ⅓ cup (90 ml) milk
- ⅓ cup (50 g) all-purpose (plain) flour
- 1 tablespoon butter, melted
- Salt

Cheese Filling

- 1 cup (250 g) ricotta cheese
- ⅔ cup (150 g) chèvre or soft fresh goat cheese
- ¾ cup (90 g) grated Parmesan cheese
- 1 tablespoon finely chopped marjoram
- 1 tablespoon finely chopped parsley
- 1 clove garlic, finely chopped
- Freshly ground pepper
- 1 tablespoon butter

Serves: 6
Preparation: 40 minutes
Cooking: 20 minutes
Level: 2

Nutritional Facts
Amount per serving
Percentage of Daily Values
based on 2,000 calories

CALORIES 365

PROTEIN 21g

FAT 24g

FIBER 2.3g

SALT 1.2g

SPICY EGGS, THAI STYLE

462

Bring the eggs to a boil in a saucepan and boil for 7 minutes. • Drain and rinse under cold running water. Shell the eggs and cut them in half lengthwise. • While the eggs are cooking, melt the butter in a large frying pan over medium heat. Add the onions, chiles, ginger, cinnamon, and turmeric and sauté until the onions have softened, about 5 minutes. • Pour in the coconut milk and lemon juice. Season with salt and mix well. Carefully place the eggs, yolk-side up, in the sauce. Simmer over medium heat for 3 minutes, or until the sauce has thickened slightly. • Garnish with the lemon zest and serve hot.

4 large eggs

1/4 cup (60 g) butter

4 large onions, thinly sliced

3 fresh red chiles, seeded and thinly sliced

2 tablespoons finely grated fresh ginger

1/2 teaspoon ground cinnamon

1/2 teaspoon ground turmeric

1/2 cup (125 ml) coconut milk

3 tablespoons freshly squeezed lemon juice

Salt

Zest of 1/2 lemon, very finely cut into strips, to garnish

Serves: 4
Preparation: 10 minutes
Cooking: 20 minutes
Level: 1

Nutritional Facts
Amount per serving
Percentage of Daily Values
based on 2,000 calories

CALORIES 463
PROTEIN 14g
FAT 38g
FIBER 2.8g
SALT 1.3g

FIERY EGGS WITH CHERRY TOMATOES

Heat the oil in a large frying pan over medium heat. Add the onion and garlic and sauté until softened, about 5 minutes. • Stir in the tomatoes and chile. Season with salt and pepper. Cook for 2 minutes. • Break the eggs into the pan. Cook until the whites are set but the yolks are still slightly runny, 5–7 minutes. • Serve hot with freshly baked bread to mop up the egg yolks and juices.

¹/₄ cup (60 ml) extra-virgin olive oil

1 onion, finely chopped

1 clove garlic, finely chopped

2 pounds (1 kg) cherry tomatoes, halved

1 fresh red or green chile, seeded and finely chopped

Salt and freshly ground black pepper

6 large eggs

Freshly baked crusty bread, to serve

Serves: 4
Preparation: 10 minutes
Cooking: 15 minutes
Level: 1

Nutritional Facts

Amount per serving
Percentage of Daily Values
based on 2,000 calories

 CALORIES 313

 PROTEIN 14g 30

 FAT 26g 3

 FIBER 3.7g 15

 SALT 1.1g

CHEESE SOUFFLÉ

466

Preheat the oven to 350°F (180°C/gas 4). Butter four 1-cup (250-ml) ramekins or soufflé dishes. • Lightly beat the egg yolks in a large bowl. • Add the milk, butter, and mustard to the egg yolks and mix well. • Stir in the bread crumbs and cheese and season with the salt and pepper. • Beat the egg whites with a pinch of salt until stiff peaks form. Fold into the yolk mixture. • Pour into the prepared dishes. Bake for 25–30 minutes, until well risen, brown on top, and set in the middle. • Serve at once.

4   large eggs, separated

1¼ cups (300 ml) milk, warmed

1   tablespoon butter, melted

1   teaspoon Djion mustard

3   cups (100 g) fresh bread crumbs

4   ounces (125 g) Cheddar or Emmental cheese, grated

Salt and freshly ground black pepper

Serves: 4
Preparation: 10 minutes
Cooking: 25–30 minutes
Level: 2

Nutritional Facts
Amount per serving
Percentage of Daily Values
based on 2,000 calories

 CALORIES **335**

 PROTEIN **21g**

 FAT **22g**

 FIBER **1.2g**

SALT **1.7g**

ZUCCHINI FRITTATA

468

Heat the oil in a large frying pan over medium heat. Add the garlic and sauté until pale gold, about 3 minutes. • Add the zucchini and sauté until tender, 5–7 minutes. Season with salt and pepper. • Beat the eggs and cheese in a medium bowl. • Pour the egg mixture into the pan and cook until the egg is almost solid, 7–8 minutes. • Slide the frittata onto a plate, flip it onto another plate, and then slide it back into the pan. Cook until golden brown and the egg is cooked through, 3–4 minutes. • Serve hot.

3 tablespoons extra-virgin olive oil

1 clove garlic, finely chopped

2 pounds (1 kg) zucchini (courgettes), thinly sliced horizontally

Salt and freshly ground black pepper

6 large eggs

1/2 cup (60 g) freshly grated pecorino or Parmesan cheese

Fresh salad greens, to serve

Serves: 4
Preparation: 10 minutes
Cooking: 20 minutes
Level: 1

Nutritional Facts
Amount per serving
Percentage of Daily Values
based on 2,000 calories

 CALORIES 317 15%

 PROTEIN 21g 46%

 FAT 24g 30%

 FIBER 2.3g 9%

 SALT 1.3g 23%

BAKED FRITTATA WITH TOMATO AND OLIVES

470

Oil a 9-inch (23-cm) baking dish. Preheat the oven to 400°F (200°C/gas 6). • Put the bell peppers and tomatoes on a plate in a microwave oven. Cook at high for 3 minutes. • Peel the vegetables. Cut the bell peppers into strips and the tomatoes into wedges. • Heat the oil in a large frying pan over low heat. Add the onions and sauté until softened, 3–4 minutes. • Add the tomatoes, bell peppers, and herbs. Season with salt. • Cook for 5 minutes. Set aside. • Beat the eggs, milk, and Gruyère in a large bowl. Pour into the fried vegetables. • Pour the mixture into the prepared dish and garnish with the black olives. • Bake for 25–30 minutes, or until set and golden on top. • Serve hot or at room temperature.

2   red bell peppers (capsicums)

2   pounds (1 kg) tomatoes

3   tablespoons extra-virgin olive oil

4   small onions, thinly sliced

1   cup (50 g) fresh aromatic herbs (oregano, basil, thyme, chervil), finely chopped

    Salt

4   large eggs

1/2   cup (125 ml) milk

1³/4 cups (200 g) grated Gruyère cheese

1   cup (100 g) black olives, pitted

Serves: 6
Preparation: 25 minutes
Cooking: 40–50 minutes
Level: 2

Nutritional Facts
Amount per serving
Percentage of Daily Values
based on 2,000 calories

 CALORIES 345

 PROTEIN 18g

 FAT 24g

 FIBER 3.7g

 SALT 1.6g

FRITTATA ROLL WITH PEAS AND PINE NUTS

Boil the peas in a pot of salted water until tender, about 5 minutes. Drain well. • Beat the eggs in a large bowl. Add the bread crumbs, pecorino, and chives. Season with salt and pepper. • Heat 2 tablespoons of oil in a large frying pan over medium heat. Add the egg mixture and cook until golden brown underneath, 3–5 minutes. • Slide the frittata onto a plate, flip it onto another plate, and then slide it back into the pan. Cook until the other side is golden brown, 2–3 minutes. • Heat the remaining 2 tablespoons oil in a small frying pan over high heat. Add the peas, pine nuts, and thyme and sauté until heated through, 2–3 minutes. • Place the cooked frittata on a cutting board and spread with the pea mixture. Sprinkle with the Parmesan and drizzle with the lemon juice. Roll up, slice, and serve hot.

1 cup (150 g) frozen peas
6 large eggs
1 cup (150 g) fine dry bread crumbs
2/3 (100 g) freshly grated pecorino cheese
2 tablespoons finely chopped fresh chives
Salt and freshly ground black pepper
1/4 cup (60 ml) extra-virgin olive oil
2 tablespoons pine nuts
1 tablespoon finely chopped fresh thyme
6 tablespoons freshly grated Parmesan cheese
1 tablespoon freshly squeezed lemon juice

Serves: 4
Preparation: 20 minutes
Cooking: 15 minutes
Level: 3

Nutritional Facts
Amount per serving
Percentage of Daily Values
based on 2,000 calories

 CALORIES 572
 PROTEIN 33g
 FAT 41g
 FIBER 5.2g
 SALT 1.5g

BASIL FRITTATA

474

Beat the eggs in a large bowl. Add the cheese and season with salt and pepper. Add the basil and mix well. • Heat the oil in a large frying pan over medium heat. Pour the egg mixture into the pan and cook until the bottom is browned, 3–5 minutes. • Slide the frittata onto a plate, flip it onto another plate, and then slide it back into the pan. Cook until the egg is cooked through and lightly browned all over, 3–4 minutes. • Transfer to a serving dish. Garnish with basil and serve hot.

12 large eggs

1 cup (120 g) freshly grated pecorino or Parmesan cheese

Salt and freshly ground black pepper

Bunch of fresh basil leaves, coarsely chopped + extra leaves, to garnish

2 tablespoons extra-virgin olive oil

Serves: 6
Preparation: 10 minutes
Cooking: 10 minutes
Level: 2

Nutritional Facts
Amount per serving
Percentage of Daily Values
based on 2,000 calories

 CALORIES **297**

 PROTEIN **22g**

 FAT **23g**

 FIBER **0g**

 SALT **0.7g**

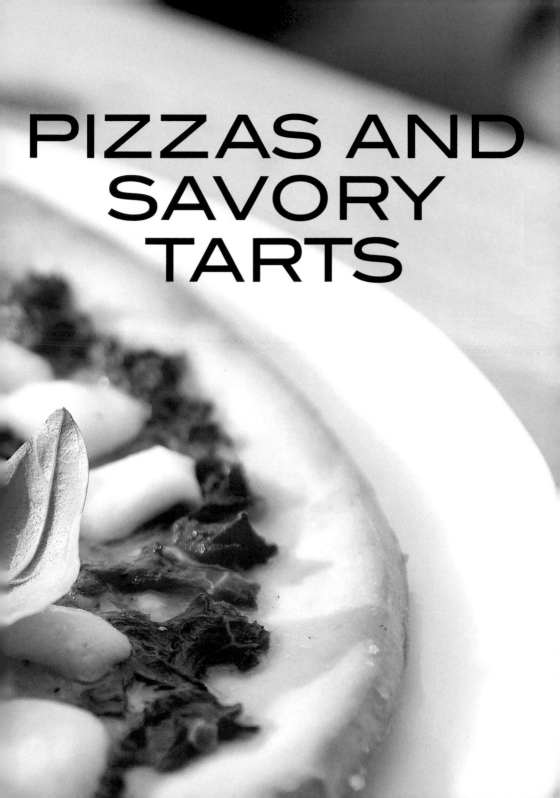

PIZZAS AND SAVORY TARTS

ONION TARTE TATIN

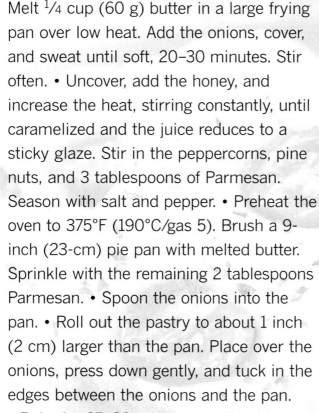

478

Melt ¹/₄ cup (60 g) butter in a large frying pan over low heat. Add the onions, cover, and sweat until soft, 20–30 minutes. Stir often. • Uncover, add the honey, and increase the heat, stirring constantly, until caramelized and the juice reduces to a sticky glaze. Stir in the peppercorns, pine nuts, and 3 tablespoons of Parmesan. Season with salt and pepper. • Preheat the oven to 375°F (190°C/gas 5). Brush a 9-inch (23-cm) pie pan with melted butter. Sprinkle with the remaining 2 tablespoons Parmesan. • Spoon the onions into the pan. • Roll out the pastry to about 1 inch (2 cm) larger than the pan. Place over the onions, press down gently, and tuck in the edges between the onions and the pan. • Bake for 25–30 minutes, until golden brown. • Let cool for 10 minutes, then run a knife around the edges. Place a plate on top and turn over. Serve warm.

¹/₄ cup (60 g) butter + 1–2 tablespoons extra for the pan

3 large white onions, sliced into wedges about ²/₃ inch (1.5 cm) thick

3 large red onions, sliced into wedges about ²/₃ inch (1.5 cm) thick

1 tablespoon honey

1 tablespoon brined green peppercorns, drained

1 tablespoon pine nuts

5 tablespoon freshly grated Parmesan cheese

Salt and freshly ground black pepper

1 sheet (8 ounces/ 250 g) ready-rolled pie pastry, thawed if frozen

Serves: 6
Preparation: 15 minutes + 10 minutes to cool
Cooking: 45–60 minutes
Level: 2

Nutritional Facts
Amount per serving
Percentage of Daily Values
based on 2,000 calories

CALORIES	PROTEIN	FAT	FIBER	SALT
387	8g	28g	2.7g	0.7g

LEEK TARTS

Preheat the oven to 375°F (190°C/gas 5). • Brush a baking sheet with melted butter. • Heat the oil in a large frying pan over medium heat, add the leeks, and sauté until the leeks are soft but not browned, 3–5 minutes. • Add the celery and cream, and simmer until the celery has softened, 6 minutes. • Stir in the parsley and leave to cool. • Roll out the pastry to about 9 inches (23 cm) square and cut into 4 squares. Place on the baking sheet • Mix the egg into the cooled leek mixture and season with salt and plenty of pepper. • Top the pieces of pastry with the leek mixture. Leave a $3/4$-inch (1.5-cm) border all around. • Bake for 30 minutes, until set and golden in places. Serve warm or at room temperature.

3 tablespoons extra-virgin olive oil

3 medium leeks, trimmed, cleaned, and coarsely chopped

2 celery stalks, trimmed and coarsely chopped

$1^1/4$ cups (300 ml) heavy (double) cream

$1/2$ cup (25 g) coarsely chopped fresh parsley, leaves only

8 ounces (250 g) chilled puff pastry (one $9^1/4$ x $9^1/2$-inch /24 x 24-cm sheet), thawed if frozen

1 large egg, lightly beaten

Salt and freshly ground black pepper

Serves: 4
Preparation: 15 minutes
Cooking: 40 minutes
Level: 2

Nutritional Facts
Amount per serving
Percentage of Daily Values
based on 2,000 calories

 CALORIES 450

 PROTEIN 9g

 FAT 34g

 FIBER 2.2g

 SALT 1.3g 24

HERB AND BLUE-CHEESE TURNOVERS

482

Pastry: Combine the flour and salt in a large bowl. Cut in the butter with a pastry blender, or pulse the mixture in a food processor, until it resembles fine bread crumbs. • Mix the herbs, egg yolk, and water in a food processor or blender. Add the herb mixture to the flour mixture. • Knead or pulse, adding enough additional water (2–3 tablespoons) to obtain a smooth, firm dough. • Press into a log, wrap in plastic wrap (cling film), and chill in the refrigerator for at least 30 minutes.

Filling: Mix the potatoes with scallions, parsley, watercress, and tarragon in a large bowl. Stir in the cheese and hard-boiled egg. • Whisk the crème fraîche with the egg yolk in a small bowl, reserving the white. Stir the crème fraîche mixture into the potato mixture. Season well with salt and pepper and set aside. • Preheat the oven to 350°F (180°C/gas 4). • Line a baking sheet with

Pastry

3	cups (450 g) all-purpose flour
1	scant teaspoon salt
1/2	cup (125 g) unsalted butter, chilled and cut into small cubes
3	tablespoons finely chopped fresh parsley
1	tablespoon finely chopped fresh tarragon
1	large egg yolk
2	tablespoons iced water + 2–3 tablespoons, if needed

Filling

1	pound (500 g) potatoes, peeled and cut in small cubes
4	scallions (spring onions), finely chopped
2	tablespoons finely chopped fresh parsley
2	tablespoons finely chopped watercress

1 tablespoon finely chopped fresh tarragon, or 1/2 teaspoon dried

1/2 cup (60 g) crumbled hard blue cheese (e.g. Stilton)

1 egg, hard-boiled, peeled, and chopped

2 tablespoons crème fraîche or sour cream

1 large egg, separated

Salt and freshly ground black pepper

Serves: 4
Preparation: 20–30 minutes + 30 minutes to chill
Cooking: 45–50 minutes
Level: 2

483

parchment paper. • Unwrap the pastry and divide into four equal pieces. • Lightly flour a work surface and roll out each piece into a circle, 8–9 inches (20–22 cm) in diameter. Use a plate as a guide and cut around it. • Divide the filling evenly among the dough circles, spooning a quarter onto one-half of each and leaving a border around the edge. Brush the edges with a little egg white, or moisten with water, and fold the dough over the filling. Crimp the edges together. Prick each turnover with a fork and brush with the remaining egg white. • Use a spatula to transfer the turnovers to the baking sheet. • Bake for 45–50 minutes, until the turnovers are golden and the filling is cooked. Serve hot or at room temperature.

(See photograph on the following page.)

Nutritional Facts
Amount per serving
Percentage of Daily Values
based on 2,000 calories

 CALORIES 780 37

 PROTEIN 14g

 FAT 32g

 FIBER 5.2g

 SALT 2g

GOAT CHEESE TURNOVERS

486

Sift the flour into a large bowl. Add half the oil and $\frac{1}{3}$ cup (90 ml) water. Mix to a smooth dough. Shape into a ball and wrap in plastic wrap (cling film). Chill in the refrigerator for 1 hour. • Stir the goat cheese in a small bowl until smooth. Add half the thyme. Season with salt and pepper. • Preheat the oven to 400°F (200°C/gas 6). • Oil a large baking sheet. • Divide the dough into eight pieces. Roll out on a floured work surface into $\frac{1}{8}$-inch (3-mm)-thick circles. • Spoon the cheese mixture onto one-half each circle. • Beat the egg white and remaining 2 tablespoons water in a small bowl and brush the edges of the pastry. Fold over the filling. Pinch the edges together to seal. • Place on the sheet. Brush with some of the remaining oil. • Bake for 5 minutes. Brush with the remaining oil. • Bake until puffed and golden brown, 5–10 minutes. • Serve hot.

$1^{2}/3$ cups (250 g) all-purpose (plain) flour

$^{1}/3$ cup (90 ml) extra-virgin olive oil

$^{1}/3$ cup (90 ml) water + 2 tablespoons

5 ounces (150 g) chèvre or other soft fresh goat cheese

2 tablespoons finely chopped fresh thyme

Salt and freshly ground black pepper

1 large egg white

Serves: 4
Preparation: 30 minutes + 1 hour to chill
Cooking: 10–15 minutes
Level: 1

Nutritional Facts
Amount per serving
Percentage of Daily Values
based on 2,000 calories

 CALORIES 473 23%
 PROTEIN 12g 26%
 FAT 27g 33%
 FIBER 2g 8%
 SALT 1.2g 21%

RICOTTA TURNOVERS

488

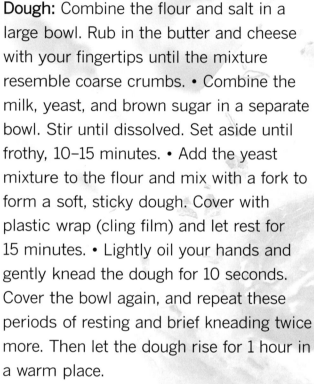

Dough: Combine the flour and salt in a large bowl. Rub in the butter and cheese with your fingertips until the mixture resemble coarse crumbs. • Combine the milk, yeast, and brown sugar in a separate bowl. Stir until dissolved. Set aside until frothy, 10–15 minutes. • Add the yeast mixture to the flour and mix with a fork to form a soft, sticky dough. Cover with plastic wrap (cling film) and let rest for 15 minutes. • Lightly oil your hands and gently knead the dough for 10 seconds. Cover the bowl again, and repeat these periods of resting and brief kneading twice more. Then let the dough rise for 1 hour in a warm place.

Filling: Heat the oil in a medium pan over medium heat. Add the scallions, garlic, crushed red pepper, and mushrooms and sauté until slightly colored, about 5 minutes. • Put the spinach in a colander and pour boiling water over to wilt the leaves. Press out as much liquid as

Dough

- 1²/₃ cups (250 g) all-purpose (plain) flour
- ¹/₂ teaspoon salt
- ¹/₄ cup (60 g) unsalted butter, cut into cubes and softened
- 2 tablespoons freshly grated Parmesan cheese
- ¹/₂ cup (125 ml) milk, warmed (110°F/43°C)
- ¹/₂ ounce (15 g) compressed fresh yeast, or 1 (¹/₄-ounce/7-g) package active dry yeast
- 1 teaspoon dark brown sugar

Filling

- 2 tablespoons extra-virgin olive oil
- 2 scallions (spring onions), trimmed and sliced
- 1 clove garlic, sliced
- ¹/₂ teaspoon crushed red pepper flakes

8   ounces (250 g)
    cremini, button,
    or chestnut
    mushrooms, sliced
1   pound (500 g) fresh
    spinach leaves
8   ounces (250 g)
    ricotta cheese
1   large egg, lightly
    beaten
    Salt and freshly
    ground black pepper

Glaze
1   small egg, lightly
    beaten

Serves: 4
Preparation: 45 minutes
    + 2 hours 15 minutes
    to rise
Cooking: 30–35 minutes
Level: 2

489

possible. • Beat the ricotta and egg in a large bowl and season with salt and a good grinding of pepper. Stir in the mushroom mixture and the spinach. • Lightly flour a work surface, place the dough on it, knead briefly with floured hands, then divide into four pieces. • Roll out each piece into a circle, about 8 inches (20 cm) in diameter. • Spoon a quarter of the filling onto one-half of each circle. Moisten the edges with a little water, fold over, and crimp the edges to seal. • Line a baking sheet with parchment paper. • Place the turnovers on the sheet and let rise for 30 minutes. • Preheat the oven to 400°F (200°C/gas 6). **Glaze:** Brush the turnovers with the egg glaze and cut 3 diagonal slits with a sharp knife in the top of each. • Bake for 30–35 minutes, until golden and crisp. Serve warm or cold.

(See photograph on the following page.)

Nutritional Facts
Amount per serving
Percentage of Daily Values
based on 2,000 calories

CALORIES	PROTEIN	FAT	FIBER	SALT
571	22g	31g	5.3g	1.7g

SWISS CHARD AND WALNUT TART

Pastry: Combine the flour, salt, and Parmesan in a bowl. Add the egg, oil, and enough water to form a smooth dough. Knead briefly on a lightly floured work surface. Form into a ball, wrap in plastic wrap (cling film), and refrigerate for 30 minutes. • Preheat the oven to 400°F (200°C/gas 6). • Unwrap the pastry and roll out into an 11-inch (28-cm) circle. Loosely wrap around the rolling pin and unroll over a 9-inch (23-cm) tart pan with a removable bottom. Gently press into the pan to line the bottom and sides. Prick all over with a fork, line with parchment paper, and fill with pie weights or dried beans. • Bake for 10 minutes, until the edges are just golden. Remove the paper and beans and bake for 5 more minutes. • Remove from the oven and set aside.

Pastry

1²/₃ cups (250 g) all-purpose (plain) flour

Pinch of salt

¹/₄ cup (30 g) finely grated Parmesan

1 large egg, beaten

5 tablespoons extra-virgin olive oil

¹/₄ cup (60 ml) warm water

Filling

¹/₄ cup (60 g) unsalted butter

2 medium onions, finely sliced

8 ounces (250 g) Swiss chard, leaves and stems separated and thinly sliced

1¹/₂ cups (150 g) walnuts, coarsely chopped

Salt and freshly ground black pepper

2 **large eggs + 1 large egg yolk**

1 **cup (250 ml) crème fraîche or sour cream**

½ **cup (60 g) freshly grated Gruyère cheese**

Serves: 6
Preparation: 35 minutes, + 60 minutes to chill
Cooking: 55 minutes
Level: 2

Filling: Decrease the oven temperature to 350°F (180°C/gas 4). • Melt the butter in a large frying pan over medium heat. Add the onions and sauté until softened, 3–4 minutes. • Add the chard stems and walnuts. Sauté until the stems begin to soften, 2–3 minutes. Mix in the chard leaves and cook until wilted, 1–2 minutes. Season to taste with salt and pepper. • With a slotted spoon, transfer the chard mixture into the pastry shell, discarding any juice. • Whisk together the eggs, egg yolk, and crème fraîche in a bowl. Stir in the cheese and pour over the chard filling, making sure it oozes down through the filling. • Bake for 25 minutes, until golden and set. • Serve hot or at room temperature.

(See photograph on the following page.)

493

WILD MUSHROOM AND HERB TART

Pastry: Prepare the pastry and bake blind following the instructions on page 492. Set aside.

Filling: Heat the oil in a large frying pan over medium heat. Add the onion and garlic and sauté until softened, 3–4 minutes. • Add the mushrooms and sauté for 2 minutes. • Remove from the heat and stir in the herbs. Set aside. • Whisk the egg and egg yolk in a bowl and beat in the crème fraîche. Season with salt and pepper and combine with the mushroom mixture. • Spoon the filling into the tart shell and sprinkle with the Gruyère cheese. • Bake for 20–25 minutes, until golden brown. • Serve warm or at room temperature.

Pastry
(see Swiss Chard and Walnut Tart, page 492)

Filling

3 tablespoons extra-virgin olive oil

1 onion, finely chopped

2 cloves garlic, crushed

8 ounces (250 g) porcini or cremini mushrooms, sliced

1/2 cup (25 g) finely chopped parsley

1/2 ounce (25 g) snipped fresh chives

2 tablespoons finely chopped fresh thyme

1 large egg + 1 large egg yolk

3/4 cup (200 ml) crème fraîche or heavy (double) cream

Salt and freshly ground black pepper

1/2 cup (50 g) grated Gruyère cheese

Serves: 6
Preparation: 25 minutes + time for the pastry
Cooking: 25–30 minutes
Level: 2

Nutritional Facts
Amount per serving
Percentage of Daily Values
based on 2,000 calories

 CALORIES **555** 27

 PROTEIN **16g** 35

 FAT **28g** 35

 FIBER **1.9g**

 SALT **0.8g**

MACEDONIAN SPINACH PIE

Steam the spinach until wilted, 1–2 minutes. Drain and chop finely. Squeeze out excess moisture. • Heat the oil in a frying pan over medium heat. Add the onion and sauté until softened, 3–4 minutes. Remove from the heat, and add the spinach, garlic, and herbs. Season with salt, pepper, and nutmeg. Stir in the cheese. • Oil a 9-inch (23-cm) spring-form pan. • Roll a pastry sheet out thinly. Cut out an 11-inch (28-cm) circle. Line the bottom and sides with the pastry. • Sprinkle with bread crumbs and spoon in the filling. • Make four hollows in the filling and break an egg into each. • Cut a 9-inch (23-cm) circle from the remaining pastry. Place on the pie. Cut two small holes in the center to let steam escape. • Beat the remaining egg and brush the pie with it. Sprinkle with sesame seeds. • Preheat the oven to 400°F (200°C/gas 6). • Bake for 30–35 minutes, until puffed and golden brown. • Serve hot.

2 pounds (1 kg) fresh spinach

2 tablespoons extra-virgin olive oil

1 white onion, finely chopped

2 cloves garlic, thinly sliced

3 tablespoons finely chopped fresh thyme

1 tablespoon finely chopped fresh oregano

2 sage leaves, chopped

Salt and freshly ground black pepper

Grating of nutmeg

5 ounces (150 g) soft goat cheese or feta cheese, diced

2 (9¼ x 9½-inch/24 x 24-cm) sheets ready-rolled puff pastry

1 tablespoon fresh bread crumbs

5 small eggs

1 tablespoon sesame seeds

Serves: 6
Preparation: 45 minutes
Cooking: 40–45 minutes
Level: 2

Nutritional Facts
Amount per serving
Percentage of Daily Values
based on 2,000 calories

 CALORIES **366**

 PROTEIN **16g** 35

 FAT **25g** 3

 FIBER **4g** · SALT **1.8g**

EASY ZUCCHINI TORTE

500

Heat 3 tablespoons of the oil in a large frying pan over medium heat. Add the onion and sauté until tender, about 5 minutes. Season with salt and pepper.
• Preheat the oven to 350°F (180°C/gas 4). Oil a 10-inch (25-cm) springform pan.
• Sift the flour and baking powder into a large bowl. Add the milk, remaining oil, eggs, zucchini, and onion. Season with salt and pepper and mix well. • Spoon the mixture into the prepared pan. • Bake for about 50 minutes, until golden brown and a skewer inserted into the center comes out clean. • Serve hot or at room temperature.

6	tablespoons (90 ml) extra-virgin olive oil
1	medium white onion, thinly sliced
	Salt and freshly ground black pepper
2	cups (300 g) all-purpose (plain) flour
2	teaspoons baking powder
1/3	cup (90 ml) milk
3	large eggs, lightly beaten
4	zucchini (courgettes), cut into tiny cubes
	Salt and freshly ground black pepper

Serves: 4
Preparation: 15 minutes
Cooking: 50 minutes
Level: 1

Nutritional Facts
Amount per serving
Percentage of Daily Values
based on 2,000 calories

CALORIES	PROTEIN	FAT	FIBER	SALT
547	16g	27g	3.6g	0.9g
26%	35%	33%	14%	16%

GERMAN ONION CAKE (ZWIEBELKUCHEN)

502

Dough: Place $1/3$ cup (90 ml) of the milk in a small bowl with the sugar and yeast. Mix well and set aside until frothy, 10–15 minutes. • Combine the flour, salt, and marjoram in a large bowl. Make a well in the center and pour in the yeast mixture and the remaining $2/3$ cup (150 ml) of milk and the melted butter. • Cut the liquid into the flour with a knife or spatula, and use your fingers to bring together the mixture to form a ball. • Lightly flour a work surface, turn the dough out, and knead for 2 minutes, adding a little more flour if needed, until a smooth but slightly damp dough is formed. • Place in a floured bowl, cover, and leave to rise for 30–40 minutes.

Topping: Heat the butter and oil in a large heavy pan over low to medium heat. Add the onions and sauté until soft, golden, and caramelized, about 30 minutes. • Stir in the marjoram and generous pinches of salt and pepper. • Beat the sour cream and eggs together in a bowl, stir in the caraway seeds, and season with salt and pepper.

Dough
- 1 cup (250 ml) milk, warmed (110°F/43°C)
- 1 teaspoon sugar
- 1 ounce (30 g) compressed fresh yeast, or 2 ($1/4$-ounce/7-g) packages active dry yeast
- $2^2/3$ cups (400 g) all-purpose (plain) flour
- 1 teaspoon salt
- 1 teaspoon dried marjoram
- $1/3$ cup (100 g) butter, melted

Topping
- 2 tablespoons (30 g) butter
- 2 tablespoons extra-virgin olive oil
- $1^1/4$ pounds (600 g) yellow onions, peeled and thinly sliced into rings
- 1 pound (500 g) red onions, peeled and thinly sliced into rings

2 tablespoons fresh marjoram, coarsely chopped, or 1 teaspoon dried

Salt and freshly ground black pepper

1/2 cup (125 ml) sour cream

3 large eggs

1 teaspoon caraway seeds

5 ounces (150 g) Emmental or Gruyère cheese, finely grated

Serves: 6
Preparation: 30–35 minutes + 40–50 minutes to rise
Cooking: 50–60 minutes
Level: 3

503

• Preheat the oven to 400°F (200°C/ gas 6). Oil a $15^{1}/_{2}$ x $11^{1}/_{2}$-inch (40 x 30-cm) or larger baking sheet. • Turn the dough out onto a floured work surface, sprinkle with flour, and knead for 2–3 minutes until smooth. Transfer the dough to the prepared baking sheet and press it out with your hands to a thickness of about 1 inch (2.5 cm) to fit the sheet. If using a larger sheet, roll the dough into a $15^{1}/_{2}$ x $11^{1}/_{2}$-inch (40 x 30-cm) rectangle. • Spoon the onions onto the dough and spread out, leaving a $^{3}/_{4}$-inch (2-cm) border all the way around the edge. Pinch the edges upward to form a rim. • Drizzle the cream mixture over the onions, starting in the middle and making sure it doesn't flow over the edges. • Bake for 20–30 minutes, until well risen and browned. Serve hot or at room temperature.

(See photograph on the following page.)

Nutritional Facts
Amount per serving
Percentage of Daily Values
based on 2,000 calories

CALORIES	PROTEIN	FAT	FIBER	SALT
707	22g	40g	4.6g	1.7g

FOCACCIA WITH SAGE AND BLACK OLIVES

Basic Focaccia and Pizza Dough:
Combine the yeast and sugar in a small bowl. Add half the warm water and stir with a fork until the yeast has dissolved. Set aside until frothy, 10–15 minutes.

• Put the flour and salt in a large bowl. Pour in the yeast mixture, most of the remaining water, and the oil. Stir until the flour is absorbed, adding more water as required. Now it is ready to knead.

• Transfer the dough to a lightly floured work surface and shape into a compact ball. Press down on the dough with your knuckles to spread it. Take the far end of the dough, fold it a short distance toward you, then push it away again with the heel of your palm. Flexing your wrist, fold it toward you again, give it a quarter turn, then push it away. Repeat, gently and with the lightest possible touch, for 8–10 minutes, until the dough is smooth and elastic, shows definite air bubbles beneath the surface, and springs back if

Basic Focaccia and Pizza Dough

1   ounce (30 g) fresh compressed yeast or 2 ($^1/4$-ounce/7-g) packages active dry yeast

1   teaspoon sugar

    About 1$^1/2$ cups (350 ml) water, warmed (110°F/ 43°C)

3$^1/3$ cups (500 g) all-purpose (plain) flour

1   teaspoon salt

$^1/4$ cup (60 ml) extra-virgin olive oil

Topping

12   sage leaves, finely chopped

$^1/2$ cup (50 g) pitted black olives, coarsely chopped

2   tablespoons extra-virgin olive oil

Serves: 4
Preparation: 30 minutes
  + 90 minutes to rise
Cooking: 20–25 minutes
Level: 2

you flatten it with your palm. • Put in a large oiled bowl and cover with a cloth. Set aside until doubled in bulk, about 1½ hours. To test, poke your finger gently into the dough; if the impression remains, it is ready. • Preheat the oven to 425°F (220°C/gas 7). • Transfer the dough to a lightly floured work surface and knead for 2–3 minutes. • Place the dough on a large oiled baking sheet and, using your hands, spread into a circle about 12 inches (30 cm) in diameter and ½ inch (1 cm) thick. Dimple the surface with your fingertips.

Topping: Sprinkle with the sage and olives, drizzle with the oil. • Bake until pale golden brown, 20–25 minutes.

• Serve hot or at room temperature.

(See photograph on the following page.)

Nutritional Facts
Amount per serving
Percentage of Daily Values
based on 2,000 calories

 CALORIES **618**

 PROTEIN **13g** 28

 FAT **22g**

 FIBER **4.2g**

 SALT **1.9g** 34

POTATO FOCACCIA WITH CHERRY TOMATOES AND OREGANO

510

Cook the potato in a small pot of salted boiling water until tender, about 10 minutes. Drain and mash until smooth.
• Prepare the focaccia dough, up to the point where it is ready to knead. Gradually work the mashed potato into the dough as you knead. Let rise in a warm place until doubled in bulk, about 2 hours. • Oil a 10-inch (25-cm) round baking pan and press the dough onto the baking pan using your fingers. Sprinkle with the tomatoes, coarse salt, and oregano. • Drizzle with the oil and let rise for 30 minutes. • Preheat the oven to 425°F (220°C/gas 7). Bake until the focaccia is golden brown, 25–30 minutes.
• Serve hot or at room temperature.

1   large baking (floury) potato, peeled and cut into small cubes

Basic Focaccia and Pizza Dough (see Focaccia with Sage and Black Olives, page 506)

20 cherry tomatoes, halved

1   teaspoon coarse sea salt

1   tablespoon finely chopped fresh oregano

2   tablespoons extra-virgin olive oil

Serves: 4
Preparation: 25 minutes + 2 hours 30 minutes to rise
Cooking: 35–40 minutes
Level: 2

Nutritional Facts
Amount per serving
Percentage of Daily Values
based on 2,000 calories

 CALORIES 665

 PROTEIN 15g

 FAT 20g

 FIBER 5.6g

 SALT 2.4g

HERB AND TOMATO FOCACCIA

Prepare the focaccia dough up to the point where the dough is ready to knead. Gradually work 2 tablespoons of the oil into the dough as you knead. Let rise in a warm place until doubled in bulk, about 2 hours. • Preheat the oven to 450°F (250°C/gas 8). Lightly oil a large baking sheet. • Turn the dough out onto a lightly floured work surface and knead for 5 minutes. Spread out into a large oval on the prepared sheet. • Mix the onion, garlic, parsley, basil, rosemary, and oregano in a small bowl. Add 2 tablespoons of the remaining oil and season with pepper. Spread the tomatoes over the focaccia and top with the herb mixture. Season with salt, and drizzle with the remaining oil. • Bake until the focaccia is golden brown, 20–25 minutes. • Serve hot or at room temperature.

Basic Focaccia and Pizza Dough (see Focaccia with Sage and Black Olives, page 506)

- 6 tablespoons extra-virgin olive oil
- 1 medium onion, very finely chopped
- 2 cloves garlic, very finely chopped
- 3 tablespoons finely chopped fresh parsley
- 2 tablespoons finely chopped fresh basil
- 1 tablespoon finely chopped fresh rosemary
- 1/2 teaspoon dried oregano

  Freshly ground black pepper
- 1 (14-ounce/400-g) can tomatoes, with juice, chopped

  Salt

Serves: 4
Preparation: 25 minutes + 2 hours to rise
Cooking: 20–25 minutes
Level: 2

Nutritional Facts
Amount per serving
Percentage of Daily Values
based on 2,000 calories

 CALORIES 780 37

 PROTEIN 14g 30

 FAT 38g 5

 FIBER 5.1g 20

 SALT 1.3g 22

FILLED ONION FOCACCIA

514

Prepare the focaccia dough and let rise in a warm place until doubled in bulk, about 1^1/$_2$ hours. • Preheat the oven to 425°F (220°C/gas 7). • Oil a 12-inch (30-cm) pizza pan. • Heat the oil in a large frying pan over medium heat. Add the onions and sauté until tender, about 10 minutes. Season lightly with salt. • Turn the dough out onto a lightly floured work surface and knead for 5 minutes. Divide into two equal portions. • Roll out each piece of dough into a 12-inch (30-cm) circle. • Line the prepared pan with one piece of dough. • Spread with the onions. Cover with the remaining dough. • Bake until golden brown, 20–25 minutes. • Serve hot or at room temperature.

Basic Focaccia and Pizza Dough (see Focaccia with Sage and Black Olives, page 506)

^{1}/$_4$ cup (60 ml) extra-virgin olive oil

4 large white onions, thinly sliced

Salt

Serves: 4
Preparation: 35 minutes + 90 minutes to rise
Cooking: 30–35 minutes
Level: 2

Nutritional Facts
Amount per serving
Percentage of Daily Values
based on 2,000 calories

 CALORIES 740 36%
 PROTEIN 14g 30%
 FAT 30g 37%
 FIBER 6g 24%
 SALT 1.2g 22%

FILLED FOCACCIA WITH GORGONZOLA AND BELL PEPPERS

Prepare the dough and let rise in a warm place until doubled in bulk, about $1^1/_2$ hours. • Preheat the oven to 400°F (200°C gas 6). • Oil a 9 x 13-inch (23 x 33-cm) baking pan. • Bake the bell peppers for 20–30 minutes, until charred all over. Put in a plastic bag and let rest for 10 minutes. Peel and seed, then slice thinly. • Turn the dough out onto a floured surface and knead for 5 minutes. • Divide in two and press one into the prepared pan. • Cover with the peppers, garlic, and Gorgonzola. Season with salt and pepper and drizzle with 2 tablespoons of oil. • Roll out the remaining dough into a rectangle large enough to cover the pan. Cover the filling with the dough. • Press the cherry tomatoes into the top at regular intervals. Sprinkle with oregano and drizzle with the remaining 2 tablespoons oil. • Bake for 25–30 minutes, until golden brown.

Basic Focaccia and Pizza Dough (see Focaccia with Sage and Black Olives, page 506)

1 large red bell pepper (capsicum)

1 large yellow pepper (capsicum)

1 clove garlic, thinly sliced

8 ounces (250 g) Gorgonzola cheese, sliced

Salt and freshly ground black pepper

4 tablespoons (60 ml) extra-virgin olive oil

12 cherry tomatoes

1 teaspoon dried oregano

Serves: 4
Preparation: 45 minutes + 90 minutes to rise
Cooking: 55–60 minutes
Level: 2

Nutritional Facts
Amount per serving
Percentage of Daily Values
based on 2,000 calories

CALORIES	PROTEIN	FAT	FIBER	SALT
974	29g	52g	5.5g	2.4g

BABY FOCACCIAS WITH OLIVES AND PINE NUTS

518

Prepare the dough and let rise in a warm place until doubled in bulk, about $1^1/_2$ hours. • Preheat the oven to 425°F (220°C/gas 7). • Bake the bell peppers for 20–30 minutes, until charred all over. • Place in a plastic bag and let rest for 10 minutes. Peel and seed, then slice thinly. • Oil two large baking sheets. • Turn the dough out onto a lightly floured work surface and knead for 5 minutes, adding the olive paste as you work. • Divide the dough into 16 equal portions and press into rounds about $1/_2$ inch (1 cm) thick. Place on the prepared baking sheets. • Top each round with some of the peppers, olives, and pine nuts. Season with salt and pepper. Drizzle with the oil. • Bake until golden brown, about 15 minutes. • Serve hot or at room temperature.

Basic Focaccia and Pizza Dough (see Focaccia with Sage and Black Olives, page 506)

1 small green bell pepper (capsicum)
1 small yellow bell pepper (capsicum)
1 small red bell pepper (capsicum)
3 tablespoons black olive paste or tapenade
16 black olives, pitted and coarsely chopped
2 tablespoons pine nuts
   Salt and freshly ground black pepper
2 tablespoons extra-virgin olive oil

Serves: 4
Preparation: 35 minutes
  + 90 minutes to rise
Cooking 35–45 minutes
Level: 2

Nutritional Facts
Amount per serving
Percentage of Daily Values
based on 2,000 calories

CALORIES	PROTEIN	FAT	FIBER	SALT
707	15g	28g	6.4g	2.2g
34%	33%	35%	26%	40%

FOCACCIA FILLED WITH ZUCCHINI AND BASMATI RICE

Prepare the dough up to the point where it is ready to knead. Gradually work in 1 tablespoon of oil. Let rise until doubled in bulk, about 2 hours. • Heat 2 tablespoons of oil in a large frying pan over medium heat. Add the zucchini and garlic and sauté until tender, 7–10 minutes. Season with salt. • Cook the rice in salted boiling water until tender, 12–15 minutes. • Drain and stir into the zucchini mixture. Let cool slightly. • Add the egg and cilantro. Mix well. • Preheat the oven to 400°F (200°C/gas 6) Oil a large baking sheet. • Turn the dough out onto a floured surface and knead for 5 minutes. • Roll into a circle about 15 inches (40 cm) in diameter. Place on the baking sheet. • Place the zucchini mixture in the center and pull the edges over the top. • Brush with the remaining oil and sprinkle with the sesame seeds. • Bake for 30–35 minutes, until golden. • Serve hot.

Basic Focaccia and Pizza Dough (see Focaccia with Sage and Black Olives, page 506)

4 tablespoons extra-virgin olive oil

4 medium zucchini (courgettes), coarsely grated

1 clove garlic, finely chopped

Salt

1/2 cup (100 g) basmati rice

1 large egg, lightly beaten

2 tablespoons finely chopped fresh cilantro (coriander)

2 tablespoons sesame seeds

Serves: 4
Preparation: 30 minutes
    2 hours to rise
Cooking: 50–55 minutes
Level: 2

Nutritional Facts
Amount per serving
Percentage of Daily Values
based on 2,000 calories

CALORIES 850 | PROTEIN 19g | FAT 35g | FIBER 5.2g | SALT 1.2g

CHEESE AND TOMATO FOCACCIA

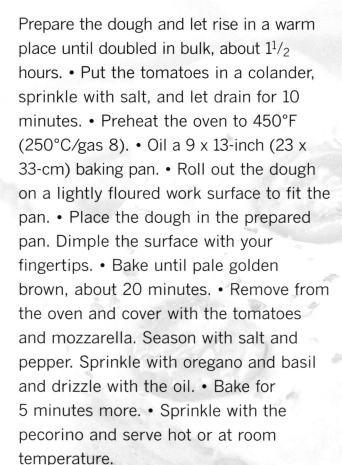

Prepare the dough and let rise in a warm place until doubled in bulk, about 1¹/₂ hours. • Put the tomatoes in a colander, sprinkle with salt, and let drain for 10 minutes. • Preheat the oven to 450°F (250°C/gas 8). • Oil a 9 x 13-inch (23 x 33-cm) baking pan. • Roll out the dough on a lightly floured work surface to fit the pan. • Place the dough in the prepared pan. Dimple the surface with your fingertips. • Bake until pale golden brown, about 20 minutes. • Remove from the oven and cover with the tomatoes and mozzarella. Season with salt and pepper. Sprinkle with oregano and basil and drizzle with the oil. • Bake for 5 minutes more. • Sprinkle with the pecorino and serve hot or at room temperature.

Basic Focaccia and Pizza Dough (see Focaccia with Sage and Black Olives, page 506)

2   cherry tomatoes, sliced

Salt

8   ounces (250 g) mozzarella cheese, thinly sliced

Freshly ground black pepper

¹/₂   teaspoon dried oregano

8   leaves fresh basil, torn

2   tablespoons extra-virgin olive oil

¹/₂   cup (60 g) shaved aged pecorino cheese

Serves: 4
Preparation: 30 minutes
  + 90 minutes to rise
Cooking: 1 hour
Level: 2

Nutritional Facts
Amount per serving
Percentage of Daily Values
based on 2,000 calories

 CALORIES 844 41%
 PROTEIN 34g 74%
 FAT 38g 47%
 FIBER 3.9g 16%
 SALT 2.4g 43%

PIZZA MARGHERITA

524

Prepare the dough and let rise in a warm place until doubled in bulk, about $1^1/_2$ hours. • Preheat the oven to 425°F (220°C/gas 7). • Oil a 12-inch (30-cm) pizza pan. • Transfer the dough to a lightly floured work surface and knead briefly. Press it into the prepared pan using your hands. • Spread the tomatoes over the dough and season with salt and pepper. Drizzle with half the oil. • Bake for 15 minutes. • Remove from the oven and top with the mozzarella. Bake for 5–10 minutes, until the crust is crisp and golden brown and the mozzarella has melted. • Drizzle with the remaining 1 tablespoon oil, and garnish with the basil. • Serve hot or at room temperature.

Basic Focaccia and Pizza Dough (see Focaccia with Sage and Black Olives, page 506)

1 (14-ounce/400-g) can tomatoes, drained and chopped

Salt and freshly ground black pepper

2 tablespoons extra-virgin olive oil

5 ounces (150 g) fresh mozzarella cheese, drained and chopped

Sprigs of fresh basil, to garnish

Serves: 4
Preparation: 30 minutes + 90 minutes to rise
Cooking: 20–25 minutes
Level: 2

Nutritional Facts
Amount per serving
Percentage of Daily Values
based on 2,000 calories

CALORIES	PROTEIN	FAT	FIBER	SALT
696	20g	28g	3.9g	1.5g

PIZZA WITH ONION AND PESTO

Prepare the dough and let rise in a warm place until doubled in bulk, about $1^1/_2$ hours. • Preheat the oven to 425°F (220°C/gas 7). • Oil a 12-inch (30-cm) pizza pan.

Pesto: Chop the basil and garlic with a pinch of salt in a food processor. Add the pine nuts, Parmesan, and pecorino and chop until smooth. Stir the oil in by hand. The pesto should be smooth and fairly dense. • Transfer the dough to a lightly floured work surface and knead briefly. Press it into the prepared pan using your hands. • Spread evenly with the tomatoes. Season with salt. • Bake for 10 minutes. Remove from the oven and add the onions. • Bake for 10–15 minutes, until the crust is crisp and the onions are lightly browned. Remove from the oven and dot with the pesto. • Serve hot.

Basic Focaccia and Pizza Dough (see Focaccia with Sage and Black Olives, page 506)

Pesto

1	large bunch basil leaves
2	cloves garlic
	Salt
2	tablespoons pine nuts
2	tablespoons freshly grated Parmesan cheese
2	tablespoons freshly grated pecorino cheese
1/4	cup (60 ml) extra-virgin olive oil

1	(14-ounce/400-g) can tomatoes, chopped, with juice
	Salt
4	small white onions, finely sliced

Serves: 4
Preparation: 30 minutes
+ 90 minutes to rise
Cooking: 20–25 minutes
Level: 2

Nutritional Facts
Amount per serving
Percentage of Daily Values
based on 2,000 calories

 CALORIES **784** 38%
 PROTEIN **20g** 43%
 FAT **31g** 38%
 FIBER **6.3g** 25%
 SALT **1.5g** 28%

PIZZA WITH APPLE AND GORGONZOLA

528

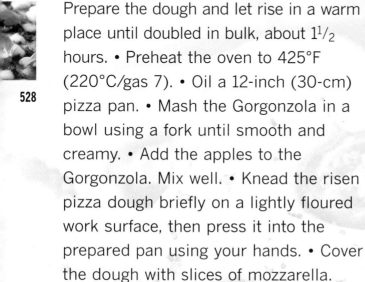

Prepare the dough and let rise in a warm place until doubled in bulk, about 1¹/₂ hours. • Preheat the oven to 425°F (220°C/gas 7). • Oil a 12-inch (30-cm) pizza pan. • Mash the Gorgonzola in a bowl using a fork until smooth and creamy. • Add the apples to the Gorgonzola. Mix well. • Knead the risen pizza dough briefly on a lightly floured work surface, then press it into the prepared pan using your hands. • Cover the dough with slices of mozzarella. Spread with the Gorgonzola and apple mixture. Season with salt and pepper. Drizzle with the oil. • Bake for 20–25 minutes, until the topping is lightly browned and the crust is crisp and golden brown. • Garnish with cilantro and serve hot.

Basic Focaccia and Pizza Dough (see Focaccia with Sage and Black Olives, page 506)

4 ounces (125 g) Gorgonzola cheese, at room temperature

2 ripe Granny Smith apples, peeled, cored, and thinly sliced

4 ounces (125 g) fresh mozzarella, thinly sliced

Salt and freshly ground black pepper

2 tablespoons extra-virgin olive oil

Sprigs of cilantro (coriander), to garnish

Serves: 4
Preparation: 30 minutes + 90 minutes to rise
Cooking: 20–25 minutes
Level: 2

Nutritional Facts
Amount per serving
Percentage of Daily Values
based on 2,000 calories

CALORIES
912
44%

PROTEIN
27g
59%

FAT
41g
51%

FIBER
5.3g
21%

SALT
2.3g
42%

PIZZA WITH ZUCCHINI FLOWERS

Prepare the dough and let rise in a warm place until doubled in bulk, about $1^1/_2$ hours. • Preheat the oven to 425°F (220°C/gas 7). • Oil a 12-inch (30-cm) pizza pan. • Knead the risen pizza dough briefly on a lightly floured work surface, then press it into the prepared pan using your hands. • Drizzle with half the oil and cover with the mozzarella. • Bake for 15 minutes. Top with the zucchini flowers and cherry tomatoes and drizzle with the remaining 1 tablespoon oil. Bake for 5–10 minutes, until the crust is crisp and golden brown. • Serve hot or at room temperature.

Basic Focaccia and Pizza Dough (see Focaccia with Sage and Black Olives, page 506)

2 tablespoons extra-virgin olive oil

6 ounces (180 g) fresh mozzarella cheese, thinly sliced

6 large zucchini flowers, rinsed and dried

12 cherry tomatoes, halved

Salt and freshly ground black pepper

Serves: 4
Preparation: 30 minutes
 + 90 minutes to rise
Cooking: 20–25 minutes
Level: 2

Nutritional Facts
Amount per serving
Percentage of Daily Values
based on 2,000 calories

CALORIES 725
PROTEIN 21g
FAT 30g
FIBER 4.3g
SALT 0.7g

BREADS

WHITE FARMHOUSE LOAF

Pour $^1/_2$ cup (125 ml) of the water into a small bowl and stir in half the butter. Add the honey and yeast and mix until dissolved. • Mix the flours and salt in a large bowl. Make a well in the center and pour in the yeast mixture. • Dust with flour and leave in a warm place for 10 minutes, until dimpled and spongy. • Add most of the remaining 1 cup (250 ml) water and the remaining butter, and mix with a spatula or your hands to form a soft dough. • Dust a work surface with flour, turn out the dough, and knead until smooth and elastic, 10–15 minutes. • Alternatively, knead with a dough hook for 5 minutes, until the dough comes away cleanly from the sides of the bowl. • Shape into a ball and place in a large lightly oiled bowl. Turn to coat with the oil and cover the bowl with plastic wrap (cling film). • Let rise in a warm place until almost doubled in bulk, 1–2 hours. • Punch the dough down with your fist so the air is

$1^1/_2$ cups (375 ml) warm water (110°F/43°C)

3   tablespoons butter, melted

1   tablespoon honey

$^1/_2$ ounce (15 g) compressed fresh yeast or 1 ($^1/_4$-ounce 7-g) package active dry yeast

$3^1/_3$ cups (500 g) white bread flour

$^2/_3$ cup (100 g) whole-wheat (wholemeal) flour

1   tablespoon salt

Serves: 8
Preparation: 30–35 minutes + 2–3 hours to rise
Cooking: 35–50 minutes
Level: 2

released, and knead briefly on a floured surface. • Preheat the oven to 425°F (220°C/gas 7). • Butter and flour a 9 x 5-inch (23 x 12-cm) loaf pan. • Flatten the dough to a thickness of about 1 inch (2.5 cm) and roll it into an oblong loaf to fit into the pan. Pinch the seam to seal, and place the loaf seam-side down into the pan. • Cover with oiled wrap and leave to rise for about 1 hour, until it is doubled in bulk. • Remove the wrap and dust flour over the loaf through a tea strainer. • Bake for 15 minutes, then reduce the heat to 400°F (200°C/gas 6). Bake for another 20–30 minutes, until the crust is golden. • Turn the loaf out of the pan and tap the underside. It is done if it makes a hollow noise. If not, return to the oven (out of the pan) and bake for 5 more minutes. • Let cool on a rack before slicing.

(See photograph on following page.)

Nutritional Facts
Amount per serving
Percentage of Daily Values
based on 2,000 calories

CALORIES	PROTEIN	FAT	FIBER	SALT
312	8g	7g	2.7g	1.9g
5%	7%	9%	1%	2%

MILK BREAD

Bring the milk to a boil in a small saucepan. Pour into a medium bowl and whisk in the crème fraîche and honey, until the mixture is lukewarm. • Add the yeast and stir until dissolved. • Beat the eggs and egg yolk in a separate bowl with a hand whisk. • Combine the flour and salt in a large bowl. • If kneading by hand, make a well in the center of the flour and pour in the milk-and-egg mixture. Bring together with a spatula to make a soft dough that leaves the bowl clean, adding more flour if very sticky or milk if dry. • Transfer to a lightly floured surface and knead until the dough feels springy, 8–10 minutes. • Alternatively, if using a dough hook, mix all the liquid ingredients into the flour at the lowest speed and then knead at a higher speed for 5 minutes, until smooth and elastic. • Clean and butter the bowl. Shape the dough into a ball and return to the bowl. Cover with a clean kitchen towel. • Let rise in a warm place until almost doubled in bulk, 1–2 hours.

1/2 cup (125 ml) milk + extra, for brushing

2/3 cup (150 ml) crème fraîche or sour cream, at room temperature

1 tablespoon honey or maple syrup

1/2 ounce (15 g) compressed fresh yeast, or 1 (1/4-ounce 7-g) package active dry yeast

2 large eggs, + 1 large yolk

3 1/3 cups (500 g) all-purpose (plain) flour

1 teaspoon salt

1 tablespoon fresh bread crumbs

Serves: 8
Preparation: 30–35 minutes + 1 1/2–2 1/2 hours to rise
Cooking: 40–50 minutes
Level 2

• Butter a 9 x 5-inch (23 x 12-cm) loaf pan and sprinkle with bread crumbs. • Punch the risen dough down so the air is released, and knead again briefly. • Flatten the dough out and roll it toward you, shaping into an oblong loaf that will fit into the pan. Pinch the seam to seal. Fit the loaf into the pan, seam-side down. • Cover with plastic wrap and leave in a warm place for 30 minutes. • Preheat the oven to 400°F (200°C/gas 6). • Uncover the loaf, and brush the top with milk. • Make a cut down the middle, about $1/2$ inch (1 cm) deep, with a sharp knife. • Bake for 40–50 minutes, until the loaf is golden brown and sounds hollow when the underside is tapped. • Cool on a rack.

(See photograph on the following page.)

■■■*For a sweet bread, knead in $3/4$ cup (135 g) of golden raisins (sultanas) before rolling the dough into a loaf.*

Nutritional Facts
Amount per serving
Percentage of Daily Values
based on 2,000 calories

 CALORIES **300**

 PROTEIN **10g**

 FAT **7g**

 FIBER **2g**

 SALT **0.7g**

QUICK NORWEGIAN BREAD

Preheat the oven to 425°F (220°C/gas 7).
• Oil a large baking sheet. • Combine both flours, baking powder, baking soda, salt, and brown sugar in a large bowl. • Stir the buttermilk and butter in a small bowl.
• Make a well in the middle of the flour mixture, and pour in the buttermilk mixture and egg. Draw the flour into the liquid with your hands until all the flour is incorporated. • Knead briefly on a lightly floured work surface, until smooth. • Divide the dough in two and shape each piece into a flat disk, about ³⁄₄ inch (2 cm) thick.
• Dust with a little rye flour using a tea strainer. Transfer to the prepared sheet, placing about 4 inches (10 cm) apart.
• Bake for 20–30 minutes, until well browned and the bottoms sound hollow when tapped. • Transfer to a rack and cover with a clean kitchen towel. • Cool for 20–30 minutes. Serve warm, with butter.

2 cups (300 g) rye flour + extra to dust

2 cups (300 g) whole-wheat (wholemeal) flour

2 teaspoons baking powder

1¹⁄₂ teaspoons baking soda

1¹⁄₂ teaspoons salt

1 tablespoon dark brown sugar

1 cup (250 ml) buttermilk

¹⁄₄ cup (60 g) unsalted butter, melted

1 large egg, lightly beaten

Butter, to serve

Serves: 8
Preparation: 15–20 minutes + 20–30 minutes to cool
Cooking: 20–30 minutes
Level: 1

Nutritional Facts
Amount per serving
Percentage of Daily Values
based on 2,000 calories

 CALORIES 336 16%

 PROTEIN 10g

 FAT 9g

 FIBER 8.1g

 SALT 1.6g

WHOLE-WHEAT LOAF

Mix the yeast and brown sugar in a small bowl with $^{1}/_{2}$ cup (125 ml) of the water. Set aside until frothy, 10–15 minutes. • Mix the flour with the salt in a large bowl and make a well in the middle. • Pour in the yeast mixture and $^{3}/_{4}$ cup (200 ml) of the remaining water. Gradually draw the flour into the water with a wooden spoon or a spatula. • Add the oil and work the dough into a rough ball with your hands. If the dough is dry, add a little more of the water (the quantity of water needed depends on the type and age of the flour). • Transfer to a lightly floured work surface and knead by hand until smooth and elastic, 10–15 minutes. Alternatively, beat with a dough hook until it will come away cleanly in your hands but is still moist, 5–6 minutes. • Shape the dough into a ball. • Clean the bowl, lightly brush with oil, and put the dough in it, turning to coat. • Cover with plastic wrap (cling film) and leave in a warm place until doubled in bulk, 1–2 hours. • Oil a 9 x 5-inch (23 x 12-cm) loaf pan or a

$^{1}/_{2}$ ounce (15 g) compressed fresh yeast or 1 ($^{1}/_{4}$-ounce/7-g) package active dry yeast

1 teaspoon brown sugar

About 1$^{1}/_{2}$ cups (375 ml) warm water (110°F/43°C)

3$^{1}/_{3}$ cups (500 g) whole-wheat (wholemeal) bread flour

1 teaspoon salt

1 tablespoon sunflower oil

2 tablespoons milk, for brushing

1 tablespoon rolled oats, for sprinkling (optional)

Serves: 8
Preparation: 20 minutes + 1$^{1}/_{2}$–2$^{1}/_{2}$ hours to rise
Cooking: 35–40 minutes
Level: 2

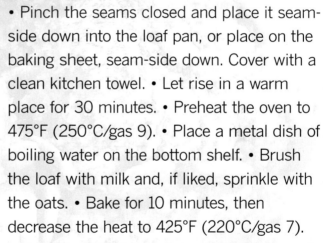

baking sheet. The dough is ready when it is almost doubled in bulk and springs back when touched with a floured finger. • Punch it down and return to the floured work surface. • Briefly knead the dough, and shape into a 9 x 12-inch (23 x 30-cm) rectangle. Roll it up into an oblong loaf.
• Pinch the seams closed and place it seam-side down into the loaf pan, or place on the baking sheet, seam-side down. Cover with a clean kitchen towel. • Let rise in a warm place for 30 minutes. • Preheat the oven to 475°F (250°C/gas 9). • Place a metal dish of boiling water on the bottom shelf. • Brush the loaf with milk and, if liked, sprinkle with the oats. • Bake for 10 minutes, then decrease the heat to 425°F (220°C/gas 7).
• Bake for 25–30 minutes, until a firm crust forms. It should sound hollow when tapped on the bottom. • Cool on a rack.

(See photograph on following page.)

545

Nutritional Facts
Amount per serving
Percentage of Daily Values
based on 2,000 calories

 CALORIES **214** 10%
 PROTEIN **8g** 7
 FAT **3g**
 FIBER **5.7g**
 SALT **0.6g**

CHEESE, CHIVE, AND SUN-DRIED TOMATO SCONE BREAD

Combine the flour, baking powder, mustard powder, salt, and pepper in a large bowl. Rub in the butter until the mixture resembles coarse bread crumbs. Stir in the sun-dried tomatoes, chives, and Cheddar, and mix well. • Beat the egg in a small bowl and whisk in ³⁄4 cup (180 ml) of buttermilk. • Make a well in the flour and mix in the egg-and-milk mixture with a fork. Stir in enough of the remaining buttermilk to bind into a soft dough. • Knead the dough on a lightly floured work surface for 30 seconds. Roll out into an oblong shape about 1 inch (2 ½ cm) thick. • Preheat the oven to 400°F (200°C/gas 6). • Brush a 13 x 9-inch (33 x 23-cm) baking pan with oil. Fit the dough in the pan. • Mark into 6–8 equal pieces with a knife. Brush with the remaining buttermilk. • Bake for 30–35 minutes, until golden. • Cool on a rack for 10 minutes. Serve warm.

2¹⁄3 cups (350 g) all-purpose (plain) flour

2 teaspoons baking powder

1 teaspoon dry mustard powder

1 teaspoon salt

Pinch of freshly ground black pepper

¹⁄2 cup (125 g) unsalted butter, chilled and cut into small cubes

¹⁄4 cup (45 g) sun-dried tomatoes, soaked in warm water for 15 minutes, drained and chopped

3 tablespoons finely chopped fresh chives

3 ounces (100 g) aged Cheddar or other hard cheese, grated

1 large egg

1 cup (250 ml) buttermilk

Serves: 8
Preparation: 10 minutes + 15 minutes to soak
Cooking: 30–35 minutes
Level: 1

Nutritional Facts
Amount per serving
Percentage of Daily Values
based on 2,000 calories

CALORIES 352
PROTEIN 10g
FAT 19g
FIBER 2g
SALT 1.2g

POLISH SOURDOUGH BREAD

Starter (stage 1): Mix the rye flour, sugar, water, and milk in a large plastic bowl. Beat with a fork or a whisk to form a smooth batter. • Cover the bowl with plastic wrap (cling film) and leave in a warm place until it smells slightly sour and has expanded, 2–3 days.

Starter (stage 2): Measure out $3/4$ cup (180 ml) of the stage 1 starter, discard the rest, and beat in the water and rye flour. • Cover the bowl and leave until pocked with tiny holes, 1–2 days.

Dough: Combine both flours and salt in a large bowl. • Dissolve the yeast in $1/3$ cup (90 ml) of warm water. Set aside until frothy. • Make a well in the center of the flour mixture and pour in the starter, butter, and yeast mixture. • Gradually pour in most of the water. Draw the flour mixture with a spatula or your fingers into the liquids, adding a little more water if needed. Mix until the flour is incorporated. • Knead until smooth and elastic, 8–12 minutes. • Shape the dough into a ball and place in a clean oiled bowl. Cover with

Starter (stage 1)

- 1 cup (150 g) rye flour
- $1/4$ cup (50 g) sugar
- $1/2$ cup (125 ml) warm water (110°F/43°C)
- $1/3$ cup (75 ml) milk, warmed (110°F/43°C)

Starter (stage 2)

- $3/4$ cup (180 ml) of the first starter
- $3/4$ cup (180 ml) warm water (110°F/43°C)
- $2/3$ cup (100 g) rye flour

Dough

- 2 cups (300 g) rye flour + extra, for dusting
- $1^1/3$ cups (200 g) white bread flour
- 2 teaspoons salt
- 1 ($1/4$-ounce/7-g) package active dry yeast, or $1/2$ ounce (15 g) compressed fresh yeast
- $1^1/3$ cups (300 ml) warm water (110°F/43°C)
- 1 tablespoon unsalted butter, melted

Serves: 8
Preparation: 30 minutes + 3–5 days for the starter, + 2–2¹/₂ hours to rise
Cooking: 35–45 minutes
Level: 3

plastic wrap (cling film). • Let rise in a warm place until doubled in bulk, 1¹/₂–2 hours. • Punch down and knead briefly. • Shape into a round loaf, about 6 inches (15 cm) across. • Grease a baking sheet and place the dough on it. • Cover with a floured kitchen towel and leave in a warm place until well risen, 30–40 minutes. • Preheat the oven to 400°F (200°C/gas 6). • Half fill a baking pan with boiling water. Place in the bottom of the oven. • Brush the loaf with water and dust with rye flour. • Make 4–5 diagonal ¹/₂-inch (1-cm) deep cuts in the top with a sharp knife. • Bake for 35–40 minutes, until browned and the bottom sounds hollow when tapped. If it does not sound hollow, lower the oven temperature to 325°F (170°C/gas 3), place the loaf upside-down, and bake for 5 minutes. • Cool on a rack.

(See photograph on the following page.)

Nutritional Facts
Amount per serving
Percentage of Daily Values
based on 2,000 calories

CALORIES	PROTEIN	FAT	FIBER	SALT
297	7g	4g	7.3g	0.6g
4%	5%	5%	9%	1%

ZUCCHINI AND CHIVE MUFFINS

554

Line a 12-cup muffin pan with paper liners. • Preheat the oven to 400°F (200°C/gas 6). • Combine the flour, baking powder, salt, and pepper in a large bowl. • Stir in the cheese. • Whisk the eggs and milk together in a small bowl. Pour into the dry ingredients and mix with a fork until well combined, adding 1 or 2 extra tablespoons of milk, if needed. • Stir in the zucchini and chives—the mixture will be lumpy. • Spoon into the muffin cups. • Sprinkle the tops with sunflower seeds. • Bake for 20–25 minutes, until risen, golden, and firm to the touch. Transfer to a rack and leave to cool.

2 cups (300 g) all-purpose (plain) flour

2¹/₂ teaspoons baking powder

¹/₂ teaspoon salt

¹/₂ teaspoon coarsely ground black pepper

1 cup (125 g) grated Gruyère, pecorino, or Parmesan cheese

2 large eggs

³/₄ cup (180 ml) milk or half-and-half (single cream) + more as needed

1 cup (150 g) finely grated zucchini (courgettes)

Bunch of chives (about 1 ounce/ 30 g), finely chopped

1 tablespoon sunflower seeds, for sprinkling

■ ■ ■ *For a change, make these muffins with peeled and grated butternut squash instead of zucchini (courgettes).*

Serves: 8
Preparation: 10–15 minutes
Cooking: 20–25 minutes
Level: 1

Nutritional Facts
Amount per serving
Percentage of Daily Values
based on 2,000 calories

CALORIES	PROTEIN	FAT	FIBER	SALT
240	13g	8g	1.5g	0.7g

RYE AND POTATO BREAD

Boil the potatoes in a pan of salted water until tender, about 20 minutes. • Drain, reserving the cooking water. • Mash the potatoes or put through a potato ricer, and leave to cool. • Combine the flours and salt in a large bowl and add the potatoes. Rub the potatoes into the flour mixture with your fingertips until it feels like crumbly pastry. • Dissolve the yeast in $1/2$ cup (125 ml) of the reserved potato water. Set aside until frothy, 10–15 minutes. • Make a well in the middle of the flour mixture and add the yeast and enough of remaining potato water to obtain a soft dough. • Work the dough until it comes together in a sticky lump. • Knead on a floured work surface until smooth and sticky, 10–15 minutes. Alternatively, knead with a dough hook, 5–8 minutes. • Grease a clean bowl with butter and add the dough. • Brush with a little melted butter and cover with plastic wrap (cling film). • Let rise in a warm place for 1–2 hours, until doubled in bulk. • Punch down to release the air. • Flour

8   ounces (250 g) potatoes, peeled and quartered

$3/4$ cup (125 g) rye or whole-wheat (wholemeal) flour

$2^1/4$ cups (330 g) white bread flour

2   teaspoons salt

1   ($1/4$-ounce/7-g) package active dry yeast, or $1/2$ ounce (15 g) compressed fresh yeast

1   cup (250 ml) reserved potato cooking water

2   tablespoons melted butter, for greasing

Serves: 8
Preparation: 30–40 minutes + $1^1/2$–$2^1/2$ hours to rise
Cooking: 50–60 minutes
Level 2

a work surface, transfer the dough, and knead briefly with floured hands; it will be very soft and sticky. • Shape into a round loaf about 8 inches (20 cm) in diameter. Butter a baking sheet and place the loaf on it. Loosely cover with plastic wrap (cling film). • Let rise for about 30 minutes. • Preheat the oven to 400°F (200°C/gas 6). • Half fill a baking pan with boiling water. Place in the bottom of the oven to create steam. • Dust the loaf with flour and make $1/2$-inch (1-cm)-deep crisscross cuts with a sharp knife. • Bake for 30–40 minutes. • Spray the top of the loaf with water after 10 minutes in the oven and twice again during baking, to ensure a crisp crust. The bread is ready when the crust is browned and the loaf sounds hollow when you tap the underside with your knuckles. • Let cool completely on a rack.

(See photograph on following page.)

Nutritional Facts
Amount per serving
Percentage of Daily Values
based on 2,000 calories

 CALORIES 231 1%
 PROTEIN 7g 5
 FAT 3g 4%
 FIBER 4g 6%
 SALT 1.2g 2

RIESKA

Preheat the oven to 425°F (220°C/gas 7).
• Combine the flour, baking powder, and
salt in a large bowl. Stir in the brown
sugar, half-and-half, buttermilk, and
butter, and mix well. • Flour your hands,
briefly knead the dough until smooth,
and shape into a ball. • Grease a baking
sheet and place the dough on it. • Flatten
into a large circle with a thickness of
$1/2$ inch (1 cm). Prick the top lightly with
a fork. • Bake for 10–15 minutes, until
golden brown. • Cut into wedges and
serve warm.

$1^{1}/_{2}$ cups (225 g) barley
    or rye flour

2   teaspoons baking
    powder

    Pinch of salt

1   scant tablespoon
    light brown sugar

$1/_{3}$ cup (90 ml) half-
    and-half (single
    cream)

$1/_{3}$ cup (90 ml)
    buttermilk or milk

2   tablespoons
    unsalted butter,
    melted

Serves: 4
Preparation: 10 minutes
Cooking: 10–15 minutes
Level 1

■ ■ ■ *This nutritious quick bread comes from Finland.*

Nutritional Facts
Amount per serving
Percentage of Daily Values
based on 2,000 calories

 CALORIES 291 | 14

 PROTEIN 6g | 13%

 FAT 10g | 12%

 FIBER 6.6g | 26%

 SALT 0.8g | 15%

562

CHILE CORN BREAD

Preheat the oven to 400°F (200°C/gas 6).
• Lightly grease a square 8-inch (20-cm) cake pan with butter and set aside. • Mix the flour, baking soda, baking powder, and salt in a large bowl. • Whisk the egg in a separate large bowl, until frothy.
• Whisk in the yogurt and half-and-half.
• Gradually stir the egg mixture into the flour mixture. • Fold in the cornmeal in batches, until well blended. • Mix the chiles and scallions into the corn batter.
• Pour into the pan. • Bake for 25–30 minutes, until a skewer inserted into the center of the bread comes out clean.
• Cool in the pan for 5 minutes. Cut into squares and serve warm.

¹/₂ cup (75 g) all-purpose (plain) flour
1 teaspoon baking soda
1 teaspoon baking powder
1 teaspoon salt
1 large egg
1 cup (250 ml) plain yogurt
²/₃ cup (150 ml) half-and-half (single cream) or milk
1³/₄ cups (275 g) yellow cornmeal
3 tablespoons finely chopped roasted chile peppers
2 scallions (spring onions), finely chopped

Serves: 4
Preparation: 15–20 minutes
Cooking: 25–30 minutes
Level: 1

Nutritional Facts
Amount per serving
Percentage of Daily Values
based on 2,000 calories

 CALORIES 408 20
 PROTEIN 12g 26
 FAT 12g
 FIBER 0.9g
 SALT 2.1g 38

WHOLE-WHEAT YOGURT BREAD

564

Preheat the oven to 400°F (200°C/gas 6). • Oil a 9 x 5-inch (23 x 12-cm) loaf pan. Combine the flour, brown sugar, salt, paprika, and baking soda in a large mixing bowl and mix well. • Gradually add the yogurt, and malt extract if using. • Stir in as much milk as needed to make a moist dough. For best results, mix everything together with your hands, although the dough is very sticky. • Dust your hands with a little flour and transfer the dough to the pan. Sprinkle the top with flour, and make a $^2/_3$-inch ($1^1/_2$-cm)-deep cut lengthwise down the center with a knife. • Sprinkle with the pumpkin and sunflower seeds. • Bake for 15 minutes. • Decrease the heat to 350°F (180°C/gas 4) and bake for 40–45 minutes more, until brown and crisp on top. • Cool on a wire rack. • Serve warm or toasted.

3 cups (450 g) whole-wheat (wholemeal) flour + extra, for sprinkling
1 tablespoon dark brown sugar
1 teaspoon salt
$^1/_2$ teaspoon sweet paprika
1 teaspoon baking soda (bicarbonate of soda)
2 cups (500 g) plain yogurt
1 teaspoon malt extract (optional)
$^1/_3$ cup (90 ml) milk
$^1/_4$ cup (45 g) pumpkin seeds
1 tablespoon sunflower seeds

Serves: 8
Preparation: 15 minutes
Cooking: 55–60 minutes
Level: 1

Nutritional Facts
Amount per serving
Percentage of Daily Values
based on 2,000 calories

 CALORIES 271 | 3

 PROTEIN 13g | 28%

 FAT 5g | 6

 FIBER 5.7g | 23%

 SALT 1.1g | 21%

QUICK BUTTERNUT AND PARMESAN BREAD

Preheat the oven to 375°F (190°C/gas 5). • Oil a baking sheet and set aside. • Mix the flour, baking powder, sage, Parmesan, butternut squash, and olives in a large bowl. • Whisk the eggs and milk in a separate bowl and stir into the flour mixture. Mix well and shape into a sticky ball. • Flour your hands, transfer the dough to the baking sheet, and pat into a round loaf. • Sprinkle the top with pumpkin seeds and Parmesan. • Bake for 45–50 minutes, until the underside sounds hollow when tapped. • Check after 30 minutes, and cover with aluminum foil if the top is browning too fast. • Cool on a rack for 10 minutes before slicing.

1¹/2 cups (225 g) all-purpose (plain) flour

¹/2 teaspoon baking powder

1 tablespoon sage, finely chopped

¹/2 cup (60 g) freshly grated Parmesan or pecorino cheese + 1 teaspoon for sprinkling

1²/3 cups (250 g) grated butternut squash or pumpkin

12 black olives, pitted and chopped

2 large eggs

1 tablespoon milk

1 tablespoon pumpkin seeds, for sprinkling

Serves: 8
Preparation: 15 minutes
Cooking: 45–50 minutes
Level 1

Nutritional Facts
Amount per serving
Percentage of Daily Values
based on 2,000 calories

CALORIES	PROTEIN	FAT	FIBER	SALT
173	8g	5g	1.6g	0.4g

ONION BREAD

Dissolve the yeast and sugar in ¹⁄₄ cup (60 ml) of water in a small bowl. Set aside until frothy, 10–15 minutes. • Combine both flours and the salt in a large bowl. • Add the beer, half the remaining water, the yeast mixture, and oil. Mix with a dough hook at low speed and then higher speed for 5 minutes, gradually adding more flour, if sticky, or water if dry, until pliable. • If kneading by hand, mix the dough in the bowl, adding extra water if dry, until you can knead it. • Knead on a floured work surface until smooth and elastic, 10–12 minutes, adding more flour a little at a time. • Lightly oil a large, clean bowl. Shape the dough into a ball and place in the bowl. Turn to coat, then cover with plastic wrap (cling film). • Let rise until doubled in bulk, 1–2 hours. • Melt the butter in a frying pan over medium heat. Add the onion and sauté until softened, 3–4 minutes. • Add the parsley and sauté for 1 minute. Let cool. • Return the dough to a work surface and knead briefly. • Flatten into a strip about 2 inches

¹⁄₂ ounce (15 g) compressed fresh yeast or 1 (¹⁄₄-ounce/7-g) package active dry yeast

1 teaspoon dark brown sugar

¹⁄₂ cup (125 ml) warm water

3¹⁄₃ cups (500 g) white bread flour + extra, to knead

1¹⁄₃ cups (200 g) whole-wheat flour + extra to dust

2 teaspoons salt

1¹⁄₃ cups (330 ml) dark beer (such as Guinness) or dark ale, at room temperature

3 tablespoons sunflower oil

2 tablespoons butter

1 medium onion, finely chopped

1 tablespoon finely chopped fresh parsley

2 teaspoons semolina, for the baking sheet

1 large egg

1   **tablespoon milk**

2   **tablespoons
    sunflower seeds,
    for sprinkling**

Serves: 8
**Preparation: 20 minutes
    + 2–3 hours to rise**
Cooking: 55–60 minutes
Level: 3

(5 cm) thick and cover with the onion mixture. Fold in half and then in three in the other direction (like a blanket), and knead in the onion filling for 2 minutes. • Divide the dough in half and shape into oblong loaves. • Line a baking sheet with parchment paper and sprinkle with semolina. • Place the loaves on the sheet. Cover with lightly oiled plastic wrap. • Set in a warm place until doubled in bulk, about 1 hour. • Preheat the oven to 400°F (200°C/gas 6). • Half fill a roasting pan with water and put in the bottom of the oven. • Beat the egg and milk in a small bowl. • Brush over the loaves and sprinkle with sunflower seeds. • Make a $1/2$-inch (1-cm)-deep cut down the center of each loaf. • Bake for 30 minutes. Decrease the heat to 375°F (190°C/gas 5) and bake for 15–25 minutes, until golden brown.

(See photograph on the following page.)

Nutritional Facts
Amount per serving
Percentage of Daily Values
based on 2,000 calories

 CALORIES **400** 9

 PROTEIN **13g** 8

 FAT **10g** 2%

 FIBER **6g** 24

 SALT **1.2g**

POLENTA BREAD WITH HERBS

Preheat the oven to 375°F (190°C/gas 5). • Grease an 8-inch (20-cm) springform pan with butter or line with parchment paper and set aside. • Combine the flour, baking powder, polenta, salt, and brown sugar in a large bowl. • Stir in the cheese, chiles, herbs, and pepper, and mix well. • In a separate bowl, whisk together the eggs, butter, creamed corn, and buttermilk. Fold into the flour-and-polenta mixture, and stir until well combined. • Spoon into the pan and bake for 45–50 minutes, until a skewer inserted in the center comes out clean. • Cool on a rack for 30–40 minutes before slicing.

1   cup (150 g) all-purpose (plain) flour
1/2 teaspoon baking powder
6   ounces (175 g) instant polenta
2   teaspoons salt
1   tablespoon light brown sugar
1   cup (250 g) chèvre or other soft fresh goat cheese, cubed
2   red chiles, seeded and finely chopped
1   teaspoon dried thyme
1   teaspoon dried oregano
1   tablespoon finely chopped fresh parsley
1/8 teaspoon freshly ground black pepper
2   large eggs, beaten
1/4 cup (60 g) butter, melted
1   (14-ounce/400-g) can creamed corn
3/4 cup (180 ml) buttermilk

Nutritional Facts
Amount per serving
Percentage of Daily Values
based on 2,000 calories

 CALORIES 360

 PROTEIN 12g

 FAT 15g

 FIBER 1.7g

 SALT 2g

Serves: 8
Preparation: 20 minutes
Cooking: 45–50 minutes
Level: 1

GREEK FETA AND SPINACH BREAD

Dough: Combine the milk and sugar in a small bowl and stir to dissolve. Mix in the yeast and set aside until frothy, 10–15 minutes. • Beat the egg and yolk together in a small bowl with a fork and stir in the oil. • Combine the flour and salt in a large bowl, make a well in the center, and pour in the yeast and egg mixtures. Mix together with a spatula or your fingers. • Transfer to a lightly floured work surface and knead, adding more flour as needed, until the dough is smooth, shiny, and no longer sticky, 10–12 minutes. Alternatively, knead in the bowl with a dough hook, about 5 minutes. • Shape the dough into a ball and put in an oiled bowl. Cover the bowl with plastic wrap (cling film). • Let rise in a warm place until doubled in bulk, about 1 hour. • Line a 12 x 17-inch (30 x 40-cm) half-sheet pan with parchment paper. • Transfer the dough to a lightly floured work surface. Punch down, knead for 1 minute, then roll out to about the size of the sheet pan. • Transfer to the sheet pan and pat down. • Cover with a

Dough

- ²/₃ cup (150 ml) milk, warmed (110°F/ 43°C)
- 1 teaspoon sugar
- ¹/₂ ounce (15 g) compressed fresh yeast or 1 (¹/₄-ounce/7-g) package active dry yeast
- 1 large egg + 1 large egg yolk
- ¹/₄ cup (60 ml) light olive oil
- 2¹/₃ cups (350 g) all-purpose (plain) flour + more as needed
- 1 scant teaspoon salt

Filling

- 8 ounces (250 g) spinach leaves
- ²/₃ cup (150 g) cream cheese or crème fraîche, at room temperature
- ¹/₂ teaspoon salt
  Freshly ground black pepper

1   tablespoon chopped fresh oregano, or 1 teaspoon dried

8   ounces (250 g) feta cheese

3/4 cup (100 g) freshly grated pecorino or Parmesan cheese

3   ounces (100 g) sun-dried tomatoes packed in oil, drained and chopped

1   small egg, lightly beaten

1   tablespoon poppy seeds

Serves: 8
Preparation: 45 minutes
  + 60–70 minutes
  to rise
Cooking: 35–45 minutes
Level: 2

kitchen towel and set aside until well-risen, 30–40 minutes.

Filling: Put the spinach in a colander and pour boiling water over it to wilt the leaves. Drain well, squeezing out excess moisture. • Spread the dough with the cream cheese, leaving a 3/4-inch (2-cm) border all around. Season with salt, pepper, and oregano. Cover with the spinach, both cheeses, and sun-dried tomatoes. • Roll up the long side into a log. Gently press the ends together. Place the log seam-side down on the baking sheet. • Cover with a kitchen towel and let rise for 30 minutes. • Preheat the oven to 400°F (200°C/gas 6). • Brush with the egg and sprinkle with poppy seeds. • Bake for 10 minutes. Decrease the temperature to 300°F (150°C/gas 2) and bake for 25–35 minutes, until deep golden brown. • Serve warm or at room temperature.

(See photograph on the following page.)

575

Nutritional Facts
Amount per serving
Percentage of Daily Values
based on 2,000 calories

CALORIES
434

PROTEIN
19g

FAT
23g

FIBER
3.4g
4%

SALT
2.4g

GRANDMA'S LIGHT RYE BREAD

Starter: Combine the yeast and water in a large bowl and stir to dissolve. Let sit until frothy, 10–15 minutes. • Add the flours and stir to form a thick batter. • Cover the bowl with plastic wrap (cling film). Leave in a warm room for 24 hours.

Dough: Add the water, salt, oil, and both flours to the starter. Stir until well mixed. • Knead until smooth and elastic, 10–15 minutes. • Shape into a round loaf. • Lightly oil a baking sheet. • Place the loaf on the baking sheet and cover with a floured kitchen towel. Let rise until doubled in bulk, 30–50 minutes. • Preheat the oven to 400°F (200°C/gas 6). • Half fill a baking pan with boiling water. Place in the bottom of the oven. • Cut a $1/2$-inch (1-cm) cross in the top with a sharp knife. • Bake for 50–60 minutes, until the loaf is golden and sounds hollow when tapped on the bottom. • Cool on a rack.

Starter

- $1^{1}/_{2}$ ounces (45 g) compressed fresh yeast or 2 ($1/4$-ounce/7-g) packages active dry yeast
- 1 cup (250 ml) warm water (110°F/43°C)
- $1/2$ cup (75 g) white bread flour
- $1/2$ cup (75 g) rye flour

Dough

- $1^{1}/_{3}$ cups (330 ml) warm water (110°F/43°C)
- 2 teaspoons salt
- 2 tablespoons corn oil or olive oil
- $3^{1}/_{3}$ cups (500 g) white bread flour
- 1 cup (150 g) rye flour

Serves: 8
Preparation: 20–30 minutes + 24 hours for the starter + 30–50 minutes to rise
Cooking: 50–60 minutes
Level: 2

Nutritional Facts
Amount per serving
Percentage of Daily Values
based on 2,000 calories

 CALORIES **365** 18%
 PROTEIN **10g** 22%
 FAT **4g** 5%
 FIBER **5.5g** 22%
 SALT **1.2g** 21%

GERMAN CARAWAY SEED BREAD

Starter: Combine the yeast and water in a large bowl and stir until dissolved. Let sit until frothy, 10–15 minutes • Add the rye flour and mix to form a thick batter. Cover the bowl tightly with plastic wrap (cling film) and leave to rise for 16 hours. **Dough:** Stir the milk, oil, salt, and 1 tablespoon of the caraway seeds into the starter mixture. • Mix in the rye and white flours. Knead the dough on a floured work surface until smooth and elastic, 10–12 minutes. • Alternatively, knead with a dough hook for 5 minutes. Add a little flour or warm milk as needed, until the dough is smooth and comes together in a ball. • Place in an oiled bowl and cover with plastic wrap (cling film). • Let rise in a warm place until almost doubled in bulk, 1–2 hours. • Lightly oil a large baking sheet. • Dust a work surface with flour and place the dough on it. Punch down to expel air, and knead briefly. • Divide in half, shape into

Starter

$1/4$ ounce (10 g) compressed fresh yeast, or 2 scant teaspoons ($1/4$ ounce 5 g) active dry yeast

1 cup (250 ml) warm water (110°F)

$1^1/4$ cups (180 g) rye flour

Dough

1 cup (250 ml) warmed milk (110°F/43°C) + extra as needed

2 teaspoons sunflower oil

$2^1/2$ teaspoons salt

2 tablespoons caraway seeds

1 cup (150 g) rye flour

3 cups (450 g) white bread white flour + extra as needed

1 large egg, lightly beaten for the glaze

Serves: 8
Preparation: 30 minutes
+ 16 hours for the
starter + 2–3 hours
to rise
Cooking: 45–65 minutes
Level: 2

2 round loaves, and place on the baking sheet about 5 inches (12 cm) apart. Cover with plastic wrap. • Let rise until doubled in bulk, about 1 hour. • Preheat the oven to 400°F (200°C/gas 6). • Half fill a baking pan with boiling water and put in the bottom of the oven to create steam. • Uncover the bread, and brush the tops with the egg. • Cut the loaves diagonally a few times with a sharp serrated knife, about $^3/_4$ inch (2 cm) deep, and sprinkle with the remaining 1 tablespoon caraway seeds. Bake for 45–60 minutes, until brown. • Test the bread by tapping the underside with your knuckles. If it sounds hollow, it is done. If not, return to the oven for 5 minutes. • Cool on a rack.

(See photograph on the following page.)

Nutritional Facts
Amount per serving
Percentage of Daily Values
based on 2,000 calories

 CALORIES 367 8%

 PROTEIN 13g 28

 FAT 5g 5%

 FIBER 7g 28

 SALT 1.6g 29

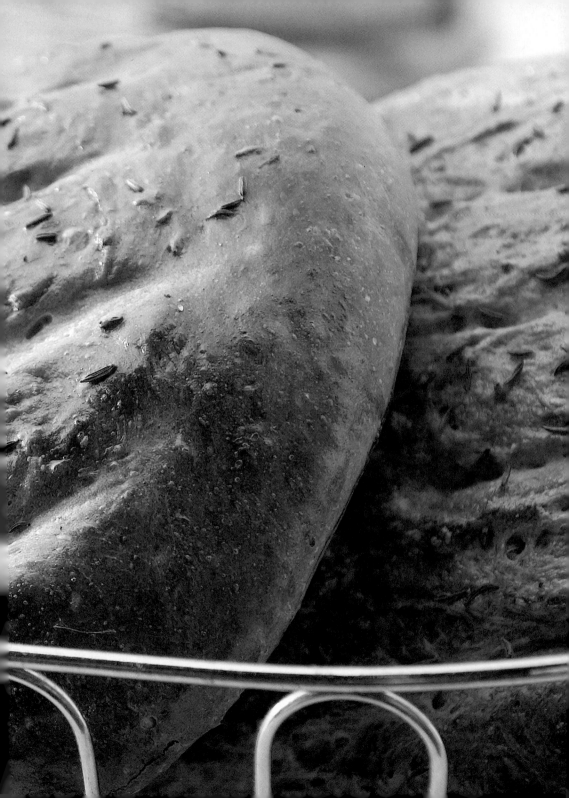

THREE-SEED LOAVES

Bread: Dissolve the yeast and sugar in 3 tablespoons of the milk in a small bowl. Set aside until frothy, 10–15 minutes. • Mix the yogurt with the remaining milk in a separate bowl and set aside. • Combine the flours and salt in a large bowl. Make a well in the center, pour in the yeast and yogurt mixtures, and add the eggs and butter. • Mix well with a spatula or your hands, to blend in the flour. • Transfer to a lightly floured surface and knead until smooth and elastic, 10–15 minutes. Alternatively, beat in the bowl with a dough hook, about 5 minutes. • Shape into a ball. • Brush the bowl with butter and return the dough to it. Cover with plastic wrap (cling film) or a damp kitchen towel. • Let rise in a warm place, until doubled in bulk, about 1 hour. • Transfer to a floured surface. Knead again briefly, then divide in two. Roll out each piece and shape with your hands into a disk about $3/4$ inch (2 cm) thick. • Line a

Bread
- $1/2$ ounce (15 g) compressed fresh yeast or 1 ($1/4$-ounce 7-g) package active dry yeast
- 1 teaspoon sugar
- $1^1/2$ cups (300 ml) milk, warmed (110°F/43°C)
- $2/3$ cup (150 g) plain yogurt, at room temperature
- $1^2/3$ cups (250 g) white bread flour
- $1^2/3$ cups (250 g) all-purpose (plain) flour
- 1 teaspoon salt
- 2 large eggs, lightly beaten
- $1/4$ cup (60 g) butter, diced and softened

Glaze
- 2 tablespoons butter, melted
- 1 tablespoon sesame seeds
- 1 tablespoon caraway seeds
- 1 tablespoon poppy seeds

large baking sheet with parchment paper and place the loaves about 4 inches (10 cm) apart.

Glaze: To glaze the bread, brush the loaves with butter and sprinkle with the seeds. • Cover with a clean kitchen towel and leave in a warm place until visibly risen, about 1 hour. • Preheat the oven to 425°F (220°C/gas 7). • Bake for 15–20 minutes, until golden brown and the undersides of the loaves sound hollow when tapped. • Leave to cool on a rack.

(See photograph on the following page.)

Nutritional Facts
Amount per serving
Percentage of Daily Values
based on 2,000 calories

CALORIES
236

PROTEIN
9g

FAT
12g

FIBER
1.1g

SALT
0.8g
5%

CORNISH SEED BREAD

Dissolve the yeast in the water in a small bowl. Set aside until frothy, 10–15 minutes. • Whisk the eggs and milk in a medium bowl. • Combine the flour and salt in a large bowl and make a well in the center. • Pour in the yeast and egg mixtures. • Draw the flour into the liquid with a spatula until all the flour is incorporated and a soft but not too sticky dough is formed. Add a little more milk if the dough is dry. • Knead the dough on a floured work surface until smooth and elastic, 5–8 minutes. • Shape into a ball. Clean the bowl, dust with flour, and put the dough in it. Cover with plastic wrap (cling film). • Let rise in a warm place until almost doubled in bulk, 1–1¹/₂ hours. • Oil a 9 x 5-inch (23 x 12-cm) loaf pan. • Transfer the dough to the floured surface, punch down to release the air, and knead for 1 minute. • Pat out with the back of your hands, sprinkle with half of the caraway and fennel seeds, and dot with

¹/₂ ounce (15 g) compressed fresh yeast or 1 (¹/₄-ounce 7-g) package active dry yeast

¹/₄ cup (60 ml) warm water (110°F/43°C)

2 large eggs

²/₃ cup (150 ml) milk, warmed (110°F/43°C) + extra as needed

3¹/₃ cups (500 g) white bread flour

1¹/₂ teaspoons salt

1 tablespoon caraway seeds, coarsely ground

1 tablespoon fennel seeds, coarsely ground

¹/₃ cup (80 g) solid vegetable shortening or white vegetable margarine, cut up into small pieces and chilled

Serves: 6
Preparation: 20 minutes + 1¹/₂–2¹/₄ hours to rise
Cooking: 30–35 minutes
Level 2

the vegetable shortening. Knead in the seeds and shortening. • Roll out the dough with a rolling pin to a thickness of about ¾ inch (2 cm). Fold the sides in underneath into a loaf shape, turn the loaf over, and pinch the seam to seal. Place seam-side down in the pan. • Cover with a damp kitchen towel and leave in a warm place until the dough has risen to the rim of the pan, 30–45 minutes. • Preheat the oven to 375°F (190°C/gas 5). Sprinkle with the remaining caraway and fennel seeds. Bake for 30–35 minutes, until the crust is golden and the underside of the loaf sounds hollow when you tap it. • Cool on a wire rack.

589

(See photograph on the following page.)

■■■ *This Cornish bread is traditionally made with lard. Solid vegetable shortening is a vegetarian alternative.*

Nutritional Facts
Amount per serving
Percentage of Daily Values
based on 2,000 calories

CALORIES	PROTEIN	FAT	FIBER	SALT
425	12g	15g	2.6g	1.4g
20	26	9	0	26

HERBY CHEESE BREAD

Bread: Combine the water and yeast in a large bowl and stir to dissolve the yeast. Let sit until frothy, 10–15 minutes. • Stir in just over half of the flour, until the mixture has the consistency of hot cereal (porridge). • Beat with a hand whisk until well mixed. Cover with plastic wrap (cling film). • Let rise in a warm place until doubled in bulk, 30–50 minutes. • Stir in the salt with a wooden spoon and gradually add more flour to form a stiff dough that you can knead. • Knead the dough on a floured work surface until smooth and elastic, about 10 minutes. • Clean and oil the bowl and place the dough in it. Cover with plastic wrap (cling film). • Let rise in a warm place until almost doubled in bulk, about 1 hour.

Filling: Combine all the ingredients in a medium bowl. • Transfer the dough to a floured surface, punch it down to release the air, and knead for 2–3 minutes. Divide in half. • Lightly oil a work surface

Bread

- 1 cup (250 ml) warm water (110°F/43°C)
- 3/4 ounce (20 g) compressed fresh yeast or 1 (1/4-ounce 7-g) package active dry yeast
- 3 1/3 cups (500 g) whole-wheat (wholemeal) flour
- 1 teaspoon salt

Filling

- 3 1/2 cups (430 g) freshly grated Cheddar or Gruyère cheese
- 1 teaspoon sweet paprika
- 1 scallion (spring onion), finely chopped
- 1 tablespoon finely chopped fresh basil or 1 teaspoon dried
- 2 tablespoons finely chopped fresh parsley
- 1 tablespoon finely chopped fresh dill, or 1 teaspoon dried

Serves: 8
Preparation: 20 minutes
    + 2 hours to rise
Cooking: 40–45 minutes
Level: 2

and roll out each half into a 4 x 12-inch (10 x 30-cm) rectangle. • Spread the dough with the filling, leaving a border all around. Reserve 2 tablespoons of filling for the topping. • Working from the short side, roll up each rectangle tightly into a log. Pinch the short edges to seal. • Oil two 8 x 4-inch (20 x 10-cm) loaf pans. Fit the dough into the pans, seam-side down. • Top with the remaining filling. Loosely cover with plastic wrap. Let rise in a warm place for about 1 hour, until risen to fill the pans. • Preheat the oven to 425°F (220°C/gas 7). • Bake the loaves for 40–45 minutes, until a crust has formed and the loaves sound hollow when you tap the bottom. • Let cool before slicing.

(See photograph on the following page.)

593

Nutritional Facts
Amount per serving
Percentage of Daily Values
based on 2,000 calories

 CALORIES **415** 20

 PROTEIN **23g** 50

 FAT **19g** 23

 FIBER **5.7g** 23

 SALT **1.4g** 26

FRUIT AND MALT BREAD

Grease two 1-pound (500-g) (8 x 4-inch (20 x 10-cm) loaf pans with butter and set aside. • Combine the water and yeast in a large bowl, and stir to dissolve the yeast. Set aside until frothy, 10–15 minutes. • Stir in just over half of the whole-wheat flour, until the mixture has the consistency of hot cereal (porridge). • Beat with a hand whisk until well mixed. Cover with plastic wrap (cling film). • Let rise in a warm place for about 1 hour, until well risen. • Stir in the salt, oil, malt extract, corn syrup, and raisins with a wooden spoon. • Gradually add more flour to form a stiff dough that comes away from the sides of the bowl. • Flour a work surface and knead the dough until smooth and elastic, 10–12 minutes. • Clean and oil the bowl. Shape the dough into a ball, return to the bowl, and cover with plastic wrap. • Let rise in a warm place until almost doubled in bulk, 50–60 minutes. • Lightly oil a work

1 cup (250 ml) warm water (110°F)

3/4 ounce (20 g) compressed fresh yeast or 1 (1/4-ounce 7-g) package active dry yeast

3 1/3 cups (500 g) whole-wheat flour

1 teaspoon salt

1 tablespoon sunflower oil

3 tablespoons malt extract (available where beer supplies are sold)

1 tablespoon dark corn syrup or maple syrup

1 cup (180 g) golden raisins (sultanas) or other seedless raisins

Serves: 8
Preparation: 20 minutes + 2 hours to rise
Cooking: 35–45 minutes
Level 2

surface and knead gently for 1–2 minutes.
• Divide the dough in half and flatten
each half into a 1¹⁄₂-inch (4-cm)-thick
rectangle, about the length of the pan.
Roll into a loaf, tuck the edges under, and
pinch the seams to seal. Fit the loaves
into the pan, seam-side down. • Cover
the pans with plastic wrap and return to
a warm place until the dough has risen
to the rim of the pans, about 1 hour.
• Preheat the oven to 400°F (200°C/gas
6). • Bake for 35–45 minutes, until the
loaves have a dark crust and shrink
slightly away from the sides of the pans.
• Remove from the pans and tap the
bottoms with your knuckles. If the loaves
sound hollow, they are done. If not,
return upside-down (out of the pan) to
the oven and bake for 5 minutes. • Leave
to cool on a rack.

(See photograph on the following page.)

597

Nutritional Facts
Amount per serving
Percentage of Daily Values
based on 2,000 calories

CALORIES	PROTEIN	FAT	FIBER	SALT
287	9g	3g	6g	0.6g
14%	20%	4%	24%	11%

SOUR CREAM GRIDDLE SCONES

Combine the flour, baking powder, and salt in a large bowl. • Rub the butter into the flour with your fingertips. • Stir in the sugar. • Make a well in the center of the flour. • Whisk the egg in a small bowl, then whisk in the sour cream. • Pour into the well and mix the flour into the liquid with a fork or round-bladed knife to make a soft dough. • Dust a work surface with flour and knead the dough for 30 seconds. • Flour your hands and pat out into a round about ½ inch (1 cm) thick. Cut into 8 equal pieces. • Heat a griddle over medium heat and melt the butter on it. • Place the scones on the griddle and cook until golden, about 10 minutes. Turn over and cook the other side, until golden. • Transfer to a rack and serve while still warm.

■ ■ ■ *If you don't have a griddle, use a heavy grill pan or frying pan for these scones.*

1²/₃ cups (250 g) all-purpose (plain) flour

1 tablespoon baking powder

Pinch of salt

1 ounce (30 g) butter, chilled and diced

1 tablespoon sugar

1 large egg

²/₃ cup (150 ml) sour cream

1 teaspoon unsalted butter, for the griddle

Serves: 4
Preparation: 10 minutes
Cooking: 18–20 minutes
Level: 1

Nutritional Facts
Amount per serving
Percentage of Daily Values
based on 2,000 calories

CALORIES
394
19%

PROTEIN
9g
20%

FAT
17g
21%

FIBER
1.9g
8%

SALT
0.9g
17%

INDEX